Postal Exam
Book

Albert B. Kim

NOVA
PRESS

Additional educational titles from Nova Press (available at novapress.net):

- ➢ **GRE Prep Course** (624 pages)
  GRE Math Prep Course (528 pages)
- ➢ **GMAT Prep Course** (624 pages, includes software)
  GMAT Math Prep Course (528 pages)
  GMAT Data Sufficiency Prep Course (422 pages)
- ➢ **Master The LSAT** (608 pages, includes software and 4 official LSAT exams)
- ➢ **The MCAT Physics Book** (444 pages)
  The MCAT Biology Book (416 pages)
  The MCAT Chemistry Book (428 pages)
- ➢ **SAT Prep Course** (640 pages, includes software)
  SAT Math Prep Course (404 pages)
  SAT Critical Reading and Writing Prep Course (350 pages)
- ➢ **ACT Math Prep Course** (402 pages)
  ACT Verbal Prep Course (248 pages)
- ➢ **Scoring Strategies for the TOEFL® iBT:** (800 pages, includes audio CD)
  Speaking and Writing Strategies for the TOEFL® iBT: (394 pages, includes audio CD)
  500 Words, Phrases, and Idioms for the TOEFL® iBT: (238 pages, includes audio CD)
  Practice Tests for the TOEFL® iBT: (292 pages, includes audio CD)
  Business Idioms in America: (220 pages)
  Americanize Your Language and Emotionalize Your Speech! (210 pages)
- ➢ **Law School Basics:** A Preview of Law School and Legal Reasoning (224 pages)
- ➢ **Vocabulary 4000:** The 4000 Words Essential for an Educated Vocabulary (160 pages)

ISBN-10: 1–889057–77–0
ISBN-13: 978–1–889057–77–4

P. O. Box 692023
West Hollywood, CA 90069

Phone: 1-310-275-3513
E-mail: info@novapress.net
Website: www.novapress.net

Table of Contents

1. PREFACE

This book is designed for the Postal Test 473 and 473-c. This version of the test has been in use since 2005.

I have scored 100% on the Postal Exam six times: twice for the Clerk and Carrier position and four times for the Distribution Clerk Machine position.

When practicing with this book, you should cut out the address-checking test, all answer sheets, and the Guide to Post Office Employment. Also, copies of the answer sheets should be made to allow additional practice. This will allow you to simulate the actual test.

This book also includes information covering the Federal Employees Retirement System. It is advisable to know this information upon hire. The Federal Employment Retirement System (FERS) is a three-tiered retirement plan. The three components of FERS work together to give you a strong financial foundation for your retirement years.

I wish you success in obtaining employment with the U.S. Postal Service.

Albert B. Kim

2. EXAMINATION OUTLINE

1) QUALIFICATION
You must be at least 18 years old or 16 years old with a high school diploma or G.E.D. There is no sexual or educational discrimination. Also, applicant must be a U.S. citizen or permanent resident.

2) TYPE OF OCCUPATION
   A. City Carrier
   A person who delivers mail to the appropriate places according to addresses by foot, cart, satchel or jeep.

   B. Mail Processing Clerk
   Sort mail by hand or machine according to memorized scheme or by ZIP code into prepared cases.

   C. Mail Handler
   Does mostly physical work.

   D. Sales, Service and Distribution Associate
   This designation is also called a window clerk. Duties include selling stamps, money orders and accepting accountable mail.

   E. PSE (see Guide to Post Office Employment, page 268)

   F. Rural Carrier Associate (see Guide to Post Office Employment, page 244)

   G. CCA (City Carrier Assistant) (see Guide to Post Office Employment, page 269)

   H. Test Battery 473
   It contains the six types of positions, which are explained above.

   I. TEST 473-C
   When the USPS accepts applications for only city carrier, it is called Test 473-C. There are four test subjects for Test 473 and Test 473-C. These are *Address Checking*, *Forms Completion*, *Coding and Memory*, and *Personal Characteristics and Experience Inventory*.

3) BENEFITS
   A. Salary
   Salary is paid every other Friday.

   B. Vacation
   Employees who have worked less than three years can take 13 days off each year. Employees who have worked more than three years but less than 15 years can take 20 days off, which is accumulated six hours at every pay period. Employees

2

who have worked at least 15 years can take 25 days vacation, which is accumulated eight hours at each pay period.

C. Sick Leave
Employees can take 13 days of sick leave a year, regardless of length of service.

D. Night Shifts
Night Shift means working during the hours of 6 P.M. to 6 A.M. In this case, regular pay plus about 8% is paid. This is called night differential.

E. Sunday Premium
Sunday shift workers get paid regular salary plus 25%. This is called Sunday Premium. Even if you work only 1 hour on Sunday, you will get 8 hours pay.

F. Holiday
There are 10 holidays a year. Full-time employees get paid for 8 hours without working for each holiday. Part-Time Flexible employees do not get paid if they do not work the holiday.

G. Health and Life Insurance
Everyone can join the health and life insurance plan. The Postal Service may inform you how soon you need to join the health and life insurance plan (usually within one or two months from the date of hire). There are many different types of health insurance available. You can change your health insurance once a year, during the open enrollment season. There is also free basic life insurance. The life insurance amount equals an employee's annual salary plus $2,000.

H. Veterans
Refer to the Guide to Post Office Employment

I. Retirement
Refer to the Guide to Post Office Employment

J. Change of Craft
Refer to the Guide to Post Office Employment

K. Transferring
Refer to the Guide to Post Office Employment

L. Cash for Suggestion
Refer to the Guide to Post Office Employment

M. Overtime Pay
Refer to the Guide to Post Office Employment

3. PROCEDURES FOR HIRING

1) INTERVIEW (call in notice)

Call in notice will be issued by the recorded date of the test result. The notice date will depend on the score and opening of that post office.

2) PHYSICAL EXAMINATION

Physical exam notice will be mailed to the applicant's home after passing the interview. You may not know whether you passed the interview on the date of interview. A notice of driving test or physical examination will be sent to your home if you pass the interview. Physical examination will be performed at the hospital designated by the post office.

3) DRIVING TEST

A driving test is given to the carriers around one to two weeks before the physical exam.

4) ORIENTATION

An orientation notice will be delivered about two weeks later to those who pass their physical exam and driving test. The orientation day is the first day of work.

4. Address Checking (Test 1)

A. No Errors	B. Address Only	C. Zip Code Only	D. Both

	Correct List			List to be Checked	
	Address	ZIP Code		Address	ZIP Code
1.	394 Wilson Ave. Zerbe, PA	17981		394 Wilson St. Zerbe, PA	17981
2	27 3rd St. Durand, MI	48428		27 3rd St. Durand, MI	48429
3.	8694 Western Ave. Elmwood, MA	02337		8694 Western Ave. Elmwood, MA	02337
4.	13288 Oxford Dr. Lusby, MD	20658-1237		13288 Oxford Dr. Lusby, MD	20658-1238
5.	692 Orion Ave. NW. Shetland, KY	40383		692 Orion Ave. NW. Shetland, KY	40383
6.	1795 Kettle Dr. Kemp, GA	30402-6194		1795 Kettle Dr. Kemp, GA	30402-6195
7.	419 E. Coral Ave. Montclair, NC	28300		419 W. Coral Ave. Montclair, NC	28304
8.	24 Flora St. Spring Grove, RI	02814		24 Flora St. Spring Grove, RE	02814
9.	4927 Ancona Rd. SE. Jones, TX	75140-3369		4927 Ancona Rd. SE. Jones, TX	75140-3369
10.	91 Chapulin Blvd. Red Oak, VA	23964		91 Chapulen Blvd. Red Oak, VA	23964
11.	24681 Ladera Cir. North Rose, NY	14516		24881 Ladera Cir. North Rose, NY	14518
12.	3920 Klamath Ct. Arch Rock, PA	17059		3820 Klamath Ct. Arch Rock, PA	17059
13.	92 Fair View St. Garden Grove, CA	92843-3692		92 Fair View St. Garden Grove, CA	92843-3694
14.	492 Fordham Dr. Carol Stream, IL	60188		492 Fordham Dr. Carol Stream, IL	60188
15.	7614 Rincom Rd. Gosport, NH	03801		7614 Rincom Rd. Gosport, NH	03801

Address Checking(Test 1)

A. No Errors	B. Address Only	C. Zip Code Only	D. Both

	Correct List			List to be Checked	
	Address	ZIP Code		Address	ZIP Code
16.	819 N. Prescott Pl. Blachly, OR	97412		818 N. Prescott Pl. Blachly, OR	97412
17.	6948 Fiesta Ct. Moussam, ME	04258		6848 Fiesta Ct. Moussam, ME	04258
18.	1296 N. Gordon Ave. Freeburg, MN	55921		1296 N. Gerdon Ave. Freeburg, MN	55821
19.	462 Pearl St. Mogadore, OH	44268-3795		462 Pearl St. Mogadore, OH	44260-3795
20.	6291 Pecan Cir. Choto Hills, TN	37777		6291 Pecan Cir. Choto Hills, TN	37777
21.	31520 Crest Dr. High Bank, NY	12981		31520 Crest Dr. High Bank, NY	12981
22.	769 W. Moco Lane Five Porks, NC	27551		769 E. Moco Lane Five Porks, NC	27551
23.	1247 127th St. East Canton, OH	44730-2647		1247 127th St. East Canton, OH	44720-2647
24.	27 Lindsay Dr. Union Valley, OK	74871		27 Lindsay Dr. Union Valley, OK	74871
25.	3294 Gretta Ave. Kamey, TX	77978		3294 Gratta Ave. Kamey, TX	77979
26.	8694 Pacific Ave. Harrod, OH	45858		8694 Pacific Ave. Harred, OH	45850
27.	278 Crocker St. SE. Bowstring, MN	56631-1159		278 Crocker St. SE Bowstring, MI	56631-1159
28.	2149 Adams Dr. Hyndman, PA	15545		2149 Adams Dr. Hyndman, PA	15545
29.	926 E. Hoover Ct. Mosshiem, TN	37818		926 E. Hoover Ct. Mosshiem, TN	37818
30.	4979 Rialto Way. Downsville, TX	76706		4989 Rialto Way. Downsville, TX	76706

Address Checking (Test 1)

A. No Errors	B. Address Only	C. Zip Code Only	D. Both

	Correct List		List to be Checked	
	Address	ZIP Code	Address	ZIP Code
31.	19 3rd St. Sylmar, NC	28779	19 3rd Way Sylmar, NC	28779
32.	462 Florence Ave. Westwilton, NH	03686-4429	462 Florence Ave. Westwilton, NH	03686-4439
33.	2694 Risa Pl. Porchtown, NJ	08344-6211	2694 Risa Pl. Porchtown, NJ	08344-6311
34.	637 Golden Ave. Chestuee, TN	37311	637 Golden Ave. Chestuee, TM	37311
35.	7695 S. Rimrock St. Ashland, GA	30521	7695 S. Rimrock St. Ashland, GA	30521
36.	584 Saddla Ct. NW. Gokonda, IL	62939-1271	584 Saddla Ct. NE. Gokonda, IL	62939-1271
37.	8194 Flint Pl. Vine Grove, KY	48175	8194 Flint Pl. Vine Grove, KY	40175
38.	46129 Willow Way. Lightsey, MS	39440	46129 Willow Way. Lightsey, MS	39440
39.	29 NE. Royal Hill Rd. Wood Lake, NE	69221-4229	29 NW. Royal Hill Rd. Wood Lake, NE	69221-4229
40.	3924 Overbrook Dr. Tunipus, RI	02837	3924 Overbrook Dr. Tunipus, RE	02837
41.	23927 N. Padua Dr. Fairmont, MN	56031	23926 N. Padua Dr. Fairmont, MN	56032
42.	379 Flores Ave. Westborough, MA	01581-1179	379 Flores Ave. Westborough, MA	01581-1179
43.	28 Dartmore St. Ockley, IN	46923	28 Dartmoor St. Ockley, IN	46923
44.	769 Safford St. Winsted, CT	06098	768 Safford St. Winsted, CT	06098
45.	4697 Fonda St. Fowler, MI	48835-2145	4697 Fonda St. Fowler, MI	48835-2245

Address Checking (Test 1)

A. No Errors	B. Address Only	C. Zip Code Only	D. Both

	Correct List		List to be Checked	
	Address	ZIP Code	Address	ZIP Code
46.	1694 Bahama Pl. Edison, CO	80864	1694 Bahama Pl. Edisom, CO	80864
47.	265 Crystal Dr. Swanton, MD	21561	265 Crystal Dr. Swanton, MC	21564
48.	284 E. Judy Cir. New Cambria, MO	63559	284 E. Judy Ct. New Cambria, MO	63558
49.	4297 N. Azita Dr. Woodcrest, CA	92504	4297 N. Azita Dr. Woodcrest, CA	92504
50.	5429 Babcock St. Denver, WV	26034-3200	5439 Babcock St. Denver, WV	26034-3200
51.	32612 26th St. Draddock, PA	15301	32612 26th St. Draddock, PA	15401
52.	P.O.Box 869 Gilbert, MN	55741	P.O.Box 879 Gilbert, MN	55741
53.	6924 Ridgewood Pl. Esom Hill, GA	30138	6924 Ridgewood Pl. Esom Hill, GA	30138
54.	4264 W. Linden Lane Garden Grove, CA	92640	4254 W. Linden Lane Garden Grove, CA	92648
55.	P.O.Box 6296 Baltimore, KY	42066-6122	P.O.Box 6298 Baltimore, KY	42066-6122
56.	7294 N. Forest Dr. Yorktown, IA	51656	7294 N. Forest Dr. Yorktown, IA	51656
57.	26948 Saturna Dr. Limestone, OH	43532	26948 Saturna Dr. Limestone, OH	43432
58.	219 Silver St. Sampson, TN	37367-1142	219 Silver St. Sampson, TN	37367-1242
59.	6296 S. 169th St. Meadville, VA	24558	6296 N. 169th St. Meadville, VA	24558
60.	361 Bergh Pl. Conway, FL	32809	361 Bergh Pl. Conway, FL	32809

END

Address Checking (Test 2)

A. No Errors	B. Address Only	C. Zip Code Only	D. Both

Correct List

	Address	ZIP Code
1.	6192 Parkview Dr. Akron, OH	44313
2	479 N. Bristol St. Pittsburgh, PA	15207
3.	12132 Oakmere Rd. San Antonio, TX	78232-1149
4.	629 SE. Woodhaven St. Asheboro, NC	27204
5.	5694 S. Deerland Rd. Memphis, TN	38109
6.	871 169th St. Laramie, WY	82718-1159
7.	4269 Cimarron St. Green Bay, WI	54313
8.	3694 Tanager Ave. Greer, SC	29650
9.	29 W. March Hare Ln. Richmond, VA	23235
10.	6642 Handley St. Huntington, WV	25604
11.	278 S. Coleman Ave. Mesa, AZ	85210-4469
12.	4327 Dogwood Rd. Costa Mesa, CA	92627
13.	324 Advent St. Newark, DE	19718
14.	12479 Pineview Dr. Grifin, GA	30223
15.	1290 Ogden Ave. Worcester, MA	01606

List to be Checked

	Address	ZIP Code
1.	6192 Parkview Dr. Akron, OH	44313
2	489 N. Bristol St. Pittsburgh, PA	15207
3.	12132 Oakmere Rd. San Entonio, TX	78232-1159
4.	629 SW. Woodhaven St. Asheboro, NC	27204
5.	5694 S. Deerland Rd. Memphis, TN	38108
6.	871 169th St. Laramie, WY	82718-1159
7.	4269 Cimarron Dr. Green Bay, WI	54313
8.	3684 Tanager Ave. Greer, SC	29650
9.	29 W. March Hare Ln. Richmend, VA	23335
10.	6642 Handley St. Huntington, WV	25704
11.	278 S. Coleman Ave. Mesa, AZ	85210-4469
12.	4328 Dogwood Rd. Costa Mesa, CA	92627
13.	324 Advent St. Newark, DE	19713
14.	12479 Pineview Dr. Grifin, GA	30223
15.	1290 Ogden Ave. Wercester, MA	01606

Address Checking (Test 2)

A. No Errors	B. Address Only	C. Zip Code Only	D. Both

<table>
<tr>
<th colspan="3">Correct List</th>
<th colspan="3">List to be Checked</th>
</tr>
<tr>
<td></td>
<td>Address</td>
<td>ZIP Code</td>
<td></td>
<td>Address</td>
<td>ZIP Code</td>
</tr>
<tr>
<td>16.</td>
<td>49 Hill St.
Columbus, MS</td>
<td>38703-6121</td>
<td></td>
<td>49 Hill St.
Columbus, MC</td>
<td>38703-6121</td>
</tr>
<tr>
<td>17.</td>
<td>7296 Millwood Ct.
Kansas City, MO</td>
<td>64138</td>
<td></td>
<td>7296 Millwood Ct.
Kansas City, MO</td>
<td>64138</td>
</tr>
<tr>
<td>18.</td>
<td>8624 E. Morgan Cir.
Minneapolis, MN</td>
<td>55405</td>
<td></td>
<td>8624 E. Morgan Cir.
Minneapolis, MN</td>
<td>55405</td>
</tr>
<tr>
<td>19.</td>
<td>327 Temple St.
Lexington, KY</td>
<td>40517</td>
<td></td>
<td>327 Temple Ct.
Lexington, KY</td>
<td>40517</td>
</tr>
<tr>
<td>20.</td>
<td>4129 Frankie Pl.
New Iberia, LA</td>
<td>70560</td>
<td></td>
<td>4129 Frankie Pl.
New Ibaria, LA</td>
<td>70560</td>
</tr>
<tr>
<td>21.</td>
<td>2774 Webb St. SW.
Rome, GA</td>
<td>30161-4229</td>
<td></td>
<td>2774 Webb St. SW
Rome, GI</td>
<td>30161-4029</td>
</tr>
<tr>
<td>22.</td>
<td>2693 N. Cherry Ln.
Evansville, IN</td>
<td>47725</td>
<td></td>
<td>2693 N. Cherry Ln.
Evansville, IN</td>
<td>48725</td>
</tr>
<tr>
<td>23.</td>
<td>26949 Pomeroy Dr.
Spring Hill, FL</td>
<td>34609</td>
<td></td>
<td>26949 Pomeroy Dr.
Spring Hill, FL</td>
<td>34609</td>
</tr>
<tr>
<td>24.</td>
<td>3695 S. Mortimer Ct.
Boise, ID</td>
<td>83712-6649</td>
<td></td>
<td>3695 N. Mortimer Ct.
Boise, ID</td>
<td>83712-6649</td>
</tr>
<tr>
<td>25.</td>
<td>9249 Tanglewood St.
Hutchinson, KS</td>
<td>67502</td>
<td></td>
<td>8249 Tanglewood St.
Hutchinson, KS</td>
<td>67502</td>
</tr>
<tr>
<td>26.</td>
<td>1948 Campero Dr.
Riverside, CA</td>
<td>92589</td>
<td></td>
<td>1948 Campero Dr.
Riverside, CA</td>
<td>92509</td>
</tr>
<tr>
<td>27.</td>
<td>289 Bennett Blvd.
Melrose Park, IL</td>
<td>60564</td>
<td></td>
<td>289 Bennett Blvd.
Melrose Park, IL</td>
<td>60564</td>
</tr>
<tr>
<td>28.</td>
<td>7692 Kingston Cir.
Atlanta, GA</td>
<td>30344</td>
<td></td>
<td>7692 Kingston Cir.
Atlanta, GA</td>
<td>30344</td>
</tr>
<tr>
<td>29.</td>
<td>76 W. Malden Pl.
Quincy, MA</td>
<td>02169-4912</td>
<td></td>
<td>76 W. Malden Pl.
Quincy, ME</td>
<td>02169-4912</td>
</tr>
<tr>
<td>30.</td>
<td>6004 Nanroyal Dr.
Saint Louis, MO</td>
<td>63138</td>
<td></td>
<td>6004 Nanroyal Dr.
Saint Louis, MO</td>
<td>63128</td>
</tr>
</table>

Address Checking (Test 2)

A. No Errors	B. Address Only	C. Zip Code Only	D. Both

	Correct List		List to be Checked	
	Address	ZIP Code	Address	ZIP Code
31.	2311 Cabrillo Dr. Sun City, CA	92586	2311 Cabrillo Dr. Sun City, CA	92588
32.	7666 Pennock Pl. Wilmington, DE	19808	7666 Pennock Pl. Wilmington, DE	19806
33.	4921 Osborne Cir. Sarasota, FL	34234	4821 Osborne Cir. Sarasota, FL	34234
34.	3192 N. Jackson Blvd. Albany, OR	97321	3192 N. Jackson Blvd. Albany, OR	97321
35.	461 Marigold Ave. State College, PA	16801-3319	466 Marigold Ave. State College, PA	16804-3319
36.	6669 County Road, SE. Cleveland, TX	77327	6669 County Road, SW. Cleveland, TX	77327
37.	7819 126th St. Bothell, WA	98012	7819 126th St. Bothell, WA	98012
38.	4761 Hodgson Ct. Madison, WI	53717	4761 Hodgson Ct. Madison, WA	53717
39.	16214 S. Alpine Rd. Johnson City, TN	37604	16214 S. Alpine Rd. Johnson City, TN	37604
40.	5649 Winston Dr. Salt Lake City, UT	84128	5648 Winston Dr. Salt Lake City, UT	84128
41.	3694 Stratford Ln. Summerville, SC	29485-4619	3694 Stratford Ln. Summerville, SO	29485-4619
42.	2667 Parasol Rd. Houston, TX	77041	2667 Parasol Rd. Houston, TX	77041
43.	7629 Canvasback St. Chester, VA	23838-4481	7639 Canvasback St. Chester, VA	23838-4481
44.	9249 Minterwood Dr. Harbor, WA	98329-3129	9249 Minterwood Dr. Harbor, WA	98329-3139
45.	7291 Lincoln Ave. Tampa, FL	33609	7291 Lincoln Ave. Tempa, FL	33609

Address Checking (Test 2)

A. No Errors	B. Address Only	C. Zip Code Only	D. Both

	Correct List		List to be Checked	
	Address	*ZIP Code*	*Address*	*ZIP Code*
46.	3684 Eastwich Pl. Lafayette, IN	47905	3694 Eastwich Pl. Lafayette, IN	47906
47.	4676 Homesdale Ct. Baltimore, MD	21206	4876 Homesdale Ct. Baltimore, MD	21206
48.	6266 S. Chastain Dr. Dallas, GA	30132	6266 S. Chastain Dr. Dallas, GA	30132
49.	22144 56th St. SE. Corona, CA	92883-1149	22144 56th St. SW. Corona, CA	92883-1149
50.	2694 Clubhouse Cir. Temecula, CA	92592	2693 Clubhouse Cir. Temecula, CA	92592
51.	769 Westwood Ln. Denver, CO	80219-6100	769 Westwood Ln. Denver, CO	80219-6109
52.	3692 Drinkward Ave. Ames, IA	52405	3698 Drinkward Ave. Ames, IA	52485
53.	869 Dorothy St. Detroit, MI	48211	869 Dorethy St. Detroit, MI	48214
54.	7769 S. Graystone Pl. Mankato, MN	56003	7769 S. Graystone Pl. Mankato, MN	56003
55.	37 Terrace Blvd. Danbury, CT	06810	37 Terrace Blvd. Danbury, CT	06818
56.	4979 323rd Dr. Miami, FL	33196-7669	4979 323rd Dr. Miami, FL	33196-7669
57.	3694 Macon Ln. Baton Rouge, LA	70817	3894 Macon Ln. Baton Rouge, LA	70817
58.	9249 Twining Ave. San Diego, CA	92154	9249 Twening Ave. San Diego, CA	92154
59.	26921 W. Clayton Cir. Caldwell, ID	83815-4669	26921 W. Clayton Cir. Caldwell, ID	83815-4668
60.	P.O. Box 4927 Davenport, IA	52806	P.O. Box 4928 Davenport, IA	52806

END

Address Checking (Test 3)

A. No Errors	B. Address Only	C. Zip Code Only	D. Both

	Correct List		List to be Checked	
	Address	**ZIP Code**	**Address**	**ZIP Code**
1.	6792 Burmont St. Utica, NY	13502	6792 Burmont St. Utica, NY	13503
2	269 N. Akcan Cir. Canton, OH	44720	269 N. Akcan Cir. Canton, OH	44720
3.	7662 Dockery Rd. Sevierville, TN	37876-2944	7662 Dockery Rd. Seviarville, TN	37876-2944
4.	8728 Garfield NW. Kennewick, WA	99336	8728 Garfield NE. Kennewick, WA	99336
5.	469 Nelson Pl. Charlottesville, VA	22902	469 Nelson Pl. Charlottesville, VA	22902
6.	2294 Commerce Dr. Rochester, NY	14623-1299	1294 Commerce Dr. Rochester, NY	14623-1299
7.	316 Tarpon Lane Wilmington, NC	28409	316 Tarpon Lane Wilmington, NC	28408
8.	9624 Ueberroth St. N. Altoona, PA	18103	9626 Ueberroth St. N. Altoona, PA	18103
9.	7694 Shadowood Ave. Bryan, TX	77803-6114	7694 Shadowood Ave. Bryam, TX	77803-6114
10.	P.O. Box 1692 Chesapeake, VA	23321	P.O. Box 1692 Chesapeake, VA	23321
11.	4927 Regatta Terrace Fort Mill, SC	29708	4927 Regatta Terrace Fort Mill, SE	29708
12.	5624 Meadowbriar Rd. Greensboro, NC	27410	5624 Meadowbriar Rd. Grensboro, NC	27410
13.	6792 Eastlawn St. Cleveland, OH	44128-7699	6792 Eastlawn St. Cleveland, OH	44128-7698
14.	4694 Desmond Dr. San Francisco, CA	94134	4694 Desmond Dr. San Francisco, CO	94134
15.	2647 Knollcrest Pl. Longwood, FL	32779	2647 Knolcrest Pl. Longwood, FL	32789

Address Checking (Test 3)

A. No Errors	B. Address Only	C. Zip Code Only	D. Both

	Correct List			List to be Checked	
	Address	*ZIP Code*		*Address*	*ZIP Code*
16.	1469 S. Beacon Road Covington, KY	41011-9647		1469 S. Beacon Road Covington, KY	41011-9647
17.	3927 Nightshade Pl. Rockville, MD	20852		3927 Nightshade Dr. Rockville, MD	20852
18.	7600 Silverbrook St. Florissant, MO	63033-4627		7600 Silverbrook St. Florissant, MO	63033-4628
19.	3128 Darby Ct. Woodland, CA	95776		3128 Darby Ct. Woodland, CA	95876
20.	5694 Foothill Dr. E. Prescott, AZ	86303		6694 Foothill Dr. E. Prescott, AZ	86308
21.	8294 E. Yaupon Ave. Jupiter, FL	32246		8294 E. Yaupon Ave. Jupiter, FL	32246
22.	1947 Donald Rd. Nampa, ID	83651-4112		1947 Donald Rd. Nampe, ID	83651-4112
23.	638 N. Walton Street Palatine, IL	60467		638 Walton Street Palatine, IL	60467
24.	P.O. Box 6194 Owensboro, KY	42301		P.O.Box 6194 Owensboro, KY	42301
25.	9645 Hawkweed Ln. Pocatello, ID	83204-4911		9645 Hawkwood Ln. Pocatello, ID	83205-4911
26.	12947 Blaino St. Peoria, ID	61605		12947 Blaine St. Peoria, ID	61605
27.	7691 Marshall Ct. Detroit, MI	48217		7691 Marshall Ct. Detroit, MI	48218
28.	4912 123rd Ave. W. Valdosta, GA	31794-6619		4912 123rd Ave. W. Valdosta, GA	31794-6619
29.	194 Portola Lane. Tustin, CA	92780		194 Portola Lane. Tusten, CA	92780
30.	4001 Olympus Dr. Littleton, CO	80124		4004 Olympus Dr. Littleton, CO	80124

Address Checking (Test 3)

A. No Errors	B. Address Only	C. Zip Code Only	D. Both

	Correct List		List to be Checked	
	Address	ZIP Code	Address	ZIP Code
31.	8198 Bobolink Dr. Cocoa, FL	32539	7198 Bobolink Dr. Cocoa, FL	32589
32.	169 S. Madison Ln. Muncie, IN	47305	169 S. Madison Ln. Muncie, IN	47305
33.	426 Potomac Cir. Rochester, MI	48306-1611	426 Pitomac Cir. Rochester, MI	48306-1611
34.	6894 Crstal Mark Pl. Dallas, GA	30721	6894 Crstal Mark Pl. Dallas, GA	30722
35.	389 Bishop Ct. Broomfield, CO	80104	369 Bishop Ct. Broomfield, CO	80104
36.	769 Oxford Ave. W. Kansas City, KS	66049	769 Oxford Ave. W. Kansas City, KS	66049
37.	9249 Connell Terrace Brockton, MA	02302	9249 Connell Terrace Brockton, MI	02302
38.	497 Redondo Way San Diego, CA	92107	497 Redondo Way San Diego, CA	92108
39.	26314 Centerbury Dr. S. Cincinnati, OH	45246-1469	26314 Centerbury Dr. S. Cincinnati, OH	45246-1489
40.	469 Elkridge Ln. York, PA	17404	469 Elkridge Ln. York, PA	17404
41.	8624 N. Blue Goose Rd. Austin, TX	78754	8634 N. Blue Goose Rd. Austin, TX	78754
42.	489 S. 35th St. Renton, WA	98055-4611	489 S. 35th St. Renton, WA	98055-4611
43.	6247 Seneca Dr. Absecon, NJ	08205	6248 Seneca Dr. Absecon, NJ	08205
44.	427 Central Ct. Reno, NV	89434	427 Centrol Ct. Reno, NV	89436
45.	76 Lamplight Pl. Edmond, OK	73034-1924	76 Lamplight Dr. Edmond, OK	73034-1934

Address Checking (Test 3)

A. No Errors	B. Address Only	C. Zip Code Only	D. Both

	Correct List		List to be Checked	
	Address	**ZIP Code**	**Address**	**ZIP Code**
46.	4619 Somerset Ln. Sevierville, TN	37862	4619 Somerset Ln. Sevierville, TN	37862
47.	762 66th St. S. Fargo, ND	58104	862 66th St. S. Fargo, ND	58104
48.	2832 Delamere St. Rock Hill, SC	29732	2832 Delamile, St. Rock Hill, SC	29732
49.	381 Tower Ave. Charleston, WV	25306-7611	381 Tower Ave. Charleston, WV	25307-7611
50.	1694 Debeers Dr. Sandy, UT	84093	1694 Debeers Dr. Sandy, UT	84093
51.	4934 W. Colonial Dr. Watertown, WI	53098	4934 W. Colonal Dr. Watertown, WI	53098
52.	P.O. Box 893 Hampton, VA	23666	P.O. Box 883 Hampton, VA	23666
53.	4936 S. Meader Way Beaverton, OR	97008-3611	4936 S. Meader Way Beaverton, OK	97008-3611
54.	764 Duxbury Dr. Dallas, TX	75218	764 Daxbury Dr. Dallas, TX	75118
55.	4291 Petersen Pl. Cheyenne, WY	82009	4291 Petersen Pl. Cheyenne, WY	82009
56.	269 Junction Street Warwick, RI	02889	269 Junction Street Warwick, RI	02887
57.	8691 Sunshine Ct. Canton, OH	44708-2647	8691 Sunshine Ct. Canton, OH	44708-2648
58.	279 79th Ave. E. Flushing, NY	11366	279 78th Ave. E. Flushing, NY	11366
59.	6492 Sedona Ct. Hobbs, NM	87401	6492 Sedona Ct. Hobbs, NM	87401
60.	5414 Vanmar Dr. Lexington, NC	27295	5414 Vanmar Dr. Lexington, NC	27295

END

Address Checking (Test 4)

A. No Errors	B. Address Only	C. Zip Code Only	D. Both

	Correct List			List to be Checked	
	Address	ZIP Code		Address	ZIP Code
1.	8629 Tarrimore Cir. Middletown, OH	45044		8629 Terrimore Cir. Middletown, OH	45044
2	369 Hearthstone Ln. Spartanburg, SC	29316-4769		369 Hearthstone Ln. Spartanburg, SC	29316-4869
3.	7892 Woolsey St. Santa Cruz, CA	91390		7692 Woolsey St. Santa Cruz, CA	91390
4.	2769 Plumosa Ave. Lehigh Acres, FL	33936		2769 Plumosa Ave. Lehigh Acres, FL	33936
5.	1927 Jericho Rd. Houma, LA	70401		1928 Jericho Rd. Houma, LA	70402
6.	7927 3rd Ave. SE. Flint, MI	48503		7927 3rd Ave. SW. Flint, MI	48530
7.	38294 N. Monterico Rd. Downey, CA	92240-7995		38294 N. Monterico Rd. Downey, CA	82240-7995
8.	276 Bryant Rd. E. Monroe, GA	30655		276 Bryant Rd. E. Monroe, GA	30655
9.	7692 Fernlake Lane Mishawaka, IN	46544		7692 Fernlake Lane Mishawaka, EN	46544
10.	46278 S. Roadway St. Jackson, MS	39213		46278 S. Roadway St. Jackson, MS	39213
11.	76 Tangly Ct. Carbondale, IL	60440		76 Tangly Ct. Carbondale, IL	50440
12.	P.O. Box 2694 Newark, DE	19713-4611		P.O. Box 3694 Newark, DE	19713-4211
13.	2697 Robinson Rd. Pine Bluff, AR	71603		3697 Robinson Rd. Pine Bluff, AR	71603
14.	927 N. Snowden Ave. Long Beach, CA	90815		927 N. Snowden Ave. Long Beach, CA	90815
15.	5492 Hawthorne Terrace Meriden, CT	06450		5492 Hawthorn Terrace Meriden, CT	06450

Address Checking (Test 4)

A. No Errors	B. Address Only	C. Zip Code Only	D. Both

	Correct List		List to be Checked	
	Address	ZIP Code	Address	ZIP Code
16.	26475 143rd Dr. S. Miami, FL	33186	26475 143rd Dr. Miami, FL	33186
17.	37 Jessica Ave. Idaho Falls, ID	83406	38 Jessica Ave. Idaho Falls, ID	82406
18.	886 Appleton Ln. Louisville, KY	40216-6411	886 Appleton Ln. Louisville, KY	40216-7411
19.	7829 N. Comanche St. Mobile, AL	36611	7829 N. Comanche St. Mobile, AL	36611
20.	5791 Pinewood Ln. Orange, CA	91762	5791 Pinewood Ln. Orange, CA	91762
21.	9648 Dexter Dr. Washington, DC	20020	8648 Dexter Dr. Washington, DC	20020
22.	56479 S. 97th Ln. Minneapolis, MN	55420	56479 S. 97th Ln. Mineapolis, MN	55446
23.	478 Hogle St. Waterloo, IA	50703	478 Hogle St. Waterloo, IA	58703
24.	P.O. Box 9298 Sebring, FL	33875	P.O.Box 9298 Sebring, FL	33875
25.	3892 Thompson Pl. Indianapolis, IN	46227-1948	3892 Thompson Pl. Indianapolis, IN	46227-1947
26.	472 W. Regent St. Kalamazoo, MI	49001	472 W. Regen St. Kalamazoo, MI	49001
27.	36914 171st Dr. S. Little Neck, NY	11432	36914 171st Dr. S. Little Neck, NY	11432
28.	94 Glenside Ln. Tulsa, OK	74131-6644	94 Glenside Ln. Tulsa, OK	84131-6644
29.	4692 Crescent Dr. Leander, TX	75077	4692 Crescent Dr. Leand, TX	75077
30.	72958 85th St. Milwaukee, WI	53214	73058 85th St. Milwaukee, WI	53114

Address Checking (Test 4)

A. No Errors	B. Address Only	C. Zip Code Only	D. Both

	Correct List		List to be Checked	
	Address	**ZIP Code**	**Address**	**ZIP Code**
31.	7126 S. Firebrand Pl. Hayward, CA	94541	7126 S. Fireband Pl. Hayward, CA	94641
32.	641 Brummel St. Springfield, IL	60076	641 Brummel St. Springfield, IL	60076
33.	2647 Carloway Road Bel Air, MD	21015-4411	2647 Carlowy Road Bel Air, MD	21015-4411
34.	16247 22nd Ave. N. Nampa, ID	83651	16247 22nd Ave. N. Nampa, ID	83654
35.	461 Tishman Terrace Palm Bay, FL	32909	461 Tishman Terrace Palm Bay, FL	32908
36.	4927 N. Bensley Ave. Chicago, IL	60617	4927 N. Bensley Ave. Chicago, IN	60617
37.	4761 Moonraker Dr. Slidell, LA	70458	4761 Moonraker Dr. Slidell, LA	60458
38.	26 59th Ln. Glendale, AZ	85301-6619	26 59th Ln. Glendale, AZ	85301-6619
39.	8694 Locust Hill Dr. Gulfport, MS	39503	8694 Locusty Hill Dr. Gulfport, MS	39503
40.	P.O. Box 2369 Lithonia, GA	30038	P.O. Box 2369 Lithonea, GA	30038
41.	9413 Roland Dr. Cranston, RI	02920-7611	9418 Roland Dr. Cranston, RI	02928-7611
42.	529 E. 92nd St. Brooklyn, NY	11209	529 E. 92nd St. Brooklyn, NY	11209
43.	6229 Cressman Rd. Allentown, PA	18104	6229 Cressman Rd. Allentown, PA	28104
44.	38249 Durham Dr. Sumter, SC	29170	38249 Durham Dr. Sumter, SC	29170
45.	769 Larkspur Ave. Lebanon, TN	37090	769 Larkspun Ave. Lebanon, TN	37090

Address Checking (Test 4)

A. No Errors	B. Address Only	C. Zip Code Only	D. Both

	Correct List		List to be Checked	
	Address	ZIP Code	Address	ZIP Code
46.	124 Country Road Garland, TX	78628-1416	126 Country Road Garland, TX	78628-2416
47.	8412 West Ave. Norfolk, VA	23504	8412 West Ave. Norfolk, VA	33504
48.	261 W. 12nd Ave. Portland, OR	97214	261 W. 12nd Ave. Portland, OR	97214
49.	4627 Borden Ave. Spokane, WA	99224	4627 Borden Ave. Spekane, WA	99224
50.	8637 Willow Hill Ln. Sandy, UT	84092	8637 Willow Hill Ln. Sandy, UT	84093
51.	762 8th St. Los Angeles, CA	90019-1144	762 8th St. Los Angeles, CA	90018-1144
52.	29481 Oak Tree Ct. Deland, FL	32724	29481 Oak Tree Ct. Deland, FL	32724
53.	4691 Spinnaker Ln. New Orleans, LA	70124	5691 Spinnaker Ln. New Orleans, LA	70124
54.	76 Almont Ave. Weymouth, MA	01604	76 Almont Dr. Weymouth, MA	01604
55.	8694 Owens Dr. SE. Austell, GA	30106-2611	8694 Owens Dr. SE. Austall, GA	30108-2611
56.	9214 Marsteller St. Warsaw, IN	47906	9214 Marsteller St. Warsaw, IN	47906
57.	46924 Shanklin Way Bakersfield, CA	93312	46924 Shanklin Way Bakersfield, CA	93412
58.	P.O.Box 8624 Fairfield, CT	06824	P.O. Box 8624 Fairfield, CO	06824
59.	7894 SE. Hurley Ln. London, KY	40744-6214	7894 SW. Hurley Ln. London, KY	40744-6224
60.	269 Golden Hook Columbia, MD	21044	269 Golden Hook Columbia, MD	21044

END

Address Checking (Test 5)

A. No Errors	B. Address Only	C. Zip Code Only	D. Both

	Correct List		List to be Checked	
	Address	ZIP Code	Address	ZIP Code
1.	783 Maple Ave. West Chester, PA	19380	793 Maple Ave. West Chester, PA	19380
2	2948 N. Ridgewood St. Rapid City, SD	57702-6119	2948 N. Ridgewood St. Rapid City, SD	57702-6119
3.	6148 King Henry Pl. Memphis. TN	38118	6149 King Henry Pl. Memphis. TN	38129
4.	469 Breese Way Appleton, WI	54913	469 Breese Way Appleton, WI	54914
5.	287 Sunnyside St. Salem, OR	97302-4611	387 Sunnyside St. Salem, OR	97302-4611
6.	36214 Cambria Blvd. Dallas, TX	75214	36214 Cambria Blvd. Dallas, TX	75214
7.	694 E. Cooper Dr. Aiken, SC	29803-7619	694 W. Cooper Dr. Aiken, SC	29803-7618
8.	8694 Jenny Dr. Danville, VA	24541	8694 Jenny Dr. Danville, VA	24541
9.	83 N. Zocalo Cir. Torrance, CA	91360	83 N. Jocalo Cir. Torrance, CA	91360
10.	769 Loretta Dr. Leesville, LA	70448-9114	769 Loretta Dr. Leesville, LA	70449-9114
11.	3927 Kenneth St. Mobile, AL	36607	3927 Kenneth St. Mobile, AL	36607
12.	2194 Andora Cir. W. Orange, CA	95966	2194 Andora Cir. W. Olange, CA	95966
13.	5931 Calvin Ave. Winter Park, FL	33542	5932 Calvin Ave. Winter Park, FL	33542
14.	278 Buena Vista Pl. Louisville, KY	40218-1419	278 Buene Vista Pl. Louisville, KY	40218-1418
15.	662 N. 54th St. Rochester, MN	55904	662 N. 54th St. Rochester, MN	55904

Address Checking (Test 5)

A. No Errors	B. Address Only	C. Zip Code Only	D. Both

	Correct List		**List to be Checked**	
	Address	ZIP Code	Address	ZIP Code
16.	1692 Moselle Ct SE. Las Vegas, NV	89144	1692 Moselle Ct SW. Las Vegas, NV	89244
17.	9429 Florence Dr. Bellevue, NE	68147-5919	9429 Florence Dr. Bellevue, NE	68147-6919
18.	P.O.Box 4254 Lancaster, PA	17602	P.O.Box 4254 Lencaster, PA	17602
19.	4248 E. Burgess Rd. Hampton, VA	22801	4248 E. Burgess Rd. Hampton, VA	22801
20.	238 Hickory Lane Willis, TX	77378-2694	238 Hickory Lane Willis, TX	77378-3694
21.	6824 6th St. W. Akron, OH	44314-1791	6824 8th St. W. Akron, OH	44314-1891
22.	3694 Fremont Ave. Buffalo, NY	14226	3694 Fremont Ave. Buffalo, NY	14226
23.	7692 Cocamo St. Palm Springs, CA	92264	6692 Cocamo St. Palm Springs, CA	92264
24.	587 Starblaza Ct. Lake Worth, FL	33463	587 Starblaza Ct. Lake Worth, FL	33463
25.	1294 Pierce Pl. Brighton, MI	48116	1294 Pierce Pl. Brighton, MA	48116
26.	58791 N. Coachman Blvd Lenexa, KS	66502-4191	58791 N. Coachman Blvd Lenexa, KS	67502-4191
27.	269 Reynolds Dr. Rockford, IL	61103	269 Reynolds Dr. Rockford, IL	61103
28.	7694 Terrapin Cir. Huntsville, AL	35806	7694 Terrapin Ct. Huntsville, AL	35806
29.	914 W. 15th Ave. Dubuque, IA	52001-5119	914 W. 15th Ave. Duboque, IA	52001-5191
30.	P.O.Box 24611 Casper, WY	82001	P.O.Box 24612 Casper, WY	82010

Address Checking (Test 5)

A. No Errors	B. Address Only	C. Zip Code Only	D. Both

	Correct List			List to be Checked	
	Address	ZIP Code		Address	ZIP Code
31.	62489 S. Candlewyck Dr. Plano, TX	75024		62489 S. Candlewyck Dr. Plano, TX	75024
32.	311 Greenbriar Pl. Anderson, SC	29625		311 Grenbriar Pl. Anderson, SC	29625
33.	2641 Jones Bridge Rd. Greeneville, TN	37743		2641 Jones Bridge Rd. Greeneville, TN	37843
34.	3644 Melinda Dr. Lynchburg, VA	24502		8644 Melinda Dr. Lynchburg, VA	24502
35.	724 Barnard Ave. N. Madison, WI	53221		724 Barnard Ave. S. Madison, WI	53226
36.	4627 Sassafras St. Warren, OH	44485-6619		4627 Sassafras St. Warren, OH	44485-6619
37.	1247 S. Wexmouth Ave. Abingdon, VA	24211		1242 S. Wexmouth Ave. Abingdon, VA	24211
38.	5869 Pringle Way Reno, NV	89502-4129		5869 Pringle Way Reno, NV	89502-5129
39.	26419 N. 4th St. Buena Park, CA	90621		26419 S. 4th St. Buena Park, CA	90621
40.	86 Khakum Pl. Greenwich, CT	06831-5114		86 Khakum Ave. Greenwich, CT	06831-5114
41.	479 NE. Belmont Ave. Newark, DE	19804		479 NW. Belmont Ave. Newark, DE	29804
42.	1469 Harbor Blvd. Alene, ID	83814		1489 Harbor Blvd. Alene, ID	84814
43.	627 Annunciation Place Kenner, LA	70508		627 Annunciation Place Kenner, LA	70508
44.	549 Kentfield Rd. Lansing, MI	48911-5119		549 Kantfield Rd. Lansing, MI	48911-5119
45.	P.O.Box 21689 Cumming, GA	30132		P.O.Box 21689 Cumming, GA	30133

Address Checking (Test 5)

A. No Errors	B. Address Only	C. Zip Code Only	D. Both

	Correct List		List to be Checked	
	Address	ZIP Code	Address	ZIP Code
46.	469 17th St. Santa Ana, CA	92703	469 17th St. Santa Ana, CA	92703
47.	9426 Newgate Ave. Holiday, FL	34691-1144	9426 Newgate Ave. Holiday, FL	34691-1144
48.	564 Fisher Road Jan Jose, CA	95127	564 Fisher Road Jan Jose, CO	95127
49.	7694 Turner St. Bridgeport, CT	06606	7694 Turner St. Bridgepart, CT	06606
50.	8611 28th Ave. S. Marion, IN	47904-6191	8611 28th Ave. S. Marion, IN	47904-6291
51.	28791 N. Winston Ave. Tulsa, OK	74112	28791 S. Winston Ave. Tulsa, OK	74113
52.	469 Cochise Pl. Amarillo, TX	79118	469 Cochise Pl. Amarillo, TX	79118
53.	6194 Roseberg Rd. Madison, WI	53719	6294 Roseberg Rd. Madison, WI	53719
54.	1694 S. Pinecrest Cir. Greer, SC	29651-3819	1694 S. Pinecrest Dr. Greer, SC	29652-3819
55.	312 Summer St. Asheville, NC	28804	312 Summon St. Asheville, NC	28804
56.	1208 239th St. Bronx, NY	10470	1208 239th St. Bronx, NY	10470
57.	4691 Debra Dr. Aberdeen, SD	57702-4190	4691 Debra Dr. Aberden, SD	57702-4190
58.	49 W. Marketview St. Champaign, IL	61820	49 W. Marketview St. Champaign, IL	61920
59.	P.O.Box 6050 Chicopee, MA	01013	P.O.Box 6050 Chicopee, MA	01012
60.	56419 Bogota Ct. Albany, GA	31707	56419 Bogita Ct. Albany, GA	31707

END

Address Checking (Test 6)

A. No Errors	B. Address Only	C. Zip Code Only	D. Both

	Correct List		List to be Checked	
	Address	**ZIP Code**	**Address**	**ZIP Code**
1.	2769 Vanbrook Ln. Springdale, AR	72802	2769 Venbrook Ln. Springdale, AR	72802
2	48 Goodland Ct. Modesto, CA	95357-6149	48 Goodland Ct. Modesto, CA	95357-6159
3.	7694 Stallone Rd. Tampa, FL	33605	7594 Stallone Rd. Tampa, FL	33606
4.	46914 W. Overton St. Newport, KY	41071	46914 W. Overten St. Newport, KY	41071
5.	3692 Powell Blvd. Evansville, IN	47713	3692 Powell Blvd. Evansville, IN	47713
6.	962 Riverwest Ave. Augusta, GA	30907-5113	962 Riverwest Ave. Augusta, GA	30907-6113
7.	P.O.Box 8292 Shreveport, LA	71109	P.O.Box 8293 Shreveport, LA	71109
8.	2694 75th Rd. N. Saint Louis, MO	64507	2694 75th Rd. S. Saint Louis, MO	64507
9.	38 Kellogg St. Wichita, KS	67209-4041	38 Kellogg St. Wichita, KS	67209-4041
10.	424 Connemara Ct. Gastonia, NC	28054	424 Connemara Ct. Gastonia, NC	28954
11.	1769 N. 68th Ave. Philadelphia, PA	19126	1769 N. 68th Ave. Philadelphia, PA	19126
12.	4791 Indianola Ct. Chesapeake, VA	23323-2611	4791 Imdianola Ct. Chesapeake, VA	23323-3611
13.	6781 Baroma Dr. SW. Columbus, OH	43228	6781 Baroma Dr. SE. Columbus, OH	43228
14.	76911 Pleasant Ct. Midland, TX	79703	76911 Pleasant Ct. Midland, TX	79803
15.	3691 Zara Blvd. Glendora, CA	91741	4691 Zara Blvd. Glendora, CA	91741

Address Checking (Test 6)

A. No Errors	B. Address Only	C. Zip Code Only	D. Both

	Correct List		List to be Checked	
	Address	ZIP Code	Address	ZIP Code
16.	26 Ridgecrest Cir. Cairo, GA	39828	26 Ridgecrest Cir. Cairo, GA	39828
17.	9247 Normandie Ave. Aurora, IL	60506-8149	9247 Normandie Ave. Aurora, IL	60506-8149
18.	P.O.Box 7692 Anchorage, AK	99516	P.O.Box 7692 Anchorage, AK	99527
19.	567 8th St. W. Stamford, CT	06905	567 8th St. W. Stamford, CT	09605
20.	8694 Phelon Lane Saginaw, MI	48601-2647	8694 Phelon Ln. Saginaw, MI	48601-2647
21.	694 Biltmore Dr. Miami, FL	33146	694 Beltmore Dr. Miami, FL	32146
22.	2694 N. Raymond Blvd. Matthews, NC	28358	2694 N. Raymond Blvd. Matthews, NC	28358
23.	766 Allancou St. Antioch, TN	37409	766 Allancou St. Antich, TN	37409
24.	3814 Davidson Place Manassas, VA	20109-3317	3914 Davidson Place Manassas, VA	20109-3317
25.	52469 Burrline Rd. Racine, WI	53402	52469 Burrline Dr. Racine, WI	53420
26.	1294 Lakeshore St. N. Mesquite, TX	75149	1294 Lakeshore St. N. Mesquite, TX	75149
27.	8891 Chelsea Dr. Chickasha, OK	73013	8891 Chelsea Dr. Chickasha, OK	83013
28.	642 40th St. Butler, PA	16001-4914	642 48th St. Butler, PA	16001-4914
29.	2694 Progress Ct. Providence, RI	02860	2694 Progress Ct. Providence, RI	03860
30.	36249 Watson Rd. Beaufort, SC	29624	36359 Watson Rd. Beaufort, SC	29624

Address Checking (Test 6)

A. No Errors	B. Address Only	C. Zip Code Only	D. Both

	Correct List			List to be Checked	
	Address	ZIP Code		Address	ZIP Code
31.	9274 Ashmore Ave. Trenton, NJ	08618		9274 Ashmire Ave. Trenton, NJ	18618
32.	462 345th Ave. S. Hillsboro, OR	97123-3619		462 345th Ave. S. Hillsboro, OR	97123-3719
33.	8692 Warbler Rd. Loveland, CO	80537		8692 Warbler Rd. Loveland, CO	80537
34.	762 Norman Blvd. Valdosta, GA	31601		763 Norman Blvd. Valdosta, GA	31601
35.	52941 Bushnell Lane Shreveport, LA	71118-6119		52941 Bushnell Lane Shreveport, LA	71118-6119
36.	P.O. Box 3624 Springfield, MO	65809		P.O. Box 3624 Springfield, MI	65809
37.	6934 Mallory Dr. SW. Fontana, CA	92335		6934 Mallory Dr. SE. Fontana, CA	92346
38.	129 Albany Ave. Hamden, CT	06120-4129		129 Albano Ave. Hamden, CT	06120-3529
39.	3429 Wrenfield St. Oviedo, FL	32765		3429 Wrenfield Ln. Oviedo, FL	32765
40.	7694 Darrow Pl. Elgin, IL	60202		7694 Darrow Pl. Elgin, IL	60202
41.	264 Saranac Ln. Louisville, KY	40214		264 Saranac Ln. Louisville, KY	40224
42.	8694 Carradale Ct. Orlando, FL	32809-1191		9694 Carradale Ct. Orlando, FL	32809-1191
43.	314 Grandview Pl. Brandon, MS	39047		314 Grandview Dr. Brandon, MS	39047
44.	5697 Kaamahu St. S. Honolulu, HI	96822		5697 Kaamahu St. S. Honolulu, HI	96822
45.	469 Hooper Dr. West Covina, CA	91791		569 Hooper Dr. West Covina, CA	91891

Address Checking (Test 6)

A. No Errors	B. Address Only	C. Zip Code Only	D. Both

	Correct List		List to be Checked	
	Address	ZIP Code	Address	ZIP Code
46.	38294 N. Coachlite Ct. Belleville, IL	62226	38294 N. Coachlisy Ct. Belleville, IL	62236
47.	7692 Seaman Ave. New York, NY	10034	7692 Seaman Ave. New York, NY	10064
48.	P.O. Box 782 Denton, TX	76208	P.O. Box 782 Denton, TX	76208
49.	624 Pennwyn Terrace Reading, PA	19606-4911	624 Pennwyn Terrace Reeding, PA	19606-4911
50.	9289 Chadwick Cir. S. Roanake, VA	24012	9289 Chadwick Ct. S. Roanake, VA	24013
51.	268 Burton Dr. Crestview. FL	32536-8611	268 Burton Dr. Crestview. GA	32536-9611
52.	784 Nordan Ln. Montgomery, AL	36106	784 Nerdan Ln. Montgomery, AL	36106
53.	39 15th St. N. Urbana, IL	62703	39 15th St. N. Urbana, IL	62703
54.	4624 Valhalla Blvd. Duluth, MN	55811	4624 Valhalla Blvd. Duluth, MN	55814
55.	629 Delevan Dr. Herndon, VA	20171-3694	628 Delevan Dr. Herndon, VA	20171-3694
56.	26411 W. Stonegate Ave. Greensboro, NC	27406	26411 E. Stonegate Ave. Greensboro, NC	28406
57.	5892 Rhonda Way Sioux Falls, SD	57108	5892 Rhonda Way Sioux Falls, SD	57108
58.	7291 90th St. Racine, WI	53403-4611	7291 98th St. Racine, WI	53403-5611
59.	361 Hortensia Ln. Laredo, TX	78046	361 Hortensia Ln. Laredo, TX	78146
60.	4692 Ogden Rd. Newark, NJ	07104	4692 Ogden Rd. Neward, NJ	07104

END

Address Checking (Test 7)

A. No Errors	B. Address Only	C. Zip Code Only	D. Both

	Correct List		List to be Checked	
	Address	ZIP Code	Address	ZIP Code
1.	4692 Charping St. Victoria, TX	76705	4692 Chirping St. Victoria, TX	76705
2	762 Francis Dr. S. Waukesha, WI	53188	762 Francis Dr. S. Waukesha, WI	54288
3.	8624 Walford Road Cleveland, OH	44128-3612	8624 Walford Road Clevaland, OH	44128-4612
4.	3248 Tropical Ave. Hollywood, FL	33021	3250 Tropical Ave. Hollywood, FL	33021
5.	12946 31st Ave. N. Newman, GA	31788	12946 31st Ave. N. Newman, GA	31788
6.	564 Koppers St. Alexandria, LA	71302-6219	564 Koppers Ln. Alexandria, LA	71302-6219
7.	P.O.Box 41297 Midland, MI	48640	P.O.Box 41286 Midland, MI	48640
8.	27 W. Siboney Terrace Hartford, CT	06811	27 W. Siboney Terrace Hartford, CT	27811
9.	769 N. Ceremony Place Tucson, AZ	85743-5619	869 N. Ceremony Place Tucson, AZ	85743-6719
10.	9211 Casson Dr. Yorba Linda, CA	92886	9211 Casson Dr. Yorba Linda, CA	92886
11.	4294 E. 107th St. Bolingbrook, IL	60440	4294 E. 107th St. Bolingbrook, IL	60440
12.	761 Franklin Ave. Slidell, LA	70663	761 Franklen Ave. Slidell, LA	70663
13.	63119 Alissa Ln. Saint Paul, MN	55119-2661	64219 Alissa Ln. Saint Paul, MN	65119-2661
14.	5971 Hillcrest Pkwy Wetumpka, AL	36092	5917 Hillcrest Pkwy Wetumpka, AL	86092
15.	869 S. Riverton Way Stockton, CA	95219	869 S. Riverton Way Stockton, CA	95281

Address Checking (Test 7)

A. No Errors	B. Address Only	C. Zip Code Only	D. Both

	Correct List			List to be Checked	
	Address	ZIP Code		Address	ZIP Code
16.	2647 Shephan Ct. Tifton, GA	31793		2647 Shephan Ct. Tifton, GA	31793
17.	369 W. 64th Pkwy Golden, CO	80403		369 W. 64th Pkwy Golden, CA	80403
18.	723 Glenora Ct. Kokomo, IN	46902		723 Glenora Ct. Kokomo, IN	46902
19.	6248 Whitaker Cir. N. Meridian, MS	39301-9129		6248 Whitaker Cir. N. Meridean, MS	39301-9129
20.	914 Lynbrook Place Concord, CA	94521		914 Lynbrook Place Concord, CA	94530
21.	469 Hightower Blvd. Pittsburgh, PA	15205		469 Hightower Blvd. Pittsbuggh, PA	26205
22.	8624 Cayuga Ct. Killeen, TX	76544-7619		8624 Cayuga Ct. Killeen, TX	76544-7619
23.	9702 Hindman Pl. Cleveland, TN	37312		9720 Hindman Pl. Cleveland, TN	37312
24.	7010 78th Ave. W. Yakima, WA	98908		7010 78th Ave. W. Yakima, WA	99808
25.	629 Ovencou St. Rochester, NY	14611-2644		629 Ovancou St. Rochester, NY	14611-2644
26.	P.O.Box 869 Clanton, AL	35068		P.O.Box 869 Clanton, AL	35068
27.	5120 W. Cypress Ave. Burbank, CA	91502		5102 W. Cypress Ave. Burbank, CA	92502
28.	2911 Westover Dr. SW. Dover, DE	19904-3912		2911 Westover Dr. SE. Dover, DE	19904-3913
29.	3694 Claude Rd. Orange Park, FL	32003		3694 Claude Rd. Orange Park, FL	31003
30.	148 W, Rosemont Dr. Paducah, KY	42001		148 E, Rosemont Dr. Paducah, KY	42002

Address Checking (Test 7)

A. No Errors	B. Address Only	C. Zip Code Only	D. Both

	Correct List		List to be Checked	
	Address	**ZIP Code**	**Address**	**ZIP Code**
31.	7611 Janetle Ave. Lucie, FL	34953	7611 Janetle Ave. Lucie, FL	34935
32.	4021 Thallas St. Davenport, IA	51503	4021 Thallas St. Davenport, IA	51503
33.	864 159th St. E. Wichita, KS	67230	864 150th St. E. Wichita, KS	67230
34.	3621 Silvercreek Ln. Ballwin, MO	63011-7611	3621 Silvercreek Pl. Ballwin, MO	63011-8611
35.	5879 Center Road Auburn, ME	04101	5879 Center Road Auburn, MD	04110
36.	7024 N. Gannon Ave. Edmond, OK	73703	7024 N. Aanon Ave. Edmond, OK	73703
37.	43 Layside Dr. Winchester, VA	22602-3210	43 Layside Dr. Winchester, VA	22602-3210
38.	61138 Beecham Place Cordova, TN	38016	61138 Beecham Place Cordova, TN	38037
39.	4629 Stewart St. York, PA	17404-5910	4692 Stewart St. York, PA	17404-5910
40.	P.O.Box 724823 Charlotte, NC	28277	P.O.Box 728423 Charlotte, NC	28267
41.	3112 White Oak Dr. Rogers, AR	72758	3112 White Oak Dr. Rogers, AR	72758
42.	9649 E. Seagoing St. Palm Coast, FL	32164-6144	9649 W. Seagoing St. Palm Coast, FL	32264-6144
43.	562 Mary Dr. SW. Flint, MI	48507	562 Mary Dr. SE. Flint, MI	48507
44.	2694 Larose Terrace Lagrange, GA	30240	2694 Larose Terrace Lagrange, GA	30240
45.	7498 Cardinal Way Anderson, IN	46011-8612	7489 Cardinal Way Anderson, IN	46012-8612

Address Checking (Test 7)

A. No Errors	B. Address Only	C. Zip Code Only	D. Both

Correct List

	Address	ZIP Code
46.	624 Trenton Ct. N. Fresno, CA	94538
47.	124 40th Ave. Saint Cloud, MN	55906
48.	4621 Gumleaf Dr. Apex, NC	27539
49.	3129 Royalpine St. Dallas, TX	75238-6914
50.	862 N. Boulder Ave. Huntington, WV	26508
51.	5829 Lost Bridge Pl. Lawton, OK	73501
52.	26141 25th St. E. Parkersburg, WV	26101-7614
53.	3691 Pescara Ct. West Jordan, UT	84084
54.	914 Rosemont Rd. Virginia Beach, VA	23453
55.	8190 Nassau St. Nashville, TN	37208-5120
56.	P.O.Box 2611 Aiken, SC	29801
57.	789 S. Kestrel Ct. Bremerton, WA	98312
58.	4624 Blount Rd. Killeen, TX	76544-3140
59.	26437 Treadwell Dr. Bronx, NY	13905
60.	5834 Hancock St. N. Hartford, CT	06451

List to be Checked

Address	ZIP Code
624 Trenton Ct. N. Fresno, CA	94528
124 40th Ave. Saint Cloud, MN	55906
4621 Gumleaf Dr. Apes NC	27539
3128 Royalpine St. Dallas, TX	75238-6814
862 N. Boulder Ave. Huntington, WV	26588
5829 Lost Bridge Pl. Lawton, OR	73501
26141 25th St. E. Parkersburg, WV	26101-7614
3691 Pescara Ct. West Jordan, UT	74084
914 Rosemont Rd. Virginia Beach, VA	23453
8190 Nassau Ln. Nashville, TN	37208-5120
P.O.Box 3611 Aiken, SC	29801
789 N. Kestrel Ct. Bremerton, WA	98421
4624 Blount Rd. Killeem, TX	76544-3240
26437 Treadwell Dr. Bronx, NY	13805
5834 Hancock St. N. Hartford, CT	06451

END

Address Checking (Test 8)

A. No Errors	B. Address Only	C. Zip Code Only	D. Both

	Correct List		List to be Checked	
	Address	ZIP Code	Address	ZIP Code
1.	7894 Easter St. Keesport, PA	15132	7894 Easter St. Kesport, PA	15132
2	4627 Crossway Dr. Franklin, TN	37064	4627 Crossway Dr. Franklin, TN	47064
3.	614 Portsmouth Pl. Burlington, NC	27215-4190	641 Portsmouth Pl. Burlington, NC	27215-4192
4.	51892 39th Ave. Lubbock, TX	79404	51792 39th Ave. Lubbock, TX	79440
5.	874 N. Yarrow Ln. Marshall, VA	20110-7611	874 N. Yarrow Ln. Marshell, VA	20110-7611
6.	1869 Comstock Street Redding, CA	96003	1869 Comstock Street Redding, CA	96003
7.	381 Lynbrook Dr. Bethesda, MD	20814	381 Lynbrook Dr. Bethesda, MD	30814
8.	P.O. Box 7921 Twin Falls, ID	83353	P.O. Box 7912 Twin Falls, ID	83353
9.	9145 Tacaro Rd. SE. Palm Bay, FL	32909-2769	9145 Tacaro Rd. SE. Palm Bay, FL	32909-2766
10.	246 Crosstown Pkwy Kalamazoo, MI	49001	246 Crosstown Pkwy Kalamazoo, MI	49001
11.	419 River Oaks Dr. Norman, OK	74403-5927	519 River Oaks Dr. Norman, OK	74503-5927
12.	5876 E. Vermont Ave. Appleton, WI	54911	5876 E. Vermont Ave. Appleten, WI	54911
13.	314 VIctoria Ln. Bend, OR	97702	314 VIctoria Ln. Bend, OR	97702
14.	871 Wellwood Dr. Anderson, SC	29621	871 Wellwood Dr. Anderson, SC	29624
15.	1494 Lantana Ct. Palmdale, CA	93551-4411	1494 Lantana St. Palmdale, CA	93551-4411

Address Checking (Test 8)

A. No Errors	B. Address Only	C. Zip Code Only	D. Both

	Correct List		List to be Checked	
	Address	ZIP Code	Address	ZIP Code
16.	26941 Frances Pl. Pensacola, FL	32506	26941 Frances Pl. Pensacola, FL	32506
17.	726 S. Cottonwood Ct. Frederick, MD	21703	726 N. Cottonwood Ct. Frederick, MD	21703
18.	849 Bloomfield Ave. Hartford, CT	06105-5617	849 Bloomfield Rd. Hartford, CT	06205-5617
19.	P.O. Box 4216 Mobile, AL	36617	P.O. Box 4216 Mobile, AZ	36617
20.	6214 W. Tobano Blvd. Jonesboro, GA	30238	6214 W. Tobano Blvd. Jonesboro, GA	30283
21.	5794 Abernathy Dr. Charlotte, NC	28216-3192	5794 Abernathy Dr. Charlotte, NC	28216-3192
22.	949 Raccoon Cir. Baytown, TX	77521	948 Raccoon Cir. Baytown, TX	77512
23.	3824 Woodoak St. Roanoke, VA	24014	2824 Woodoak St. Roanoke, VA	24014
24.	1291 N. Votech Dr. Johnstown, PA	15904-8614	1291 N. Votech Dr. Johnstown, PA	15904-8624
25.	368 Curtis Ct. S. Kingsport, TN	37664	368 Curtis Ct. S. Kingsport, TN	37664
26.	5219 Barefoot Lane. Goshen, IN	46142	5219 Barifoot Lane. Goshen, IN	46142
27.	38294 Duncannon Rd. Baltimore, MD	21014-1149	38284 Duncannon Rd. Baltimore, MD	21014-1194
28.	469 187th St. E. Bradenton, FL	34211	469 187th St. W. Bradenton, FL	34211
29.	2621 Livingston Pl. Ventura, CA	93003	2621 Livingston Pl. Ventura, CA	93003
30.	6284 Pinehurst Ln. Battle Creek, MI	49015	6284 Pinehurst Ln. Battle Creek, MI	49815

Address Checking (Test 8)

A. No Errors	B. Address Only	C. Zip Code Only	D. Both

	Correct List		List to be Checked	
	Address	ZIP Code	Address	ZIP Code
31.	362 Woodside Dr. Belleville, IL	62223	362 Woodside Dr. Belleville, IL	62232
32.	7694 N. Rockenn St. Metairie, LA	70001	7694 N. Rockenn St. Metairie, LA	70001
33.	866 Aragon Ave. NE. Saint Louis, MD	63138	866 Aragon Ave. NW. Saint Louis, MD	63238
34.	3624 Beverly Blvd. Los Angeles, CA	90026-3194	3628 Beverly Blvd. Los Angeles, CA	90026-3194
35.	8291 41st St. Anderson, IN	46013	8294 41st St. Anderson, IN	46013
36.	5917 Oswego Ct. E. Charlotte, NC	28226-7154	5917 Oswego Ct. E. Charlotte, NC	28226-7156
37.	6311 Campfire Cir. Dallas, TX	75232	6311 Campfire Cir. Dallas, TX	75232
38.	26327 Kincheloe Ln. Klamath Falls, OR	97603	26326 Kincheloe Ln. Klamath Falls, OR	97603
39.	1249 Narberth Way. Toms River, NJ	08757	1249 Norberth Way. Toms River, NJ	08757
40.	589 Big Bend Dr. Dayton, OH	45427-6149	589 Big Bend Dr. Dayton, OH	45472-6149
41.	3327 15th St. E. Arlington, VA	22202	3327 15th St W. Arlington, VA	23202
42.	419 Ponderosa Pl. Gaffney, SC	29340	419 Ponderosa Pl. Gaffney, SC	29340
43.	2617 Morrison Ave. Bismarck, ND	58504-2947	2617 Morrison Ave. Bismarck, ND	58504-3947
44.	8611 S. Harvard Ct. Seattle, WA	98122	8612 S. Harvard Ct. Seattle, WA	98122
45.	469 N. Woodmont St. Detroit, MI	48228	469 S. Woodmont St. Detroit, MI	48228

Address Checking (Test 8)

A. No Errors	B. Address Only	C. Zip Code Only	D. Both

	Correct List		List to be Checked	
	Address	*ZIP Code*	*Address*	*ZIP Code*
46.	7621 Emporia Ct. Denver, CO	80247	7621 Emporia Ct. Denver, CA	80246
47.	P.O.Box 8624 Macon, GA	31216	P.O.Box 8624 Macon, GA	31216
48.	46126 89th Cir. N. Osseo, MN	55369-9113	46126 89th Cir. N. Osseo, MN	55369-9112
49.	2849 Las Palomas Ln. Moreno Valley, CA	92557	2849 Las Palomas Ln. Moreno Valley, CA	92557
50.	264 Kristin St. Shreveport, LA	71119	264 Kristin St. Shriveport, LA	71119
51.	4417 N. Sorrento Pl. Providence, RI	02909	4417 N. Sorrinto Pl. Providence, RI	02908
52.	3694 Fontenay Dr. Austin, TX	78744-1248	3694 Fontenay Dr. Austin, TX	78744-1348
53.	964 Raintree Ct. Bristol, VA	20147	964 Raintree Ct. Bristol, VA	20147
54.	7219 Wooten Cir. Rocky Mount, NC	27801	7219 Wooten Cir. Rocky Mount, NC	27801
55.	28 W. Chester Ave. Staten Island, NY	10304	20 W. Chester Ave. Staten Island, NY	10304
56.	629 Dunsford Dr. Bella Vista, AR	72714-3101	629 Dunsford Dr. Bella Vista, AR	72724-3101
57.	5819 Palomino Ct. W. Ontario, CA	91761	5819 Palomino Cir. W. Ontario, CA	91761
58.	18769 Demmond St. Elgin, IL	60123	18769 Dammond St. Elgin, IL	60123
59.	769 Weisman Road. Silver Spring, MD	20902	769 Weisman Road. Silver Spring, MD	20902
60.	8694 8th Street E. Bradenton, FL	34208-2611	8684 8th Street E. Bradenton, FL	34208-2612

END

Address Checking (Test 9)

A. No Errors	B. Address Only	C. Zip Code Only	D. Both

	Correct List			List to be Checked	
	Address	*ZIP Code*		*Address*	*ZIP Code*
1.	486 Hedden Pl. Vero Beach, FL	32966		486 Hedden Pl. Vero Beach, FL	32966
2	5879 Lapine Road. West Monroe, LA	71292-1411		5889 Lapine Road. West Monroe, LA	71292-1511
3.	7611 Goodrich St. W. Greenville, MS	38701		7611 Goodrich St. W. Greenville, MS	38601
4.	3624 Breezewalk Dr. Vallejo, CA	94591		3624 Breejewalk Dr. Vallejo, CA	94591
5.	8219 Rockway Ave. Waterbury, CT	06705-4811		8219 Rockway Ave. Waterbery, CT	06705-4811
6.	2611 S. Old Banyan Way. Naples, FL	34109		2611 S. Old Banyan Ave. Naples, FL	34109
7.	279 NW. 105th St. Chicago, IL	60628		289 NW. 105th St. Chicago, IL	60682
8.	6641 Purington St. Somerset, MA	02726		6641 Purington St. Somerset, MA	02726
9.	3829 Stadier Ct. Port Collins, CO	80528		3829 Stadier Ct. Port Collins, CO	80538
10.	61 Kramer Cir. Mesa, AZ	85203-5611		61 Kramer Cir. Mesa, AK	85203-5711
11.	4439 Garfield Pl. Danville, IL	61832		4439 Garfield Pl. Danville, IL	61832
12.	584 N. Bradshaw St. Overland Park, KS	66210		584 N. Bredshaw St. Overland Park, KS	66210
13.	56419 Caprice Dr. Norwalk, CT	06902-4817		54619 Caprice Dr. Norwalk, CT	06802-4817
14.	P.O.Box 25897 South Bend, IN	46601		P.O.Box 25897 South Bend, IN	46604
15.	1291 River Stone Ct. Clarkston, MI	48348		1291 River Stone Ct. Clarkston, MI	48248

Address Checking (Test 9)

A. No Errors	B. Address Only	C. Zip Code Only	D. Both

	Correct List		List to be Checked	
	Address	ZIP Code	Address	ZIP Code
16.	3924 E. 63rd Ct. Tulsa, OK	74136	3924 W. 63rd Ct. Tulsa, OK	74136
17.	7691 Avondale Pl. Charleston, SC	29407-6617	7691 Avondale Pl. Charlesten, SC	29407-6627
18.	9627 Hardwick Ct. Allen, TX	75013	9627 Hardwick Ct. Allen, TX	75013
19.	269 35th Ave. W. Lynnwood, WA	98037	269 35th Ave. W. Lynnwood, WA	98038
20.	6248 Rock Royal Rd. Trenton, NJ	08628	6248 Rock Royal Dr. Trenton, NJ	08628
21.	138 S. Nobles Ln. Kinston, NC	28501	138 S. Nobles Ln. Kinston, NC	38501
22.	27692 Silver Creek Ct. Midlothian, VA	23113-4121	27692 Silvar Creek Ct. Midlothian, VA	23113-4123
23.	867 Osceola St. Lebanon, PA	17042	867 Osceola St. Lebanon, PA	17042
24.	9624 Gencharn St. Charleston, WV	25303	9624 Gencharn St. Charleston, WV	25403
25.	6294 Presidential Ct. Port Myers, FL	33919-5611	6249 Presidential Ct. Port Myers, FL	33919-6511
26.	762 N. Martens Dr. Hammond, LA	70401	762 N. Martens Dr. Hammon, LA	70401
27.	8262 Ramsey Cir. Saint Paul, MN	55102	8262 Ramsey Cir. Saint Paul, MN	55102
28.	4024 Clubhouse Dr. Amherst, MA	01003	4024 Clubhouse Dr. Amherst, MA	01004
29.	562 Olohana St. Honolulu, HI	96815-1191	562 Olohana St. Honolulu, HI	96815-1181
30.	7841 Van Sheriff Ct. Helena, MT	59602	7941 Van Sheriff Ct. Helena, MT	59602

Address Checking (Test 9)

A. No Errors	B. Address Only	C. Zip Code Only	D. Both

	Correct List		List to be Checked	
	Address	**ZIP Code**	**Address**	**ZIP Code**
31.	31417 Montclair Rd. Cocaa, FL	32922	31427 Montclair Rd. Cocaa, FL	32921
32.	489 Caminito Doha San Diego, CA	92131	489 Caminito Doha San Diego, CA	92131
33.	6829 E. Teeter Rd. Russellville, AR	72802-2114	6829 E. Teter Rd. Russellville, AR	72802-2114
34.	262 William St. Decatur, IL	62523	262 William St. Decatur, IL	62423
35.	7624 Lemuel Ave. Chicopee, MA	01013	7624 Lemuel Ave. Chicopee, MD	01031
36.	824 Bowser Ave. Fort Wayne, IN	46803-5619	824 Bowser Ave. Fort Wayne, IN	46803-5619
37.	47 N. Humboldt St. Manhattan, KS	66502	47 S. Humboldt St. Manhattan, KS	66502
38.	P.O.Box 479 Marshall, TX	75670	P.O.Box 479 Marshall, TX	74670
39.	319 Aberdeen Ln. Spartanburg, SC	29303	319 Aberdeen Ln. Spertanburg, SC	29303
40.	9279 N. Calvert Ave. Portland, OR	97217-3619	9297 N. Calvert Ave. Portland, OR	98217-3619
41.	7800 Lane Garden Ct. Dayton, OH	45404	7800 Lane Garden Ct. Dayton, OH	45404
42.	4624 Yucatan Dr. Warwick, RI	02889	4624 Yucatan Dr. Warwick, RI	02898
43.	1928 S. Maltage Dr. Liverpool, NY	13090-4911	1918 S. Maltage Dr. Liverpool, NY	13090-4911
44.	2629 Pioneers Ct. Lincoln, NE	68520	2629 Pioneers Ct. Lancoln, NE	68520
45.	36914 Carolina Ave. Cherry Hill, NJ	08003	36914 Carolina Ave. Cherry Hill, NJ	08003

Address Checking (Test 9)

A. No Errors	B. Address Only	C. Zip Code Only	D. Both

Correct List

	Address	ZIP Code
46.	469 Rue Le Mans Dr. Clarksville, TN	37042
47.	567 Weedy St. Green Bay, WI	54313-3103
48.	4627 Sperry Ave. N. Stratford, CT	06615
49.	9411 Capitol Cir. Lansing, MI	48933
50.	6429 Norwick Dr. Lutz, FL	33559-7614
51.	8611 Oakhurst Ave. Gastonia, NC	28052
52.	3690 Hollow Oak Ln. Centreville, VA	20121
53.	26 S. Rowland St. Las Vegas, NV	89108
54.	914 Luceme Ct. Saint Louis, MO	63136-2614
55.	1765 Singer Hill Ln. Cedar Rapids, IA	52411
56.	729 Escalera St. Laramie, WY	82072
57.	8214 Poradia Rd. Orangeburg, SC	29118-3611
58.	31249 W. Mccomb Rd. Norman, OK	73026
59.	P.O.Box 2149 Everett, WA	98203
60.	4627 Albany Ave. Lorain, OH	44055-6414

List to be Checked

Address	ZIP Code
469 Rue Le Mans Dr. Clarksville, TX	47042
567 Weedy St. Green Bay, WI	54312-3103
4628 Sperry Ave. N. Stratford, CT	06615
9411 Capitol Cir. Lansing, MI	48933
6429 Norwick Rd. Lutz, FL	33559-7624
8711 Oakhurst Ave. Gastonia, NC	28025
3690 Hollow Oak Ln. Centreville, VA	20122
26 S. Rowland St. Las Vegas, NV	89108
914 Lucemi Ct. Saint Louis, MO	63136-2614
1765 Singer Hill Ln. Cedar Rapids, IN	52411
729 Escalera St. Laramie, WY	82072
8214 Poradia Rd. Oramgeburg, SC	29118-4611
31249 W. Mccomb Rd. Norman, OK	83026
P.O.Box 2149 Everett, WA	98230
4628 Albany Ave. Lorain, OH	44055-6414

END

5. Correct Answers for Address Checking

Test 1

1. B	11. D	21. A	31. B	41. D	51. C
2. C	12. B	22. B	32. C	42. A	52. B
3. A	13. C	23. C	33. C	43. B	53. A
4. C	14. A	24. A	34. B	44. B	54. D
5. A	15. A	25. D	35. A	45. C	55. B
6. C	16. B	26. D	36. B	46. B	56. A
7. D	17. B	27. B	37. C	47. D	57. C
8. B	18. D	28. A	38. A	48. D	58. C
9. A	19. C	29. A	39. B	49. A	59. B
10. B	20. A	30. B	40. B	50. B	60. A

Test 2

1. A	11. A	21. D	31. C	41. B	51. C
2. B	12. B	22. C	32. C	42. A	52. D
3. D	13. C	23. A	33. B	43. B	53. D
4. B	14. A	24. B	34. A	44. C	54. A
5. C	15. B	25. B	35. D	45. B	55. C
6. A	16. B	26. D	36. B	46. D	56. A
7. B	17. A	27. A	37. A	47. B	57. B
8. B	18. A	28. A	38. B	48. A	58. B
9. D	19. B	29. B	39. A	49. B	59. C
10. C	20. B	30. C	40. B	50. B	60. B

Correct Answers for Address Checking

Test 3

1. C	11. B	21. A	31. D	41. B	51. B
2. A	12. B	22. B	32. A	42. A	52. B
3. B	13. C	23. B	33. B	43. B	53. B
4. B	14. B	24. A	34. C	44. D	54. D
5. A	15. D	25. D	35. B	45. D	55. A
6. B	16. A	26. B	36. A	46. A	56. C
7. C	17. B	27. C	37. B	47. B	57. C
8. B	18. C	28. A	38. D	48. B	58. B
9. B	19. C	29. B	39. C	49. C	59. A
10. A	20. D	30. B	40. A	50. A	60. A

Test 4

1. B	11. C	21. B	31. D	41. D	51. C
2. C	12. D	22. D	32. A	42. A	52. A
3. B	13. B	23. C	33. B	43. C	53. B
4. A	14. A	24. A	34. C	44. A	54. B
5. D	15. B	25. C	35. C	45. B	55. D
6. D	16. B	26. B	36. B	46. D	56. A
7. C	17. D	27. A	37. C	47. C	57. C
8. A	18. C	28. C	38. A	48. A	58. B
9. B	19. A	29. B	39. B	49. B	59. D
10. A	20. A	30. D	40. B	50. C	60. A

Correct Answers for Address Checking

Test 5

1. B	11. A	21. D	31. A	41. D	51. D
2. A	12. B	22. A	32. B	42. D	52. A
3. D	13. B	23. B	33. C	43. A	53. B
4. C	14. D	24. A	34. B	44. B	54. D
5. B	15. A	25. B	35. D	45. C	55. B
6. A	16. D	26. C	36. A	46. A	56. A
7. D	17. C	27. A	37. B	47. A	57. B
8. A	18. B	28. B	38. C	48. B	58. C
9. B	19. A	29. D	39. B	49. B	59. C
10. C	20. C	30. D	40. B	50. C	60. B

Test 6

1. B	11. A	21. D	31. D	41. C	51. D
2. C	12. D	22. A	32. C	42. B	52. B
3. D	13. B	23. B	33. A	43. B	53. A
4. B	14. C	24. B	34. B	44. A	54. C
5. A	15. B	25. D	35. A	45. D	55. B
6. C	16. A	26. A	36. B	46. D	56. D
7. B	17. A	27. C	37. D	47. C	57. A
8. B	18. C	28. B	38. D	48. A	58. D
9. A	19. C	29. C	39. B	49. B	59. C
10. C	20. B	30. B	40. A	50. D	60. B

Correct Answers for Address Checking

Test 7

1. B	11. A	21. D	31. C	41. A	51. B
2. C	12. B	22. A	32. A	42. D	52. A
3. D	13. D	23. B	33. B	43. B	53. C
4. B	14. D	24. C	34. D	44. A	54. A
5. A	15. C	25. B	35. D	45. D	55. B
6. B	16. A	26. A	36. B	46. C	56. B
7. B	17. B	27. D	37. A	47. A	57. D
8. C	18. A	28. D	38. C	48. B	58. D
9. D	19. B	29. C	39. B	49. D	59. C
10. A	20. C	30. D	40. D	50. C	60. A

Test 8

1. B	11. D	21. A	31. C	41. D	51. D
2. C	12. B	22. D	32. A	42. A	52. C
3. D	13. A	23. B	33. D	43. C	53. A
4. D	14. C	24. C	34. B	44. B	54. A
5. B	15. B	25. A	35. B	45. B	55. B
6. A	16. A	26. B	36. C	46. D	56. C
7. C	17. B	27. D	37. A	47. A	57. B
8. B	18. D	28. B	38. B	48. C	58. B
9. C	19. B	29. A	39. B	49. A	59. A
10. A	20. C	30. C	40. C	50. B	60. D

Correct Answers for Address Checking

Test 9

1. A	11. A	21. C	31. D	41. A	51. D
2. D	12. B	22. D	32. A	42. C	52. C
3. C	13. D	23. A	33. B	43. B	53. A
4. B	14. C	24. C	34. C	44. B	54. B
5. B	15. C	25. D	35. D	45. A	55. B
6. B	16. B	26. B	36. A	46. D	56. A
7. D	17. D	27. A	37. B	47. C	57. D
8. A	18. A	28. C	38. C	48. B	58. C
9. C	19. C	29. C	39. B	49. A	59. C
10. D	20. B	30. B	40. D	50. D	60. B

6. Forms Completion (Test 1)

SENDER: *COMPLETE THIS SECTION*	*COMPLETE THIS SECTION ON DELIVERY*
■ Complete items 1,2 and 3. Also complete item 4 If Restricted Delivery is desired. ■ Print your name and address on the reverse so that we can return the card to you. ■ Attach this card to the back of the mailpiece, or on the front if space permits.	3a. Signature
	3b. Received by *(Printed Name)* 3c. Date of Delivery
1. Articles addressed to:	3d. Is delivery address different from item 1? □ Yes If YES, enter delivery address below: □ No
	Service Type 4a.□ Certified Mail 4d.□ Express Mail 4b.□ Registered 4e.□ Return Receipt for Merchandise 4c.□ Insured Mail 4f. □ C.O.D.
	5. Restricted Delivery? *(Extra Fee)* □ Yes
2. Article Number *(Transfer from service label)*	

Domestic Return Receipt

Forms Completion (Test 1)

1. Which of these should be a correct entry for Box 3c?

    A. 92653

    B. $29.35

    C. 3/28/04

    D. a. check mark

2. Where should you write the article numbers?

    A. Box 3a

    B. Box 3d

    C. Box 2

    D. Box 1

3. If you want to send mail by restricted delivery, where should you make a check mark?

    A. Box 2

    B. Box 3a

    C. Box 3d

    D. Box 5

4. Where should you write your signature?

    A. Box 2

    B. Box 3a

    C. Box 3b

    D. Box 1

5. The carrier Henry Edward tried to deliver a registered letter with restricted delivery on May 12, 2013. The customer has two different addresses. Where should the customer make a check mark and write except writing the date?

    A. Enter a check mark in Box 3d, 4b, 5, write in Box1, 2, 3a and 3b.

    B. Enter a check mark in Box 3d, 4b, 5, write in Box1, 2, 3a and 3c.

    C. Enter a check mark in Box 3d, 4b, write in Box1, 2, 3a and 3b.

    D. Enter a check mark in Box 3d, 4b, 5, write in Box1, 2, 3b and 3c.

6. You want to send a registered mail. Where should you indicate this?

    A. Box 4b, and 3d

    B. Box 3b

    C. Box 2

    D. Box 4b

Forms Completion (Test 1)

		1. Today's Date	2. Sender's Name

3. Item is at: ___ Post Office *(See back)* ___ _____	Available for Pick-up After 4a. Date: 4b. Time:	We will redeliver or you or your agent can pick up. See reverse.

5a. ___ Letter 5b. ___ Large envelope, magazine, catalog, etc 5c. ___ Parcel 5d. ___ Restricted Delivery 5e. ___ Perishable Item 5f. ___ Other:	**For Delivery:** *(Enter total number of items delivered by service type)* **For Notice Left:** *(Check applicable items)* 6a. ___ Express Mail (We will attempt to deliver on the next delivery day unless you instruct the post office to hold it.) 6b. ___ Certified 6c. ___ Recorded Delivery 6d. ___ Firm Bill	6e. ___ Registered 6f. ___ Insured 6g. ___ Return Receipt for Merchandise 6h. ___ Delivery Confirmation 6i. ___ Signature Confirmation	7. ☐ **If checked, you or your agent must be present at time of delivery to sign for Item** **8. Article Number(s)**

Article Requiring Payment 9a. ☐ Postage Due 9b. ☐ COD 9c. ☐ Customers	9d. Amount Due $	**Notice Left Section** 10. Customer Name and Address

11. ☐ **Final Notice:** Article will be returned to sender on	12. Delivered By and Date

Delivery Notice/Reminder/Receipt

Forms Completion (Test 1)

7. A carrier tried to deliver a certified letter with return receipt on April 27, 2013, but there is no one at the address. The carrier can't leave the mail if there is no one home. Where should the carrier make a check mark and what should be written to have the customer pick up the mail except writing the name and address?

   A. Box 1, 5b, 6g, 4a and 4b
   B. Box 6b and 4a
   C. Box 1, 5a, 6b, 6g, 4a and 4b
   D. Box 3

8. Which of these would be a correct entry for Box 8?

   A. 909-425-2137
   B. $39.27
   C. 4/27/03
   D. 0303 1910 0001

9. Which of these would be a correct entry for Box 1?

   A. $14.50
   B. 90005
   C. 7/29/03
   D. 310-460-2134

10. A carrier left a notice after he or she attempted to deliver a parcel. Where should the carrier enter a check mark?

   A. Box 6e
   B. Box 3
   C. Box 2
   D. Box 5c

11. A customer has to pay $40.50 to receive a COD. Which of these would be a correct entry?

   A. Place a check mark in Box 9b and write the amount in the Box 9d.
   B. Place a check mark in Box 6f and write the amount beside the Box 6f.
   C. Place a check mark in Box 5f and write the amount beside the Box 5f.
   D. Place a check mark in Box 9b and don't write the amount.

12. The carrier, John Hudson delivered a parcel on April 24, 2013. Where should he indicate it except writing the name and address?

   A. Box 1, 4a and 4b
   B. Box 1, 5C, 4a and 4b
   C. Box 10
   D. Box 1, 4a, 4b and 11

Forms Completion (Test 1)

Registered No.			Date Stamp
To Be Completed By Post Office	1. Reg. Fee	3. Return Receipt	
	2. Handling Charge	5. Restricted Delivery	
	4. Postage		
	6. Received by		
	7a. Customer Must Declare Full Value $	☐ 7b. With Postal Insurance ☐ 7c. Without Postal Insurance	Domestic Insurance up to $25,000 is included in the fee. International Indemnity is limited. *(See Reverse.)*

To Be Completed By Customer (Please Print) All Entries Must Be in Ballpoint or Typed	FROM	8.
	TO	9.

Receipt for Registered Mail

Forms Completion (Test 1)

13. The clerk Edward Frazer received a registered mail with restricted delivery from a customer. The customer applied for some compensation if the mail is lost. Where should the clerk indicate this request?

    A. Box 4 and 7b
    B. Box 5, 6, 7a and 7b
    C. Box 5, 2, 7a and 7b
    D. Box 3, 7a and 7b

14. Which of these would be a correct entry for Box 2?

    A. 4/26/03
    B. 92456
    C. $4.50
    D. 310-241-5629

15. The registered mail fee is $15.40 and the handling fee is $4.20. Where should the clerk write these amounts?

    A. Box 7a and 7c
    B. Box 3 and 5
    C. Box 7b and 7c
    D. Box 1 and 2

16. Where should a customer write his/her address?

    A. Box 9
    B. Box 8
    C. Box 6
    D. None of the above

17. A customer was going to send a book by registered mail with return receipt. But he or she decided that the book does not much value. Where should the postal clerk indicate that?

    A. Box 2 and 7b
    B. Box 3 and 7c
    C. Box 7b and 7a
    D. Box 1

18. Where does the customer need to write the recipient's name?

    A. Box 9
    B. Box 8
    C. Box 6
    D. Box 4

Forms Completion (Test 1)

CERTIFIED MAIL™ RECEIPT
(Domestic Mail Only; No Insurance Coverage Provided)

1. Postage	$
2. Certified Fee	
3. Return Receipt Fee (Endorsement Required)	
4. Restricted Delivery Fee (Endorsement Required)	
5. Total Postage & Fees	$

Postmark Here

6. Sent To

7. Street, Apt. No.; or PO Box No.

8. City, State, ZIP+4

Forms Completion (Test 1)

19. Which of these would be a correct entry for Box 1?

    A. 3/29/13
    B. 90124
    C. $3.95
    D. 310-247-5938

20. The recipient's name is Bill Benton. Where should he write his name?

    A. Box 8
    B. Box 2
    C. Box 6
    D. Box 5

21. A number should be written in the three boxes. In which box the customer should not write a number?

    A. Box 6
    B. Box 2
    C. Box 4
    D. Box 5

22. A customer wants to send a certified parcel with return receipt and with restricted delivery. The parcel weights 5 pounds. And the customer wants to buy insurance. Which of these would be a correct indication of this by the clerk?

    A. Write the fees in Box 2 and 5
    B. Write the fees in Box 1, 2, 3, 4 and the customer needs to act more.
    C. Write the fees in Box 2 and 3
    D. Write the fees in Box 1, 2, 3, 4, 5 and the customer needs to act more.

23. Where should a clerk write the total postage & fees?

    A. Box 1
    B. Box 5
    C. Box 2
    D. Box 4

24. Which of these would be a correct entry for Box 7?

    A. Richard Lee
    B. 324 S. Vermont Ave.
    C. $5.26
    D. 6/29/13

Forms Completion (Test 1)

Authorization to Hold Mail

NOTE: *Complete and give to your letter carrier or mail to the post office that delivers your mail.*

Postmaster: Please hold mail for:		
1. Name(s)	3. ☐	**A.** Please deliver all accumulated mail and resume normal delivery on the ending date shown below.
2. Address *(Number, street, apt./suite no., city, state, ZIP+4)*	4. ☐	**B.** I will pick up all accumulated mail when I return and understand that mail delivery will not resume until I do so.

5. Beginning Date	6. Ending Date *(May only be changed by the customer in writing)*	7. Customer Signature _____

For Post Office Use Only

8. Date Received	
9. Clerk	11. Bin Number
10. Carrier	12. Route Number

(Complete this section only if customer selected option B)

13. ☐ Accumulated mail has been picked up.	14. Resume Delivery of Mail *(Date)*	15. By _____

Forms Completion (Test 1)

25. The date to start holding the mail is March 21, 2005, and the end date is April 19, 2005.
A carrier received the application on March 20, 2005 and a carrier has to deliver again on
April 20, 2005 by customer's intention. Where should the carrier and the customer indicate this information?

    A. Box 7 and 15
    B. Box 5, 6, 8, 14 and 15
    C. Box 6 and 8
    D. Box 5 and 6

26. The carrier's name is Ron Jordan and his route number is 25. Where should the carrier write his name and
route number?

    A. Box 9 and 11
    B. Box 12 and 15
    C. Box 14 and 15
    D. Box 10 and 11

27. Which of these would be a correct entry for Box 3?

    A. 92644
    B. $26.10
    C. A check mark
    D. 323-269-5149

28. Where should a customer's name be entered?

    A. Box 15
    B. Box 9
    C. Box 1
    D. Box 12

29. A carrier received an application for authorization to hold mail on April 4, 2013. Where should the carrier
write his/her name and date received?

    A. Box 5 and 6
    B. Box 6 and 11
    C. Box 1 and 14
    D. Box 8 and 15

30. A customer doesn't want to pick up his/her accumulated mail. Where should the customer indicate that?

    A. Box 3
    B. Box 11
    C. Box 2
    D. Box 14

END

Forms Completion (Test 2)

DELIVERY EMPLOYEE - Remove Copies 1 & 2 at Time of Delivery

Collect the amount shown be-low if customer pays by **CHECK** made payable to the mailer.	Collect the amount shown below if customer pays in **CASH** (includes MO fee).	
1. Check Amount $	2. Cash Amount $	
3a. ☐ Registered Mail 3b. ☐ Express Mail	3c. ☐ Form 3849-D Requested	**COD**
3d. Date of Mailing ☐ 3e. Remit COD Charges to Sender via Express Mail	3f. EMCA No.	

4. FROM:	5. TO:	
6a. Delivered By	6b. Date Delivered	6c. Received: *(Print Name and Sign)*
7a. Check Number	7b. MO Number	7c. Date Payment Sent to Mailer — 7d. Date Form 3849-D Sent

Copy 1 - Delivery Unit

Forms Completion (Test 2)

1. A carrier's name is Neva Mabel. She has delivered a COD on August 5, 2012. The company is waiting the COD charge. The postal employee received the payment by a check and will send the payment to the sender. Where should Neva Mabel indicate this situation?

    A. Writing in Box 1, 6a, 6b and entering a check mark 3e
    B. Writing in Box 1, 6a, 6b, 7a and entering a check mark 3e
    C. Writing in Box 6a and 7a
    D. Writing in Box 6a, 6b and 7a

2. Which of these would be a correct entry for Box 4?

    A. $15.60
    B. 310-266-1459
    C. 1240 S. Western Ave.
    D. 6/16/05

3. Bill Newton received a COD on September 5, 2012. He paid $30.50 by a check. Where should the postal employee write this?

    A. Box 6c, 1 and 7a
    B. Box 7c, 1 and 6b
    C. Box 3e, 1 and 7a
    D. Box 6c, 2 and 7a

4. If the postal employee received $40 for the payment by cash, where should the postal employee indicate this?

    A. Box 3d and 5
    B. Box 2 and 7b
    C. Box 6a
    D. None of the above

5. Which of these would be a correct entry for Box 3d?

    A. 92024
    B. $14.26
    C. Kent Ned
    D. 2/26/04

6. Which of these would be a correct entry for Box 6a?

    A. 714-319-2469
    B. Jason Fuller
    C. 5/26/03
    D. 720 N. Oxford Ave.

Forms Completion (Test 2)

Forwarding Order Change Notice

Check One
16a. ☐ Entire Family
16b. ☐ Individual

1. Carrier Route No.	2. Carrier/Clerk Initials	3. Receiving Employee Initials	4. Original Order Date	5. This Order Date	6. Expiration Date

7. *Print* Last Name or Name of Business / Firm *(If more than one last name fill out an additional form.)*

8. *Print* First Name of Each Individual Covered By This Order *(Separate each name by a space.)*

9. Original Address	9a. *Print* Number and Street	Apt. / Suite No.	9b. P.O. Box No.	9c. Rural Route No.	9d. Rural Box No.
	9e. *Print* City		9f. State	9g. ZIP + 4	
10. Cancel Forwarding Order	10a. *Print* Number and Street	Apt. / Suite No.	10b. P.O. Box No.	10c. Rural Route No.	10d. Rural Box No.
	10e. *Print* City		10f. State	10g. ZIP + 4	
11. New Forwarding Order	11a. *Print* Number and Street	Apt. / Suite No.	11b. P.O. Box No.	11c. Rural Route No.	11d. Rural Box No.
	11e. *Print* City		11f. State	11g. ZIP + 4	

12a. Discontinue Forwarding *(Check One):* 12b. ☐ Moved no order 12c. ☐ Refuses to pay postage due on ALL fourth-class
12d. ☐ No such number 12e. ☐ No such street. Check forwarding Order.

13. Post Office	14. Station / Branch	15. By *(Route Number and Name)*

(Previous Edition Usable)

Forms Completion (Test 2)

7. A customer turned in a forwarding order change notice originally on July 25, 2012. Where should the customer write this?

    A. Box 6
    B. Box 4
    C. Box 5
    D. Box 14

8. Which of these would be a correct answer for Box 6?

    A. 92104-2119
    B. $26.15
    C. July 25, 2004
    D. 212-314-5194

9. Kosey Russ divorced recently and lived with a cousin. He moved out from his cousin's house on September 27, 2005. He will submit a forwarding order change notice. Which of these would be a correct indication by Kosey Russ except writing the addresses and the dates?

    A. Enter a check mark in Box 16b, write a first name in Box 8 and a last name in Box 7.
    B. Write in Box 16a and write a first name in Box 8.
    C. Enter a check mark in Box 16b and write a first name in Box 7.
    D. Enter a check mark in Box 16a and write a first name in Box 7.

10. Where should a customer write the fee to submit a forwarding order change notice?

    A. Box 5
    B. Box 10d
    C. Box 2
    D. None of the above

11. A customer is living on carrier route number 17. Where should the carrier write that number?

    A. Box 6
    B. Box 9c
    C. Box 1
    D. None of the above

12. A carrier attempted to deliver by the forwarding order change notice. However the carrier could not find the street number. Where should the carrier indicate that?

    A. Box 5
    B. Box 12d
    C. Box 2
    D. Box 12e

Forms Completion (Test 2)

Customs Declaration

1a. ☐ Gift   1b. ☐ Commercial Sample

1c. ☐ Documents   1d. ☐ Other

2a. Quantity and detailed description of contents (1)	2b. Weight lb. oz.		2c. Value (US $)
3a. For Commercial items only If known, HS tariff number and country of origin of goods (5)	3b. Total Weight		3c. Total Value (US $)

4. Date and Sender's Signature (8)

Customs Declaration CN 22 - Sender's Declaration

I, undersigned, whose name and address are given on the item, certify that the particulars given in this declaration are correct and that this item does not contain any dangerous article or articles prohibited by legislation or by postal or customs regulations. This copy will be retained at the post office for 30 days.

5. Sender's Name & Address

6. Addressee's Name & Address

7. Date and Sender's Signature

Forms Completion (Test 2)

13. The sender's name is Richard Knox and the address is 362 N. Kingston St., Burbank, CA. Where should the sender's name and address be written?

    A. Box 6
    B. Box 4
    C. Box 7
    D. Box 5

14. The sender is sending a gift. Where should the sender make a check mark?

    A. Box 2b
    B. Box 1a
    C. Box 3c
    D. Box 1d

15. A company is selling electric products globally. This company is going to send two products which weigh 26 lbs and have a value of $200.00. The company has to fill out a customs declaration form. Where should the company indicate this information?

    A. Enter a check mark in Box 1d, write in Box 2a, 2b, 2c, 3b and 3c
    B. Enter a check mark in Box 1b, write in Box 2b, 2c, 3b and 3c
    C. Enter a check mark in Box 1d, write in Box 2a, 2c and 3c
    D. Write in Box 3a, enter a check mark in Box 3b and 3c

16. Which of these would be a correct answer for Box 2c?

    A. 2/16/04
    B. $260.00
    C. 213-362-5247
    D. 710 S. Normandie Ave.

17. Where should the company write the addressee's name and address?

    A. Box 5 and 6
    B. Box 7
    C. Box 6
    D. Box 2a

18. Peter Owen is the sender. Where should he sign the customs declaration?

    A. Box 5
    B. Box 6
    C. Box 2a
    D. Box 4 and 7

Forms Completion (Test 2)

	Item Description	☐ 1a. Registered Article	☐ 1b. Letter	☐ 1c. Printed Matter	☐ 1d. Other	☐ 1e. Recorded Delivery	☐ 1f. Express Mail Inter-national

Completed by the office of origin:

2a. Insured Parcel	2b. Insured Value	3. Article Number

4. Office of Mailing	5. Date of Posting

6. Addressee Name or Firm

7. Street and No.

8. Place and Country

Completed at destination:

☐ 9. The article mentioned above was duly delivered.	10. Date	
11. Signature of Addressee	12. Office of Destination Employee Signature	

Forms Completion (Test 2)

19. Where should the addressee write his/her signature?

    A. Box 12
    B. Line 3
    C. Line 11
    D. Box 2

20. A parcel insured for $400 is being sent by International Express Mail. The item is fragile. When the item was delivered safely, where should that information be entered?

    A. Enter a check mark in Box 1a, 2a, 2b, 9 and 10
    B. Enter a check mark in Box 1f, 9, write in Box 2a, 2b and put the mark "fragile"
    C. Enter a check mark in Box 1f, 2a, 2b, 9 and put the mark "fragile"
    D. Enter a check mark in Box 1d, 2a, 2b, and put the mark "fragile"

21. Which of these would be a correct entry for Box 3?

    A. 415-269-3134
    B. 2301 0370 0001
    C. $24.95
    D. 11/24/13

22 Where should the country of the addressee be entered?

    A. Box 5
    B. Box 2b
    C. Box 10
    D. Box 8

23. Where should an employee write his/her signature?

    A. Line 12
    B. Line 11 and line 12
    C. Box 8
    D. Box 2a

24. A company's name is Garden Moving Service. Where should the employee of the company write the company's name?

    A. Box 7 and 8
    B. Line 3
    C. Box 6
    D. Box 10

Forms Completion (Test 2)

RETURN RECEIPT FOR MERCHANDISE

1. Postage	$
2. Return Receipt for Merchandise fee (Endorsement Required)	
3. Special Handling Fee	
4. **Total Postage & Fees**	$
5. Waiver of Signature	☐ YES ☐ NO

9.

Postmark
Here

6. Sent To

7. Street, Apt. No.; or PO Box No.

8. City, State, ZIP+4

Forms Completion (Test 2)

25. A Company is going to sell computer parts. The company is sending the goods by registered mail with return receipt. The company applied for waiver of signature and the special handling. Which of these would be a correct indication this?

    A. Write the fee in Box 2, 3, and enter a check mark in Box 5.
    B. Write the fee in Box 2, 3, enter a check mark in Box 5 and needs one more action.
    C. Enter a check mark in Box 5 and write the fee in Box 3
    D. Enter a check mark in Box 5, write the fee in Box 1 and needs one more action.

26. The return receipt fee is $1.00. Where should the customer write the fee?

    A. Box 1
    B. Box 4
    C. Box 2
    D. Box 7

27. Where should the recipient's name be written?

    A. Box 5
    B. Box 8
    C. Box 7
    D. Box 6

28 A number will be written except which box?

    A. Box 6
    B. Box 3
    C. Box 8
    D. Box 1

29. Which of these would be a correct entry for Box 7?

    A. 323-729-3102
    B. $49.95
    C. 7024 N. Ganon Ave
    D. 5/24/13

30. The customer will apply the special handling. Where should the customer write the fee?

    A. Box 3
    B. Box 2
    C. Box 9
    D. Box 8

END

Forms Completion (Test 3)

Postage and Delivery Confirmation fees must be paid before mailing.
Article Sent To: (to be completed by mailer)

1. Name *(Please Print Clearly)*	
2. Address	
3. Zipcode	

4.

DELIVERY CONFIRMATION NUMBER:

Postmark
Here

POSTAL CUSTOMER
Keep this receipt. For inquiries:
Access internet web site at *www.usps.com*
or call 1-800-222-1811

CHECK ONE (POSTAL USE ONLY)

5. ☐	**Priority Mail Service**	
6. ☐	**First-Class Mail Parcel**	
7. ☐	**Package Services Parcel**	

_____
8. Date of Delivery

Forms Completion (Test 3)

1. Which of these would be a correct entry for Line 8?

   A. 323-290-4191
   B. $38.20
   C. 04-27-05
   D. 32779

2. The customer's name is Mark Primo. He lives at 816 S. Normandie Ave. #510 LA, CA 90006. He is going to send a priority letter with delivery confirmation. A carrier delivered the letter on May 13, 2006. Where would Mark Primo enter all of this information?

   A. Write in Box 1 and 2
   B. A check mark in Box 5, write in Box 1, 2 and 3
   C. Write in Box 1, 2 and 3
   D. Write in Box 1, 2, 3, 5 and line 8

3. A customer is going to send a letter by Priority Mail. Which box should the postal employee check?

   A. Box 5
   B. Box 7
   C. Box 4
   D. None of the above

4 The customer's name is Allen Horst. Where should the customer's name be entered?

   A. Box 8
   B. Box 1
   C. Box 4
   D. Box 2

5. Where should the customer write the customer's address?

   A. Box 3
   B. Line 8
   C. Box 1
   D. Box 2

6. The customer is going to send a first class parcel with delivery confirmation. Where should the customer indicate that information?

   A. Box 3
   B. Box 6
   C. Box 2
   D. None of the above

Forms Completion (Test 3)

Mailing Label

Express Mail

Post Office To Addressee

DELIVERY (POSTAL USE ONLY)				
17. Delivery Attempt Mo. Day	Time	18a. ☐ AM 18b. ☐ PM	19. Employee Signature	
20. Delivery Attempt Mo. Day	Time	21a. ☐ AM 21b. ☐ PM	22. Employee Signature	
23. Delivery Date Mo. Day	Time	24a. ☐ AM 24b. ☐ PM	25. Employee Signature	

ORIGIN (POSTAL SERVICE USE ONLY)

1. PO ZIP Code	2. Day of Delivery ☐ Next ☐ 2nd ☐ 2nd Del. Day	3. Postage $
4. Date Accepted Mo Day Year	5. Scheduled Day of Delivery Month Day	6. Return Receipt Fee $
	8. Scheduled Time of Delivery ☐ Noon ☐ 3PM	9. COD Fee $ / 10. Insurance Fee $
7. Time Accepted ☐ AM ☐ PM	11. Military ☐ 2nd Day ☐ 3rd Day	12. Total Postage & Fees $
13. Flat Rate☐ or Weight lbs ozs	14. Int'l Alpha Country Code	15. Acceptance Emp. Initials

CUSTOMER USE ONLY
PAYMENT BY ACCOUNT

26a. ☐ WAIVER OF SIGNATURE

26b. _____
MAILER SIGNATURE

16a. FROM: (PLEASE PRINT)   16b.PHONE (   )_____

27a. TO: (PLEASE PRINT)   27b.PHONE (   )_____

27c.
ZIP + 4 (U.S. ADDRESSES ONLY. DO NOT USE FOR FOREIGN POSTAL CODES.)

☐ ☐ ☐ ☐ ☐ + ☐ ☐ ☐ ☐

FOR INTERNATIONAL DESTINATIONS, WRITE COUNTRY NAME BELOW.

Forms Completion (Test 3)

7. Where should a clerk enter his/her initials to receive an Express Mail?

   A. Box 19 and 27b
   B. Box 15
   C. Box 15 and 27b
   D. Box 19

8. The scheduled time of delivery is 3PM on June 27, 2004. A carrier already has delivered an Express Mail that afternoon. Where should the carrier indicate this?

   A. Box 17, 24, 25b and 26
   B. Box 24 and 27a
   C. Box 5, 8, 23, 24b and 25
   D. Box 7 and 27a

9. A carrier attempted to deliver an express mail the first time at 3PM on March 2, 2005. Where should the carrier indicate this?

   A. Box 20, 18b and 19
   B. Box 24, 25b and 26
   C. Box 17, 18b and 19
   D. Box 2 and Box 3

10. Where should a sender's information be written?

    A. Box 27a and 27b
    B. Line 26b
    C. Box 12
    D. Box 16a, and 16b

11. A customer paid the postage, $15.90, the return receipt fee $1.00 and the insurance fee $4.00. The customer wanted waiver of signature. Where would he/she indicate this information?

    A. A postal employee writes in Box 3, 6, 10, 12, the customer will do for box 26a and 26b
    B. A postal employee writes in Box 3, 6, 10, 12, and 26a
    C. A postal employee writes in Box 12, the customer will do for box 26a and 26b
    D. A customer needs to do all for this.

12. A number can be entered in all boxes except which?

    A. Box 12
    B. Box 26a and 26b
    C. Box 1
    D. Box 27c

Forms Completion (Test 3)

		1. Today's Date	2. Sender's Name

3. Item is at: ___ Post Office *(See back)* ___ _____	Available for Pick-up After 4a. Date: 4b. Time:	We will redeliver or you or your agent can pick up. See reverse.

For Delivery / Notice Left	For Pickup	Article Number
5a. ___ Letter 5b. ___ Large envelope, magazine, catalog, etc 5c. ___ Parcel 5d. ___ Restricted Delivery 5e. ___ Perishable Item 5f. ___ Other:	**For Delivery:** *(Enter total number of items delivered by service type)* **For Notice Left:** *(Check applicable items)* 6a. ___ Express Mail (We will attempt to deliver on the next delivery day unless you instruct the post office to hold it.) 6b. ___ Certified 6c. ___ Recorded Delivery 6d. ___ Firm Bill 6e. ___ Registered 6f. ___ Insured 6g. ___ Return Receipt for Merchandise 6h. ___ Delivery Confirmation 6i. ___ Signature Confirmation	7. ☐ **If checked, you or your agent must be present at time of delivery to sign for Item** **8. Article Number(s)** **Notice Left Section** 10. Customer Name and Address

Article Requiring Payment 9a. ☐ Postage Due 9b. ☐ COD 9c. ☐ Customers	9d. Amount Due $	
11. ☐ **Final Notice:** Article will be returned to sender on		12. Delivered By and Date

Delivery Notice/Reminder/Receipt

Forms Completion (Test 3)

13. The carrier wants the customer to pick up his/her mail. Where should the carrier write this information?

    A. Box 1
    B. Box 12
    C. Box 4a and 4b
    D. Box 4d

14. The carrier left a notice for the customer about the delivery confirmation. Where should the carrier make a check mark to indicate that?

    A. Box 6e
    B. Box 6h
    C. Box 3
    D. Box 5f

15. Which of these would be a correct entry for Box 10?

    A. Jose Joel and 24 Kingsley Ave, LA
    B. $4.26
    C. 5/24/04
    D. 562-314-5298

16. A company sent goods by certified mail with a return receipt. The carrier tried to deliver the goods. There was no one at the customer's house. So the carrier left a notice. Where would the carrier indicate this information?

    A. Write in Box 1, 2, 10, 4a, 4b, a check mark in Box 6b and 6i
    B. Write in Box 1, 2, a check mark in Box 6b and 6g
    C. A check mark in Box 6g and write in Box 12
    D. Write in Box 1, 2, 4a, 4b, 10, 12, a check mark in Box 5c, 6b and 6g

17. Which of these would be a correct entry for Box 9d?

    A. $12.10
    B. 92634
    C. 714-214-0239
    D. 724 S. Western Ave.

18. A carrier has attempted to deliver an express mail. Which box would the carrier check?

    A. Box 6e
    B. Box 6a
    C. Box 5d
    D. Box 6i

Forms Completion (Test 3)

INSURED MAIL RECEIPT

1. Postage	$	10a. ☐ Fragile 10b. ☐ Liquid 10c. ☐ Perishable
2. Insurance Fee		11. Insurance Coverage
3. Restricted Delivery Fee (Domestic Only: endorsement required)		
4. Special Handling Fee		12. Postmark Here
5. Return Receipt Fee (Except for Canada: endorsement required)		
6. Total Postage & Fees	$	

7. Sent To

8. Street, Apt. No.;
or PO Box No.

9. City, State, ZIP+4, County

Forms Completion (Test 3)

19. A customer paid postage of $2.50 and the insurance of $1.20. Where would the clerk indicate that?

    A. Box 5 and 6
    B. Box 1 and 4
    C. Box 1, 2 and 6
    D. None of the above

20. Which of these would be a correct entry for Box 7?

    A. 729 S. Harvard Ave.
    B. 805-274-5100
    C. 2/16/04
    D. John Yoo

21. A customer's name is Douglas Kurt. He wants to mail a gift to his friend. He told the clerk the gift is fragile, and he wants to have a return receipt. Also, he expects to get compensation if the gift is lost. Where would the clerk enter this information?

    A. Write in Box 1, 2, 5, 11 and a check mark in Box 10a
    B. Write in Box 1, 4, 5 and a check mark in Box 10a
    C. Write in Box 1, 2, 5, 6, 11 and a check mark in Box 10a
    D. Write in Box 1, 5, 6 and a check mark in Box 10c

22. The customer and the clerk can write numbers in all boxes except which?

    A. Box 10c
    B. Box 6
    C. Box 8
    D. Box 1

23. A customer is going to send an insured mail with return receipt. Where should the clerk write the fees?

    A. Box 1, 3, 5 and 6
    B. Box 1, 2, 5 and 6
    C. Box 1, 2, 4 and 6
    D. Box 5 and 6

24. Where can the customer see the postmark?

    A. Box 12
    B. Box 7
    C. Box 4
    D. None of the above

Forms Completion (Test 3)

Application Cards

Tear off this Page, fill it out, and turn it in to your post office.

Application for Post Office Box or Caller Service - Part 1

Customer: Complete items 1, 3-6, 14-16, and 18-19	Post Office: Complete items 2, 7-13, 17 and 20
1. Name(s) to which box number(s) is(are) assigned	2. Box or caller numbers _____ through _____
3. Name of person applying, title (if representing an organization), and name of organization *(if different from item 1)*	4a. Will this box be used for: ☐ Personal Use ☐ Business Use *(Optional)*
5. Address *(Number, Street, apt./ste. no., city, state, and ZIP code).* When address changes, cross out address here and put new address on back.	4b. Email Address *(Optional)* 6. Telephone Number *(Include area code)*

7. Date application received	8. Box size needed	9. ID and physical address verified by *(initials)*	10. Date of Service _____ through _____
11. Two types of identification are required. One item must contain a photo. Write in identifying information (type of ID and No.)		12. Check eligibility for carrier delivery ☐ a. City ☐ b. Rural ☐ c. HCR ☐ d.None	13. Service assigned ☐ a. Box ☐ b. Caller ☐ c. Reserve No.
		14. List name(s) and age(s) of minors or names of other persons **receiving mail** in individual box. Other persons must present two forms of vaild ID. If applicant is a firm, name each member **receiving mail**. Each member must have verifiable ID upon request.	
		15. Signature of applicant *(Same as item 3)* I agree to comply with all postal rules regarding post office box or caller service. _____	

Forms Completion (Test 3)

25. Where should a customer describe the Box size?

    A. Box 4a
    B. Box 9
    C. Box 6
    D. None of the above

26. Which of these would be a correct entry for Box 7?

    A. 698 Wilshire Pl., LA
    B. 3/8/05
    C. $24.50
    D. Gary Rene

27. A Customer submitted an application card to rent a post office box on February 24, 2005. Where should the customer write this date?

    A. Box 9
    B. Box 6
    C. Box 7
    D. None of the above

28. Where should the customer write the name of the person to whom a P.O. Box will be assigned?

    A. Box 2 and 14
    B. Box 1
    C. Box 5
    D. Box 1 and 3

29. Where should an applicant write his/her signature?

    A. Box 9
    B. Box 13
    C. Line 15
    D. Box 3

30. The customer's name is Henry Young, and he needs a post office box for business. He needs a medium size P.O. Box. A clerk required two types of IDs. Henry Young requested a six month rental. Where should Henry Young indicate this?

    A. Write in Box 1, 3, 14 and 15
    B. Write in Box 1, 2, 14, 15, 11 and a check mark in Box 4a
    C. Write in Box 1, 3, 5, 11, 14, 15 and a check mark in 13
    D. Write in Box 1, 3, 5, 6, 14 and 15

END

Forms Completion (Test 4)

DELIVERY EMPLOYEE - Remove Copies 1 & 2 at Time of Delivery

Collect the amount shown below if customer pays by **CHECK** made payable to the mailer.	Collect the amount shown below if customer pays in **CASH** (includes MO fee).	
1. Check Amount **$**	2. Cash Amount **$**	

3a. ☐ Registered Mail	3b. ☐ Express Mail	3c. ☐ Form 3849-D Requested	**COD**
3d. Date of Mailing	3e. ☐ Remit COD Charges to Sender via Express Mail	3f. EMCA No.	

4. FROM:	5. TO:

6a. Delivered By	6b. Date Delivered	6c. Received By: *(Print Name and Sign)*	
7a. Check Number	7b. MO Number	7c. Date Payment Sent to Mailer	7d. Date Form 3849-D Sent

Forms Completion (Test 4)

1. A carrier delivered a COD to a customer on March 4, 2013. Where should the carrier write this information?

  A. Box 7a and 7b
  B. Box 6a and 6b
  C. Box 7c
  D. Box 5

2. Which of these would be a correct entry for Box 6c?

  A. 213-469-2140
  B. 92651
  C. Bill Henson
  D. $46.20

3. A customer paid for the COD by cash in the amount of $50.10. Where should the carrier write this information?

  A. Box 2
  B. Box 7c
  C. Box 6b
  D. None of the above

4. A publisher sent two books to a customer on March 10, 2006 by COD and registered mail. A carrier delivered the books and received the payment by check. The post office sent the payment to the publisher on March 15, 2006. Which of these would be correct entries by the carrier?

  A. Write in Box 1, 6a, 6b, 7c and enter a check mark in Box 3a
  B. Write in Box 1, 6a, 6b, 7c and enter a check mark in Box 3b
  C. Write in Box 1, 6a, 3b, 6b, 6c and 7c
  D. Write in Box 1, 6a, 6b, 7a, 7c and enter a check mark in Box 3a

5. Which of these would be a correct entry for Box 7a?

  A. 91741-2159
  B. 2159
  C. $21.49
  D. 46 N. Vermont Ave.

6. A carrier may write the amount of money in two boxes and may write the date in one box. In which box will the carrier not write the amount and date?

  A. Box 3d
  B. Box 1
  C. Box 2
  D. Box 6c

Forms Completion (Test 4)

Finance Copy

Express Mail

Post Office To Addressee

DELIVERY (POSTAL USE ONLY)			
17. Delivery Attempt Mo. Day	Time	18a. ☐ AM 18b. ☐ PM	19. Employee Signature
20. Delivery Attempt Mo. Day	Time	21a. ☐ AM 21b. ☐ PM	22. Employee Signature
23. Delivery Date Mo. Day	Time	24a. ☐ AM 24b. ☐ PM	25. Employee Signature

CUSTOMER USE ONLY
PAYMENT BY ACCOUNT
26. ☐ **Waiver of Signature**

27. **No Delivery**
☐ **Weekend**   **Holiday** ☐

ORIGIN (POSTAL SERVICE USE ONLY)

1. PO ZIP Code	2. Day of Delivery ☐ Next ☐ 2nd ☐ 2nd Del. Day	3. Postage $	
4. Date Accepted Mo. Day Year	5. Scheduled Day of Delivery Month Day	6. Return Receipt Fee $	
7. Time Accepted ☐ AM ☐ PM	8. Scheduled Time of Delivery ☐ Noon ☐ 3PM	9. COD Fee $	10. Insurance Fee $
	11. Military ☐ 2nd Day ☐ 3rd Day	12. Total Postage & Fees $	
13. Flat Rate ☐ or Weight lbs. ozs.	14. Int'l Alpha Country Code	15. Acceptance Emp. Initials	

16a. FROM: (PLEASE PRINT)   16b.PHONE (   )_____

28a. TO: (PLEASE PRINT)   28b.PHONE (   )_____

28c.
ZIP + 4 (U.S. ADDRESSES ONLY. DO NOT USE FOR FOREIGN POSTAL CODES.)
☐☐☐☐☐ + ☐☐☐☐
FOR INTERNATIONAL DESTINATIONS, WRITE COUNTRY NAME BELOW.

Forms Completion (Test 4)

7. A customer paid the total postage and fee of $29.50. Where should the customer write that amount?

   A. Box 6
   B. Box 10
   C. Box 12
   D. None of the above

8. A carrier delivered an express mail at 3PM on January 6, 2013. Where should the carrier write this?
   A. Box 17, 18b and 19
   B. Box 23, 24b and 25
   C. Box 20, 21b and 23
   D. None of the above

9. A postal clerk accepted an express mail at 2PM on May 14, 2013. The customer ordered a return receipt. The carrier attempted to deliver the express mail in the afternoon and the customer requested no weekend delivery. Where should the postal worker indicate all this information?

   A. Write in Box 4, 6, 7, 12, 15, 17, 18b and a check mark in Box 27
   B. Write in Box 4, 7, 12, 15, 17, 18b and a check mark in Box 28a
   C. Write in Box 4, 6, 7, 15, 17, 19 and enter a check mark in Box 18b
   D. Write in Box 3, 4, 6, 7, 12, 15, and 18b

10. Yolanda Winter sent an express mail. Where should Yolanda Winter write the sender's name?

    A. Box 16b
    B. Box 16a
    C. Box 28b
    D. Box 19

11. A customer is going to send an express mail with return receipt. The customer needs to pay the return receipt fee. Where should a clerk write the amount of return receipt fee?

    A. Box 3
    B. Box 12
    C. Box 5
    D. Box 6

12. Which of these would be a correct entry for Box 28c?

    A. $26.30
    B. 818-451-2194
    C. 30907-6113
    D. 2/16/13

Forms Completion (Test 4)

OFFICIAL MAIL FORWARDING CHANGE OF ADDRESS ORDER			OFFICIAL USE ONLY
Please PRINT items 1-10 in blue and black ink. Your signature is required in item 9.			Zone/Route ID No.
Change of Address for: (Read Attached Instructions) 1a. ☐ Individual (#5) 1b. ☐ Entire Family (#5) 1c. ☐ Business (#6)	Is This Move Temporary?	2a. ☐ YES 2b. ☐ NO	Date Entered on Form 3982 M M D D Y Y
3. Start Date (ex. 02/27/05) M M D D Y Y	4. If TEMPORARY move, print date to discontinue forwarding: (ex. 03/27/05) M M D D Y Y		
5a. LAST Name & Jr./Sr./etc			Expiration Date M M D D Y Y
5b. FIRST Name and MI			Clerk/Carrier Endorsement
6. If BUSINESS Move, Print Business Name			
PRINT OLD MAILING ADDRESS BELOW: HOUSE/BUILDING NUMBER AND STREET NAME (INCLUDE ST., AVE., CT., ETC.) OR PO BOX			
7a. OLD Mailing Address			
7b. OLD APT or Suite	7c. For Puerto Rico Only: If address is in PR, print urbanization name, if appropriate.		
7d. OLD CITY		7e. STATE	7f. ZIP
PRINT NEW MAILING ADDRESS BELOW: HOUSE/BUILDING NUMBER AND STREET NAME (INCLUDE ST., AVE., CT., ETC.) OR PO BOX			
8a. NEW Mailing Address			
8b. NEW APT/Ste or PMB	8c. For Puerto Rico Only: If address is in PR, print urbanization name, if appropriate.		
8d. NEW CITY		8e. STATE	8f. ZIP
9. Print and Sign Name (see conditions on reverse) Print: _____ ► Sign:	10. Date Signed: (ex. 01/27/05) M M D D Y Y	OFFICE USE ONLY	

Forms Completion (Test 4)

13. The start date for mail forwarding is March 23, 2013. Where should the customer enter this date?

    A. Box 10
    B. Box 3
    C. Box 7d
    D. Box 1b

14. A customer is moving temporarily. Where should the customer make a check mark for that information?

    A. A check mark in the Box 4
    B. A check mark in the Box 2a
    C. Writing "Temporary" in Box 6
    D. None of the above

15. Ron Smith and Nick Kerry are roommates. Nick Kerry is going to move to another apartment. But it is only temporary situation. He will back into Ron Smith's apartment at a later date. In which boxes should Nick Kerry write numbers?

    A. Box 3, 4, 7a, 7b, 7e, 8a and 8b
    B. Box 3, 4, 7a, 7b, 7d, 7e, 8a and 8b
    C. Box 3, 4, 7a, 7b, 7f, 8a, 8b, 8f and 10
    D. Box 1, 2a, 3, 4, 7a, 7b, 7e, 8a, 8b and 10

16. Which of these would be a correct entry for Box 8a?

    A. $16.24
    B. 310-270-4159
    C. Evelyn Lorliss
    D. 269 Alameda Ave.

17. A customer is going to move his or her business. Where should the customer make a check mark?

    A. Box 2a
    B. Box 1c
    C. Box 3
    D. None of the above

18. The customer can write a date in each of the boxes except which?

    A. Box 8c
    B. Box 3
    C. Box 4
    D. Box 10

Forms Completion (Test 4)

Authorization to Hold Mail

NOTE: *This service is limited to a 30-day period. See DMM.*

Postmaster: Please hold mail for:	
1. Name(s)	2. Begin Holding Mail Date
3. Address *(Number, street, apt./suite no., city, state, ZIP+4)*	

4a. ☐ I will pick up all accumulated mail when I return and understand that mail delivery will not resume until I do. *(This is suggested if your return date may change or if no one will be at home to receive mail.)*		
4b. ☐ Please deliver all accumulated mail and resume normal delivery on the ending date shown here.		4c. Resume Delivery Date
5. Customer Signature		

For Post Office Use Only

6. Date Received	
7a. Clerk	7b. Bin Number
8a. Carrier	8b. Route Number

(The following section applies only if customer selected option A)

Note to Carrier: Accumulated mail has been picked up.	▶ 9. Resume Delivery of Mail *(Date)*
10. By	

Forms Completion (Test 4)

19. Where should the customer write his/her address?

    A. Box 6
    B. Box 9
    C. Box 3
    D. Box 5

20. Where should the customer sign?

    A. Box 10
    B. Box 5
    C. Box 4c
    D. Box 9

21. Which of these would be a correct entry for Box 4c?

    A. 909-420-2148
    B. $16.24
    C. 2/14/04
    D. Larry Lee

22. John Parker will take a vacation from June 10, 2005 to July 9, 2005. And he will leave home at 11AM on June 11, 2005 and stay in Las Vegas for 5 days. And he will leave Las Vegas at 8PM. It will take 7 hours to get from Las Vegas to his home. What date should John Parker write in Box 2 and 4c?

    A. June 10, 2005 in Box 2 and June 15, 2005 in Box 4c
    B. June 11, 2005 in Box 2 and June 15, 2005 in Box 4c
    C. June 10, 2005 in Box 2 and June 16, 2005 in Box 4c
    D. June 11, 2005 in Box 2 and June 16, 2005 in Box 4c

23. The carrier will resume delivery of the customer's mail on April 11, 2005. Where should the carrier write this date?

    A. Box 9
    B. Box 4c and 9
    C. Box 6
    D. Box 8a

24. The customer will pick up all his/her accumulated mail. Where should the customer make a check mark about this?

    A. Box 4b
    B. Box 4a
    C. Box 9
    D. Box 2

Forms Completion (Test 4)

Application for Post Office Box or Caller Service - Part 2

Special Orders

1. Postmaster: The following named persons or representatives of the organization listed below are authorized to **accept mail** addressed to this (these) post office box(es) or caller number(s). All names listed must have verifiable ID. *(Continue on reverse side).*

2. Name(s) of applicant(s)

Customer note: The Postal Service may consider it valid evidence that a person is authorized to remove mail from the box if that person possesses a key or combination to the box.

3. Name of box customer

4. Other authorized representative

5. Other authorized representative

6. Post office date stamp

7. Box or caller number to which this card applies

Will this box be used for Express Mail reshipment? *(Check one)*

8a. Yes ☐   8b. No ☐

9. Signature of applicant *(Same as item 3)* I agree to comply with all postal rules regarding post office box or caller service.

▶

Forms Completion (Test 4)

25. Which of these would be a correct entry for Box 6?

    A. 3/23/05
    B. $38.25
    C. making a date stamp
    D. 415-541-2102

26. A customer wants to use a post office box for express mail reshipment. Where should the customer make a check mark?

    A. Box 8a
    B. Box 8b
    C. Box 5
    D. Box 2

27. Royce Yynan is going to apply for rental of a post office box for Leo Hunter. Where will the name of the renter of the post office box be entered?

    A. Box 3
    B. Box 2
    C. Box 9
    D. Box 4

28. Francis Minor operates an insurance company, and he wants to apply to rent a post office box for business. He wants to authorize another person beside himself to remove his mail from the post office box. What should Francis Minor do to authorize that person?

    A. Write the name of an authorized person in Box 1
    B. Write the name of an authorized person in Box 2
    C. Write the name of an authorized person in Box 4
    D. Write the name of a customer in Box 4

29. Which of these would be a correct answer for Box 7?

    A. 212-490-1147
    B. 90247-4119
    C. $18.00
    D. 783

30. The customer has a representative. Where should the customer write the representative's name?

    A. Box 2
    B. Box 4
    C. Box 3
    D. Box 7

END

Forms Completion (Test 5)

	1. Today's Date	2. Sender's Name

3. Item is at:

_____ Post Office *(See back)*

_____ _____

Available for Pick-up After

4a. Date:

4b. Time:

We will redeliver or you or your agent can pick up. See reverse.

For Delivery / Notice Left Section	For Delivery & Notice

5a. _____ Letter

5b. _____ Large envelope, magazine, catalog, etc

5c. _____ Parcel

5d. _____ Restricted Delivery

5e. _____ Perishable Item

5f. _____ Other:

For Delivery: *(Enter total number of items delivered by service type)*
For Notice Left: *(Check applicable items)*

6a. _____ Express Mail (We will attempt to deliver on the next delivery day unless you instruct the post office to hold it.)

6b. _____ Certified

6c. _____ Recorded Delivery

6d. _____ Firm Bill

6e. _____ Registered

6f. _____ Insured

6g. _____ Return Receipt for Merchandise

6h. _____ Delivery Confirmation

6i. _____ Signature Confirmation

7. ☐ If checked, you or your agent must be present at time of delivery to sign for Item

8. Article Number(s)

Notice Left Section

10. Customer Name and Address

Article Requiring Payment

9a. ☐ Postage Due   9b. ☐ COD   9c. ☐ Customers

9d. Amount Due

$

11. ☐ **Final Notice:** Article will be returned to sender on

12. Delivered By and Date

Delivery Notice/Reminder/Receipt

Forms Completion (Test 5)

1. A carrier attempted to deliver a certified letter. But there was no one home. So the carrier left a notice. If the customer wants to pick up the letter, what should the customer do?
    - A. Needs to see the reverse side.
    - B. Needs to call the post office.
    - C. Needs to meet with a carrier.
    - D. None of the above

2. Which of these would be a correct entry for Box 6h?
    - A. Certified
    - B. Delivery Confirmation
    - C. Insured
    - D. Firm Bill

3. Which of these should be written by the carrier in Box 2?
    - A. 04/07/05
    - B. 3970 W. 8th St. LA
    - C. Larry Moon
    - D. at 3:30 PM

4. Which of these would be a correct entry for Box 4b?
    - A. 213-382-2102
    - B. 03:00 PM
    - C. 92501
    - D. 7/24/04

5. A carrier has delivered a parcel by certified mail with a return receipt as the company requested. The company said the merchandise is perishable. Where should the carrier indicate this except the numbers and name?
    - A. Box 5c, 6b and 6g
    - B. Box 5c, 6d and 6g
    - C. Box 5c, 5e, 6b and 6g
    - D. Box 5e, 6b, 6d and 6g

6. Which of these would be a correct entry for Box 11?
    - A. 5/11/04
    - B. A check mark
    - C. 714-624-3110
    - D. None of the above

Mailing Label

Express Mail

Post Office To Addressee

ORIGIN (POSTAL SERVICE USE ONLY)		
1. PO ZIP Code	2. Day of Delivery □ Next □ 2nd □ 2nd Del. Day	3. Postage $
4. Date Accepted Mo Day Year	5. Scheduled Day of Delivery Month Day	6. Return Receipt Fee $
	8. Scheduled Time of Delivery □ Noon □ 3PM	9. COD Fee $ / 10. Insurance Fee $
7. Time Accepted □ AM □ PM	11. Military □ 2nd Day □ 3rd Day	12. Total Postage & Fees $
13. Flat Rate□ or Weight lbs ozs	14. Int'l Alpha Country Code	15. Acceptance Emp. Initials

16a. FROM: (PLEASE PRINT)   16b.PHONE (   )_____

DELIVERY (POSTAL USE ONLY)			
17. Delivery Attempt Mo. Day	Time	18a. □ AM 18b. □ PM	19. Employee Signature
20. Delivery Attempt Mo. Day	Time	21a. □ AM 21b. □ PM	22. Employee Signature
23. Delivery Date Mo. Day	Time	24a. □ AM 24b. □ PM	25. Employee Signature

CUSTOMER USE ONLY

PAYMENT BY ACCOUNT

26a. □ WAIVER OF SIGNATURE

26b. _____
MAILER SIGNATURE

27a. TO: (PLEASE PRINT)   27b.PHONE (   )_____

27c.
ZIP + 4 (U.S. ADDRESSES ONLY. DO NOT USE FOR FOREIGN POSTAL CODES.)

☐ ☐ ☐ ☐ ☐ + ☐ ☐ ☐ ☐

FOR INTERNATIONAL DESTINATIONS, WRITE COUNTRY NAME BELOW.

Forms Completion (Test 5)

7. Which of these would be a correct entry for Box 27b?

    A. 02/14/04
    B. 92799
    C. 213-692-1192
    D. $14.50

8. A carrier delivered an express letter at 11:00 AM on June 21, 20   12. Where should the carrier indicate this?

    A. Box17, 18a and 19
    B. Box 20, 21b and 23
    C. Box 17, 18b and 19
    D. Box 23, 24a and 25

9. Which of these would be a correct entry for Box 16b?

    A. 310-274-2564
    B. $21.30
    C. 92651-1144
    D. 7800 Whilshire Blvd

10. A customer wants to send an express parcel with a return receipt. The clerk said the fees are $17.50. Where should the clerk write these fees?

    A. Box 6 and 12
    B. Box 3 and 12
    C. Box 3, 6 and 12
    D. Box 3, 6, 12 and 15

11. A carrier attempted to deliver an express letter at 2:00 PM on November 23, 2005. Where should the carrier indicate this?

    A. Box 17, 18a and 19
    B. Box 20, 21b, and 22
    C. Box 17, 18b and 19
    D. Box 23, 24b and 25

12. A clerk received 15 parcels from a company named Sun Jewel on July 10, 2012. An employee of Sun Jewel asked for a waiver of signature. Where should the clerk indicate this?

    A. Box 27a and 27b
    B. Box 16a and 16b
    C. Box 26a and 26b
    D. None of the above

Forms Completion (Test 5)

DELIVERY EMPLOYEE - Remove Copies 1 & 2 at Time of Delivery

Collect the amount shown below if customer pays by **CHECK** made payable to the mailer.	Collect the amount shown below if customer pays in **CASH** (includes MO fee).	
1. Check Amount $	2. Cash Amount $	**COD**
3a. ☐ Registered Mail 3b. ☐ Express Mail 3c. ☐ Form 3849-D Requested		
3d. Date of Mailing	☐ 3e. Remit COD Charges to Sender via Express Mail 3f. EMCA No.	
4. FROM:		5. TO:
6a. Delivered By	6b. Date Delivered	6c. Received: *(Print Name and Sign)*
7a. Check Number	7b. MO Number	7c. Date Payment Sent to Mailer 7d. Date Form 3849-D Sent

Forms Completion (Test 5)

13. Which of these would be a correct entry for Box 1?

     A. 4/26/02
     B. 909-247-6140
     C. $41.22
     D. John Kim

14. A carrier delivered a COD by express mail. Where should the carrier indicate this?

     A. Box 3e and 6a
     B. Box 3b and 6b
     C. Box 3b and 6c
     D. None of the above

15. A carrier Brad Johnson delivered a COD on June 25, 2013. And the customer paid by check. Which of these would be a correct indication of this by the carrier?

     A. Box 2, 6a, 6b and 7a
     B. Box 1, 6a and 7a
     C. Box 2, 6b and 7c
     D. Box 1, 6a, 6b and 7a

16. Which of these would be a correct entry for Box 6b?

     A. 91401
     B. $26.40
     C. 3/1/04
     D. 714-209-3114

17. A postal employee needs to write a date in each of the boxes below except which?

     A. Box 7a
     B. Box 6b
     C. Box 7c
     D. Box 3d

18. A clerk Edward Lee received a book by COD from a bookstore on March 26, 2005. And the carrier, Brad Johnson, delivered that book on March 27, 2005 and received the money by check. Which of these would be a correct entry by the carrier and who is the pay to order on the check?

     A. Box 1, 6a, 6b, 7a and post master
     B. Box 1, 6a, 6b and Brad Johnson
     C. Box 1, 6a, 6b, 7a and the name of book store
     D. None of the above

Forms Completion (Test 5)

Customs Declaration and Dispatch Note

FROM	1. Sender's Name 2. Business 3a. Street 3b.City 3c.State 3d.Zip code 3e.Country	15. Sender's Customs Reference	16. Insured Number	
			17. Insured Amount (US$)	18. SDR Value
TO	4. Addressee's Name 5. Business 6a. Street	19. Importer's Reference - optional *(if any)* *(Tax code/VAT no./Importer code)*		
	6b. Postal Code 6c. City 6d. Country	20. Importer's Telephone/Fax/Email *(if known)*		

7a. Detailed Description of Contents	7b. Qty	7c. Net Weight lb.	oz.	7e. Value (US $)		
Check One 8a.☐ Airmail/Priority 8b.☐ Surface/Nonpriority	7d. Total Gross Wt.			7f. Total Value	7g. Postage and Fees	
Check One 9a.☐ Gift 9b.☐ Commercial sample 9c.☐ Other 9d.☐ Documents 9e.☐ Returned goods Explanation:						
10. Comments *(e.g., goods subject to quarantine, sanitary/phytosanitary inspection, or other restrictions)*						
11. License Number(s)	12. Certificate Number(s)	13. Invoice Number				
	14. Date and Sender's signature					

Forms Completion (Test 5)

19. The Rolands department store will send a diamond to a customer. The toal value is $500. Where should an employee of the department store indicate the total value?

    A. Box 7b
    B. Box 9b
    C. Box 7f
    D. Box 7g

20. Which of these would be a correct entry for Box 7e?

    A. 909-452-6149
    B. 92521
    C. $14.50
    D. 629 N. Alameda St. LA

21. Where should the sender's business name be entered?

    A. Box 2
    B. Box 4
    C. Box 6d
    D. Box 16

22. The department store is going to send three rings. Where should the company write the quantity?

    A. Box 7c
    B. Box 8a
    C. Box 7d
    D. Box 7b

23. A company in England is going to sell goods to the U.S.A. An employee of the company has to declare for customs at the airport. The employee knows the phone number of the importer. The goods will be sent non priority. Which of these would be a correct indication of the contents?

    A. Box 7a, 7b, 7c, 7d, 7e, 7f and 9c
    B. Box 7a, 7b, 7c, 7d, and 14
    C. Box 7a, 7b, 7c, 7d, 7e, 7f, 8b and 9c
    D. Box 7a, 7b, 7c, 7d, 7e, 7f, 8b and 14

24. Which of these would be a correct entry for Box 20?

    A. 805-264-510
    B. $26.30
    C. Bill Johnson
    D. 6/16/03

Forms Completion (Test 5)

Mailing Permit Application and Customer Profile *(See instructions on reverse)*	**A. Applicant Information** *(Please print or type)*	
	1. Individual or Company Name	2. Date
Two types of identifications are required. One must contain a photograph of the addressee(s). Social security cards, credit cards, and birth certificates are unacceptable as identification. The agent must write in identifying information. Subject to verification.	3. Applicant's Signature ▶	4. Email Address
5a. Enter first ID number	6. Address *(Street and number, apt, or suite no., city, state and ZIP+4)*	
5b. Enter second ID number	7. Other Names Under Which Company Does Business *(if applicable)*	8. How can we Contact You? ☐ Phone ☐ Email ☐ Mail
	9. Federal Agency Cost Code *(if applicable)* _ _ _ _ _ _ _ .	10. Will present Plant Verified Drop shipment (PVDS)? ☐ Yes ☐ No
	11. Contact Person	12. Telephone *(include area code)*

Forms Completion (Test 5)

25. An applicant can write a number except which?

    A. Box 2
    B. Box 12
    C. Box 5b
    D. Box 3

26. An applicant can be contacted by the phone. Where should the applicant make a check mark?

    A. Box 4
    B. Box 11
    C. Box 8
    D. Box 1

27. Which of these would be a correct entry for Box 11?

    A. 949-213-4192
    B. $12.40
    C. 2/16/03
    D. Larry Lee

28. Where should an applicant write his or her signature?

    A. Box 3
    B. Box 5b
    C. Box 1
    D. Box 9

29. Nona Jocelyn is working with an online bookstore. As an employee of that online bookstore, she tries to apply for mailing permit for company business. And she has to fill out the forms. But she found out that she needs to present some IDs to get the permit.
    Which of these would be a correct presentation for IDs for this situation?

    A. Credit card and social security card
    B. Driver's license and student ID
    C. Driver's license and social security card
    D. U.S. passport and birth certificate

30. Which of these would be a correct entry for Box 12?

    A. 91329-1149
    B. 4/26/05
    C. 405-278-7210
    D. $26.17

END

7. Correct Answers for Forms Completion

Test 1

1. C	11. A	21. A
2. C	12. B	22. D
3. D	13. B	23. B
4. B	14. C	24. B
5. A	15. D	25. B
6. D	16. B	26. B
7. C	17. B	27. C
8. D	18. A	28. C
9. C	19. C	29. D
10. D	20. C	30. A

Test 2

1. B	11. C	21. B
2. C	12. B	22. D
3. A	13. D	23. A
4. B	14. B	24. C
5. D	15. A	25. B
6. B	16. B	26. C
7. B	17. C	27. D
8. C	18. D	28. A
9. A	19. C	29. C
10. D	20. B	30. A

Test 3

1. C	11. A	21. C
2. C	12. B	22. A
3. A	13. C	23. B
4. B	14. B	24. A
5. D	15. A	25. D
6. D	16. D	26. B
7. B	17. A	27. D
8. C	18. B	28. B
9. C	19. C	29. C
10. D	20. D	30. D

Test 4

1. B	11. D	21. C
2. C	12. C	22. D
3. A	13. B	23. A
4. D	14. B	24. B
5. B	15. C	25. C
6. D	16. D	26. A
7. D	17. B	27. A
8. B	18. A	28. C
9. C	19. C	29. D
10. B	20. B	30. B

Test 5

1. A	11. C	21. A
2. B	12. D	22. D
3. C	13. C	23. C
4. B	14. D	24. A
5. C	15. D	25. D
6. B	16. C	26. C
7. C	17. A	27. D
8. D	18. C	28. A
9. A	19. C	29. B
10. C	20. C	30. C

8. Coding and Memory (Test 1)
Coding Section (Step 1)

CODING GUIDE	
Address Range	**Delivery Route**
45-450 Lake Dr. 1400-2400 Toledo Rd.	A
451-900 Lake Dr. 2401-3700 Toledo Rd. 70-350 N. Jamaica Ct.	B
4000-8000 Shady St. 351-750 N. Jamaica Ct. 39-179 W. Darden Ave.	C
All mail that doesn't fall in one of the address range listed above	D

Coding and Memory (Test 1)
Coding Section (Step 1)

Sample Questions

Address	Delivery Route
1. 469 Lake Dr.	A B C D
2. 154 W. Darden Ave.	A B C D
3. 1360 Toledo Rd.	A B C D
4. 4600 Shady St.	A B C D

Sample Answer Grid

1.	Ⓐ	Ⓑ	Ⓒ	Ⓓ
2.	Ⓐ	Ⓑ	Ⓒ	Ⓓ
3.	Ⓐ	Ⓑ	Ⓒ	Ⓓ
4.	Ⓐ	Ⓑ	Ⓒ	Ⓓ

The correct answers for sample questions

1. (B) 2.(C) 3.(D) 4.(C)

Coding and Memory (Test 1)
Coding Section (Step 2)

CODING GUIDE	
Address Range	**Delivery Route**
45-450 Lake Dr. 1400-2400 Toledo Rd.	A
451-900 Lake Dr. 2401-3700 Toledo Rd. 70-350 N. Jamaica Ct.	B
4000-8000 Shady St. 351-750 N. Jamaica Ct. 39-179 W. Darden Ave.	C
All mail that doesn't fall in one of the address range listed above	D

Coding and Memory (Test 1)

Coding Section (Step 2)

Sample Questions

	Address	Delivery Route			
1.	754 N. Jamaica Ct.	A	B	C	D
2.	392 Lake Dr.	A	B	C	D
3.	178 W. Darden Ave.	A	B	C	D
4.	2369 Toledo Rd.	A	B	C	D
5.	6012 Shady St.	A	B	C	D
6.	42 Lake Dr.	A	B	C	D
7.	469 S. Normandie Ave.	A	B	C	D
8.	3800 Toledo Rd.	A	B	C	D

Sample Answer Grid			
1. (A)	(B)	(C)	(D)
2. (A)	(B)	(C)	(D)
3. (A)	(B)	(C)	(D)
4. (A)	(B)	(C)	(D)
5. (A)	(B)	(C)	(D)
6. (A)	(B)	(C)	(D)
7. (A)	(B)	(C)	(D)
8. (A)	(B)	(C)	(D)

The correct answers for sample questions

1. (D) 2.(A) 3.(C) 4.(A) 5.(C) 6.(D) 7.(D) 8.(D)

Coding and Memory (Test 1)
Coding Section (Step 3)

CODING GUIDE	
Address Range	**Delivery Route**
45-450 Lake Dr. 1400-2400 Toledo Rd.	A
451-900 Lake Dr. 2401-3700 Toledo Rd. 70-350 N. Jamaica Ct.	B
4000-8000 Shady St. 351-750 N. Jamaica Ct. 39-179 W. Darden Ave.	C
All mail that doesn't fall in one of the address range listed above	D

Coding and Memory (Test 1)
Coding Section (Step 3)

Questions

	Address	Delivery Route			
1.	48 W. Darden Ave.	A	B	C	D
2.	2900 Toledo Rd.	A	B	C	D
3.	475 Lake Dr.	A	B	C	D
4.	250 N. Jamaica Ct.	A	B	C	D
5.	2875 Appleton Way	A	B	C	D
6.	657 W. Jamaica Ct.	A	B	C	D
7.	35 Lake Dr.	A	B	C	D
8.	1469 Toledo Rd.	A	B	C	D
9.	189 W. Darden Ave.	A	B	C	D
10.	49 Preston Ave.	A	B	C	D
11.	340 S. Jamaica Ct.	A	B	C	D
12.	2450 Toledo Rd.	A	B	C	D
13.	129 Chelsea Cir.	A	B	C	D
14.	4120 Shady St.	A	B	C	D
15.	66 W. Darden Ave.	A	B	C	D
16.	2644 Bardes Ct.	A	B	C	D
17.	1722 Toledo Rd.	A	B	C	D
18.	8100 Shady St.	A	B	C	D

Coding and Memory (Test 1)
Coding Section (Step 3)

CODING GUIDE	
Address Range	**Delivery Route**
45-450 Lake Dr. 1400-2400 Toledo Rd.	A
451-900 Lake Dr. 2401-3700 Toledo Rd. 70-350 N. Jamaica Ct.	B
4000-8000 Shady St. 351-750 N. Jamaica Ct. 39-179 W. Darden Ave.	C
All mail that doesn't fall in one of the address range listed above	D

Coding and Memory (Test 1)
Coding Section (Step 3)

Questions

	Address	Delivery Route			
19.	5624 Shady St.	A	B	C	D
20.	869 Granvue Dr.	A	B	C	D
21.	490 Lake Dr.	A	B	C	D
22.	3714 Toledo Rd.	A	B	C	D
23.	275 N. Jamaica Ct.	A	B	C	D
24.	21 W. Darden Ave.	A	B	C	D
25.	6194 Oakcliff Ln.	A	B	C	D
26.	760 Lake Dr.	A	B	C	D
27.	3900 Shady St.	A	B	C	D
28.	187 Rinker Way	A	B	C	D
29.	854 N. Jamaica Ct.	A	B	C	D
30.	2900 Toledo Rd.	A	B	C	D
31.	127 W. Darden Ave.	A	B	C	D
32.	219 E. Freemont	A	B	C	D
33.	412 Lake Dr.	A	B	C	D
34.	5612 Shady St.	A	B	C	D
35	71 N. Jamaica Ct.	A	B	C	D
36.	1200 Toledo Rd.	A	B	C	D

Coding and Memory (Test 1)
Memory Section (Step 1)

CODING GUIDE	
Address Range	**Delivery Route**
45-450 Lake Dr. 1400-2400 Toledo Rd.	A
451-900 Lake Dr. 2401-3700 Toledo Rd. 70-350 N. Jamaica Ct.	B
4000-8000 Shady St. 351-750 N. Jamaica Ct. 39-179 W. Darden Ave.	C
All mail that doesn't fall in one of the address range listed above	D

Coding and Memory (Test 1)
Memory Section (Step 2)

Sample Questions

	Address	Delivery Route			
1.	569 Lake Dr.	A	B	C	D
2.	96 W. Darden Ave.	A	B	C	D
3.	2360 Toledo Rd.	A	B	C	D
4.	62 N. Jamaica Ct.	A	B	C	D
5.	9249 Shady St.	A	B	C	D
6.	924 Lake Dr.	A	B	C	D
7.	1390 Toledo Rd.	A	B	C	D
8.	6290 Shady St.	A	B	C	D

Sample Answer Grid

	A	B	C	D
1.	Ⓐ	Ⓑ	Ⓒ	Ⓓ
2.	Ⓐ	Ⓑ	Ⓒ	Ⓓ
3.	Ⓐ	Ⓑ	Ⓒ	Ⓓ
4.	Ⓐ	Ⓑ	Ⓒ	Ⓓ
5.	Ⓐ	Ⓑ	Ⓒ	Ⓓ
6.	Ⓐ	Ⓑ	Ⓒ	Ⓓ
7.	Ⓐ	Ⓑ	Ⓒ	Ⓓ
8.	Ⓐ	Ⓑ	Ⓒ	Ⓓ

The correct answers for sample questions

1. (B) 2.(C) 3.(A) 4.(D) 5.(D) 6.(D) 7.(D) 8.(C)

Coding and Memory (Test 1)
Memory Section (Step 3)

CODING GUIDE	
Address Range	**Delivery Route**
45-450 Lake Dr. 1400-2400 Toledo Rd.	A
451-900 Lake Dr. 2401-3700 Toledo Rd. 70-350 N. Jamaica Ct.	B
4000-8000 Shady St. 351-750 N. Jamaica Ct. 39-179 W. Darden Ave.	C
All mail that doesn't fall in one of the address range listed above	D

Coding and Memory (Test 1)
Memory Section (Step 4)

Questions

	Address	Delivery Route			
37.	4026 Shady St.	A	B	C	D
38.	349 N. Jamaica Ct.	A	B	C	D
39.	43 Lake Dr.	A	B	C	D
40.	2694 Lanco St.	A	B	C	D
41.	2369 Toledo Rd.	A	B	C	D
42.	780 W. Darden Ave.	A	B	C	D
43.	780 Lake Dr.	A	B	C	D
44.	8230 Shady St.	A	B	C	D
45.	926 Roswell Rd.	A	B	C	D
46.	79 E. Darden Ave.	A	B	C	D
47.	2500 Toledo Rd.	A	B	C	D
48.	1625 Reba Rd.	A	B	C	D
49.	650 N. Jamaica Ct.	A	B	C	D
50.	914 Lake Dr.	A	B	C	D
51.	3800 Shady St.	A	B	C	D
52.	3690 Toledo Rd.	A	B	C	D
53.	57 Fargo Ave.	A	B	C	D
54.	68 N. Jamaica Ct.	A	B	C	D

Coding and Memory (Test 1)
Memory Section (Step 4)

Questions

	Address	Delivery Route			
55.	124 Lake Dr.	A	B	C	D
56.	1390 Toledo Rd.	A	B	C	D
57.	6200 Shady St.	A	B	C	D
58.	769 Cavan Ln.	A	B	C	D
59.	350 W. Jamaica Ct.	A	B	C	D
60.	180 W. Darden Ave.	A	B	C	D
61.	310 Henry Pl.	A	B	C	D
62.	460 Lake Dr.	A	B	C	D
63.	626 N. Jamaica Ct.	A	B	C	D
64.	2890 Shady St.	A	B	C	D
65.	460 Hunt Dr.	A	B	C	D
66.	150 W. Darden Ave.	A	B	C	D
67.	3610 Toledo Rd.	A	B	C	D
68.	8003 Shady St.	A	B	C	D
69.	789 Bell Dr.	A	B	C	D
70.	660 N. Jamaica Ct.	A	B	C	D
71.	449 Lake Dr.	A	B	C	D
72.	2200 Toledo Rd.	A	B	C	D

END

Coding and Memory (Test 2)
Coding Section (Step 1)

CODING GUIDE	
Address Range	**Delivery Route**
22-170 Hoover Ave. 60-180 Toucan Rd.	A
171-270 Hoover Ave. 181-300 Toucan Rd. 850-949 W. Canyon Dr.	B
8600-12000 E. Randal Dr. 34-145 Vermont Ave. 950-1050 W. Canyon Dr.	C
All mail that doesn't fall in one of the address range listed above	D

Coding and Memory (Test 2)
Coding Section (Step 1)

Sample Questions

	Address	Delivery Route			
1.	126 Hoover Ave.	A	B	C	D
2.	1012 W. Canyon Dr.	A	B	C	D
3.	320 Toucan Rd.	A	B	C	D
4.	46 Vermont Ave.	A	B	C	D

Sample Answer Grid			
1. (A)	(B)	(C)	(D)
2. (A)	(B)	(C)	(D)
3. (A)	(B)	(C)	(D)
4. (A)	(B)	(C)	(D)

The correct answers for sample questions

1. (A) 2.(C) 3.(D) 4.(C)

Coding and Memory (Test 2)
Coding Section (Step 2)

CODING GUIDE	
Address Range	**Delivery Route**
22-170 Hoover Ave. 60-180 Toucan Rd.	A
171-270 Hoover Ave. 181-300 Toucan Rd. 850-949 W. Canyon Dr.	B
8600-12000 E. Randal Dr. 34-145 Vermont Ave. 950-1050 W. Canyon Dr.	C
All mail that doesn't fall in one of the address range listed above	D

Coding and Memory (Test 2)
Coding Section (Step 2)

Sample Questions

	Address	Delivery Route			
1.	8629 E. Randal Dr.	A	B	C	D
2.	429 Toucan Rd.	A	B	C	D
3.	920 W. Canyon Dr.	A	B	C	D
4.	272 Hoover Ave.	A	B	C	D
5.	156 Vermont Ave.	A	B	C	D
6.	260 Toucan Rd.	A	B	C	D
7.	126 Hoover Ave.	A	B	C	D
8.	8590 E. Randal Dr.	A	B	C	D

Sample Answer Grid

	A	B	C	D
1.	Ⓐ	Ⓑ	Ⓒ	Ⓓ
2.	Ⓐ	Ⓑ	Ⓒ	Ⓓ
3.	Ⓐ	Ⓑ	Ⓒ	Ⓓ
4.	Ⓐ	Ⓑ	Ⓒ	Ⓓ
5.	Ⓐ	Ⓑ	Ⓒ	Ⓓ
6.	Ⓐ	Ⓑ	Ⓒ	Ⓓ
7.	Ⓐ	Ⓑ	Ⓒ	Ⓓ
8.	Ⓐ	Ⓑ	Ⓒ	Ⓓ

The correct answers for sample questions

1. (C) 2.(D) 3.(B) 4.(D) 5.(D) 6.(B) 7.(A) 8.(D)

Coding and Memory (Test 2)
Coding Section (Step 3)

CODING GUIDE	
Address Range	**Delivery Route**
22-170 Hoover Ave. 60-180 Toucan Rd.	A
171-270 Hoover Ave. 181-300 Toucan Rd. 850-949 W. Canyon Dr.	B
8600-12000 E. Randal Dr. 34-145 Vermont Ave. 950-1050 W. Canyon Dr.	C
All mail that doesn't fall in one of the address range listed above	D

Coding and Memory (Test 2)
Coding Section (Step 3)

Questions

	Address	Delivery Route			
1.	1040 E. Canyon Dr.	A	B	C	D
2.	179 Toucan Rd.	A	B	C	D
3.	270 Hoover Ave.	A	B	C	D
4.	280 Toucan Rd.	A	B	C	D
5.	8650 E. Randal Dr.	A	B	C	D
6.	27 S. Milton St.	A	B	C	D
7.	128 Vermont Ave.	A	B	C	D
8.	21 Hoover Ave.	A	B	C	D
9.	12010 E. Randal Dr.	A	B	C	D
10.	140 Toucan Rd.	A	B	C	D
11.	894 E. Canyon Dr.	A	B	C	D
12.	3184 N. Walnut St.	A	B	C	D
13.	46 Vermont Ave.	A	B	C	D
14.	180 Hoover Ave.	A	B	C	D
15.	392 Eden Ln.	A	B	C	D
16.	947 W. Canyon Dr.	A	B	C	D
17.	311 Toucan Rd.	A	B	C	D
18.	38 Duvall St.	A	B	C	D

Coding and Memory (Test 2)
Coding Section (Step 3)

CODING GUIDE	
Address Range	**Delivery Route**
22-170 Hoover Ave. 60-180 Toucan Rd.	A
171-270 Hoover Ave. 181-300 Toucan Rd. 850-949 W. Canyon Dr.	B
8600-12000 E. Randal Dr. 34-145 Vermont Ave. 950-1050 W. Canyon Dr.	C
All mail that doesn't fall in one of the address range listed above	D

Coding and Memory (Test 2)
Coding Section (Step 3)

Questions

	Address	Delivery Route			
19.	137 Vermont Ave.	A	B	C	D
20.	290 Toucan Rd.	A	B	C	D
21.	89 Hoover Ave.	A	B	C	D
22.	10017 E. Randal Dr.	A	B	C	D
23.	845 W. Canyon Dr.	A	B	C	D
24.	41 Mallard Dr.	A	B	C	D
25.	139 Vermont Ave.	A	B	C	D
26.	71 Toucan Rd.	A	B	C	D
27.	259 Hoover Ave.	A	B	C	D
28.	7614 Fairway Dr.	A	B	C	D
29.	151 Vermont Ave.	A	B	C	D
30.	172 Hoover Ave.	A	B	C	D
31.	124 Toucan Rd.	A	B	C	D
32.	1950 W. Canyon Dr.	A	B	C	D
33.	9010 E. Randal Dr.	A	B	C	D
34.	76 Obispo Ave.	A	B	C	D
35	181 Hoover Ave.	A	B	C	D
36.	741 Gilbert Ave.	A	B	C	D

Coding and Memory (Test 2)
Memory Section (Step 1)

CODING GUIDE	
Address Range	**Delivery Route**
22-170 Hoover Ave. 60-180 Toucan Rd.	A
171-270 Hoover Ave. 181-300 Toucan Rd. 850-949 W. Canyon Dr.	B
8600-12000 E. Randal Dr. 34-145 Vermont Ave. 950-1050 W. Canyon Dr.	C
All mail that doesn't fall in one of the address range listed above	D

Coding and Memory (Test 2)
Memory Section (Step 2)

Sample Questions

	Address	Delivery Route			
1.	143 Vermont Ave.	A	B	C	D
2.	292 Toucan Rd.	A	B	C	D
3.	169 Hoover Ave.	A	B	C	D
4.	820 W. Canyon Dr.	A	B	C	D
5.	11824 E. Randal Dr.	A	B	C	D
6.	380 Toucan Rd.	A	B	C	D
7.	970 W. Canyon Dr.	A	B	C	D
8.	254 Hoover Ave.	A	B	C	D

Sample Answer Grid			
1. (A)	(B)	(C)	(D)
2. (A)	(B)	(C)	(D)
3. (A)	(B)	(C)	(D)
4. (A)	(B)	(C)	(D)
5. (A)	(B)	(C)	(D)
6. (A)	(B)	(C)	(D)
7. (A)	(B)	(C)	(D)
8. (A)	(B)	(C)	(D)

The correct answers for sample questions

1. (C) 2.(B) 3.(A) 4.(D) 5.(C) 6.(D) 7.(C) 8.(B)

Coding and Memory (Test 2)
Memory Section (Step 3)

CODING GUIDE	
Address Range	**Delivery Route**
22-170 Hoover Ave. 60-180 Toucan Rd.	A
171-270 Hoover Ave. 181-300 Toucan Rd. 850-949 W. Canyon Dr.	B
8600-12000 E. Randal Dr. 34-145 Vermont Ave. 950-1050 W. Canyon Dr.	C
All mail that doesn't fall in one of the address range listed above	D

Coding and Memory (Test 2)
Memory Section (Step 4)

Questions

	Address	Delivery Route			
37.	120 Vermont Ave.	A	B	C	D
38.	175 Toucan Rd.	A	B	C	D
39.	1051 W. Canyon Dr.	A	B	C	D
40.	269 Hoover Ave.	A	B	C	D
41.	930 E. Canyon Dr.	A	B	C	D
42.	319 Harvey Ave.	A	B	C	D
43.	11200 E. Randal Dr.	A	B	C	D
44.	19700 E. Randal Dr.	A	B	C	D
45.	298 Toucan Rd.	A	B	C	D
46.	279 Garvin Ln.	A	B	C	D
47.	24 Hoover Ave.	A	B	C	D
48.	890 E. Canyon Dr.	A	B	C	D
49.	24 Vermont Ave.	A	B	C	D
50.	9149 Camilla St.	A	B	C	D
51.	102 Vermont Ave.	A	B	C	D
52.	362 Evans Dr.	A	B	C	D
53.	974 E. Canyon Dr.	A	B	C	D
54.	169 Hoover Ave.	A	B	C	D

Coding and Memory (Test 2)
Memory Section (Step 4)

Questions

	Address	Delivery Route			
55.	137 Toucan Rd.	A	B	C	D
56.	274 Hoover Ave.	A	B	C	D
57.	9200 W. Randal Dr.	A	B	C	D
58.	97 Vermont Ave.	A	B	C	D
59.	616 Salut Ct.	A	B	C	D
60.	948 W. Canyon Dr.	A	B	C	D
61.	194 Hoover Ave.	A	B	C	D
62.	8690 E. Randal Dr.	A	B	C	D
63.	249 Chalon Ct.	A	B	C	D
64.	35 Vermont Ave.	A	B	C	D
65.	69 Toucan Rd.	A	B	C	D
66.	4769 Emest Dr.	A	B	C	D
67.	964 W. Canyon Dr.	A	B	C	D
68.	18 Hoover Ave.	A	B	C	D
69.	269 Toucan Rd.	A	B	C	D
70.	39 Beta Dr.	A	B	C	D
71.	64 Vermont Ave.	A	B	C	D
72.	12014 E. Randal Dr.	A	B	C	D

END

Coding and Memory (Test 3)
Coding Section (Step 1)

CODING GUIDE	
Address Range	**Delivery Route**
20-199 Kline Dr. 15-35 E. 53rd St.	A
200-400 Kline Dr. 36-60 E. 53rd St. 1-99 Genoa Ave.	B
1-30 Lagarto Pl. 100-200 Genoa Ave. 1000-2000 Crown Ct.	C
All mail that doesn't fall in one of the address range listed above	D

Coding and Memory (Test 3)
Coding Section (Step 1)

Sample Questions

Address	Delivery Route			
1. 198 Genoa Ave.	A	B	C	D
2. 420 Kline Dr.	A	B	C	D
3. 34 E. 53rd St.	A	B	C	D
4. 20 Lagarto Pl.	A	B	C	D

Sample Answer Grid			
1. Ⓐ	Ⓑ	Ⓒ	Ⓓ
2. Ⓐ	Ⓑ	Ⓒ	Ⓓ
3. Ⓐ	Ⓑ	Ⓒ	Ⓓ
4. Ⓐ	Ⓑ	Ⓒ	Ⓓ

The correct answers for sample questions

1. (C) 2.(D) 3.(A) 4.(C)

Coding and Memory (Test 3)
Coding Section (Step 2)

CODING GUIDE	
Address Range	**Delivery Route**
20-199 Kline Dr. 15-35 E. 53rd St.	A
200-400 Kline Dr. 36-60 E. 53rd St. 1-99 Genoa Ave.	B
1-30 Lagarto Pl. 100-200 Genoa Ave. 1000-2000 Crown Ct.	C
All mail that doesn't fall in one of the address range listed above	D

Coding and Memory (Test 3)
Coding Section (Step 2)

Sample Questions

	Address	Delivery Route			
1.	800 Crown Ct.	A	B	C	D
2.	225 Kline Dr.	A	B	C	D
3.	66 E. 53rd St.	A	B	C	D
4.	146 Genoa Ave.	A	B	C	D
5.	38 Lagarto Pl.	A	B	C	D
6.	74 Kline Dr.	A	B	C	D
7.	89 Genoa Ave.	A	B	C	D
8.	1200 Crown Ct.	A	B	C	D

Sample Answer Grid

1.	Ⓐ	Ⓑ	Ⓒ	Ⓓ
2.	Ⓐ	Ⓑ	Ⓒ	Ⓓ
3.	Ⓐ	Ⓑ	Ⓒ	Ⓓ
4.	Ⓐ	Ⓑ	Ⓒ	Ⓓ
5.	Ⓐ	Ⓑ	Ⓒ	Ⓓ
6.	Ⓐ	Ⓑ	Ⓒ	Ⓓ
7.	Ⓐ	Ⓑ	Ⓒ	Ⓓ
8.	Ⓐ	Ⓑ	Ⓒ	Ⓓ

The correct answers for sample questions

1. (D) 2.(B) 3.(D) 4.(C) 5.(D) 6.(A) 7.(B) 8.(C)

Coding and Memory (Test 3)
Coding Section (Step 3)

CODING GUIDE	
Address Range	**Delivery Route**
20-199 Kline Dr. 15-35 E. 53rd St.	A
200-400 Kline Dr. 36-60 E. 53rd St. 1-99 Genoa Ave.	B
1-30 Lagarto Pl. 100-200 Genoa Ave. 1000-2000 Crown Ct.	C
All mail that doesn't fall in one of the address range listed above	D

Coding and Memory (Test 3)
Coding Section (Step 3)

Questions

	Address	Delivery Route			
1.	234 Kline Dr.	A	B	C	D
2.	26 Lagarto Pl.	A	B	C	D
3.	17 W. 53rd St.	A	B	C	D
4.	48 Kline Dr.	A	B	C	D
5.	1230 Crown Ct.	A	B	C	D
6.	729 Center St.	A	B	C	D
7.	59 E. 53rd St.	A	B	C	D
8.	123 Genoa Ave.	A	B	C	D
9.	812 Oxford Rd.	A	B	C	D
10.	366 Kline Dr.	A	B	C	D
11.	37 W. 53rd St.	A	B	C	D
12.	86 Genoa Ave.	A	B	C	D
13.	860 Crown Ct.	A	B	C	D
14.	224 Genoa Ave.	A	B	C	D
15.	33 E. 53rd St.	A	B	C	D
16.	39 Lagarto Pl.	A	B	C	D
17.	19 Kline Dr.	A	B	C	D
18.	87 Genoa Ave.	A	B	C	D

Coding and Memory (Test 3)
Coding Section (Step 3)

CODING GUIDE	
Address Range	**Delivery Route**
20-199 Kline Dr. 15-35 E. 53rd St.	A
200-400 Kline Dr. 36-60 E. 53rd St. 1-99 Genoa Ave.	B
1-30 Lagarto Pl. 100-200 Genoa Ave. 1000-2000 Crown Ct.	C
All mail that doesn't fall in one of the address range listed above	D

Coding and Memory (Test 3)
Coding Section (Step 3)

Questions

	Address	Delivery Route			
19.	1469 Sarco Ct.	A	B	C	D
20.	894 Crown Ct.	A	B	C	D
21.	26 Lagarto Pl.	A	B	C	D
22.	19 E. 53rd St.	A	B	C	D
23.	125 Kline Dr.	A	B	C	D
24.	57 E. 53rd St.	A	B	C	D
25.	569 Heather Ave.	A	B	C	D
26.	178 Genoa Ave.	A	B	C	D
27.	96 Kline Dr.	A	B	C	D
28.	55 Lagarto Pl.	A	B	C	D
29.	37 W. 53rd St.	A	B	C	D
30.	26 Riata St.	A	B	C	D
31.	104 Genoa Ave.	A	B	C	D
32.	389 Kline Dr.	A	B	C	D
33.	16397 Western Ave.	A	B	C	D
34.	1020 Crown Ct.	A	B	C	D
35	34 E. 53rd St.	A	B	C	D
36.	28 Lagarto Pl.	A	B	C	D

Coding and Memory (Test 3)
Memory Section (Step 1)

CODING GUIDE	
Address Range	**Delivery Route**
20-199 Kline Dr. 15-35 E. 53rd St.	A
200-400 Kline Dr. 36-60 E. 53rd St. 1-99 Genoa Ave.	B
1-30 Lagarto Pl. 100-200 Genoa Ave. 1000-2000 Crown Ct.	C
All mail that doesn't fall in one of the address range listed above	D

Coding and Memory (Test 3)
Memory Section (Step 2)

Sample Questions

	Address	Delivery Route			
1.	37 E. 53rd St.	A	B	C	D
2.	1890 Crown Ct.	A	B	C	D
3.	180 Kline Dr.	A	B	C	D
4.	211 Genoa Ave.	A	B	C	D
5.	26 Lagarto Pl.	A	B	C	D
6.	261 Genoa Ave.	A	B	C	D
7.	180 Kline Dr.	A	B	C	D
8.	57 E. 53rd St.	A	B	C	D

Sample Answer Grid

	A	B	C	D
1.	Ⓐ	Ⓑ	Ⓒ	Ⓓ
2.	Ⓐ	Ⓑ	Ⓒ	Ⓓ
3.	Ⓐ	Ⓑ	Ⓒ	Ⓓ
4.	Ⓐ	Ⓑ	Ⓒ	Ⓓ
5.	Ⓐ	Ⓑ	Ⓒ	Ⓓ
6.	Ⓐ	Ⓑ	Ⓒ	Ⓓ
7.	Ⓐ	Ⓑ	Ⓒ	Ⓓ
8.	Ⓐ	Ⓑ	Ⓒ	Ⓓ

The correct answers for sample questions

1. (B) 2.(C) 3.(A) 4.(D) 5.(C) 6.(D) 7.(A) 8.(B)

Coding and Memory (Test 3)
Memory Section (Step 3)

CODING GUIDE	
Address Range	**Delivery Route**
20-199 Kline Dr. 15-35 E. 53rd St.	A
200-400 Kline Dr. 36-60 E. 53rd St. 1-99 Genoa Ave.	B
1-30 Lagarto Pl. 100-200 Genoa Ave. 1000-2000 Crown Ct.	C
All mail that doesn't fall in one of the address range listed above	D

Coding and Memory (Test 3)
Memory Section (Step 4)

Questions

	Address	Delivery Route			
37.	187 Genoa Ave.	A	B	C	D
38.	27 E. 53rd St.	A	B	C	D
39.	56 Kline Dr.	A	B	C	D
40.	49 Lagarto Pl.	A	B	C	D
41.	124 W. Alameda Ave.	A	B	C	D
42.	1240 Crown Ct.	A	B	C	D
43.	72 E. 53rd St.	A	B	C	D
44.	241 Dawson Rd.	A	B	C	D
45.	16 Lagarto Pl.	A	B	C	D
46.	129 Genoa Ave.	A	B	C	D
47.	394 Trout Way	A	B	C	D
48.	314 Kline Dr.	A	B	C	D
49.	1914 Crown Ct.	A	B	C	D
50.	78 Lagarto Pl.	A	B	C	D
51.	25 W. 53rd St.	A	B	C	D
52.	729 N. Hill St.	A	B	C	D
53.	1800 Crown Ct.	A	B	C	D
54.	198 Kline Dr.	A	B	C	D

Coding and Memory (Test 3)
Memory Section (Step 4)

Questions

	Address	Delivery Route			
55.	86 Kline Dr.	A	B	C	D
56.	11 Genoa Ave.	A	B	C	D
57.	972 Crown Ct.	A	B	C	D
58.	290 W. Cade Ct.	A	B	C	D
59.	42 E. 53rd St.	A	B	C	D
60.	56 Lagarto Pl.	A	B	C	D
61.	165 Kline Dr.	A	B	C	D
62.	769 N. Bolton Cir.	A	B	C	D
63.	95 Lagarto Pl.	A	B	C	D
64.	98 Genoa Ave.	A	B	C	D
65.	369 Eugene Dr.	A	B	C	D
66.	38 W. 53rd St.	A	B	C	D
67.	1518 Crown Ct.	A	B	C	D
68.	769 Cherry Pl.	A	B	C	D
69.	112 Genoa Ave.	A	B	C	D
70.	446 Kline Dr.	A	B	C	D
71.	32 E. 53rd St.	A	B	C	D
72.	3600 Crown Ct.	A	B	C	D

END

Coding and Memory (Test 4)
Coding Section (Step 1)

CODING GUIDE	
Address Range	**Delivery Route**
40-299 Redwood Dr. 30-399 Baldwin Ave.	A
300-500 Redwood Dr. 400-900 Baldwin Ave. 4-50 W. 72nd St.	B
900-2000 Naples Ct. 25-200 Beckett Pl. 51-100 W. 72nd St.	C
All mail that doesn't fall in one of the address range listed above	D

Coding and Memory (Test 4)
Coding Section (Step 1)

Sample Questions

	Address	Delivery Route			
1.	280 Baldwin Ave.	A	B	C	D
2.	46 W. 72nd St.	A	B	C	D
3.	24 Beckett Pl.	A	B	C	D
4.	417 Redwood Dr.	A	B	C	D

Sample Answer Grid

1.	Ⓐ	Ⓑ	Ⓒ	Ⓓ
2.	Ⓐ	Ⓑ	Ⓒ	Ⓓ
3.	Ⓐ	Ⓑ	Ⓒ	Ⓓ
4.	Ⓐ	Ⓑ	Ⓒ	Ⓓ

The correct answers for sample questions

1. (A) 2.(B) 3.(D) 4.(B)

Coding and Memory (Test 4)
Coding Section (Step 2)

CODING GUIDE	
Address Range	**Delivery Route**
40-299 Redwood Dr. 30-399 Baldwin Ave.	A
300-500 Redwood Dr. 400-900 Baldwin Ave. 4-50 W. 72nd St.	B
900-2000 Naples Ct. 25-200 Beckett Pl. 51-100 W. 72nd St.	C
All mail that doesn't fall in one of the address range listed above	D

Coding and Memory (Test 4)

Coding Section (Step 2)

Sample Questions

	Address	Delivery Route			
1.	78 W. 72nd St.	A	B	C	D
2.	216 Beckett Pl.	A	B	C	D
3.	416 Redwood Dr.	A	B	C	D
4.	575 Baldwin Ave.	A	B	C	D
5.	1025 Naples Ct.	A	B	C	D
6.	3 W. 72nd St.	A	B	C	D
7.	280 Redwood Dr.	A	B	C	D
8.	910 Baldwin Ave.	A	B	C	D

Sample Answer Grid			
1.	Ⓐ Ⓑ Ⓒ Ⓓ		
2.	Ⓐ Ⓑ Ⓒ Ⓓ		
3.	Ⓐ Ⓑ Ⓒ Ⓓ		
4.	Ⓐ Ⓑ Ⓒ Ⓓ		
5.	Ⓐ Ⓑ Ⓒ Ⓓ		
6.	Ⓐ Ⓑ Ⓒ Ⓓ		
7.	Ⓐ Ⓑ Ⓒ Ⓓ		
8.	Ⓐ Ⓑ Ⓒ Ⓓ		

The correct answers for sample questions

1. (C) 2.(D) 3.(B) 4.(B) 5.(C) 6.(D) 7.(A) 8.(D)

Coding and Memory (Test 4)
Coding Section (Step 3)

CODING GUIDE	
Address Range	**Delivery Route**
40-299 Redwood Dr. 30-399 Baldwin Ave.	A
300-500 Redwood Dr. 400-900 Baldwin Ave. 4-50 W. 72nd St.	B
900-2000 Naples Ct. 25-200 Beckett Pl. 51-100 W. 72nd St.	C
All mail that doesn't fall in one of the address range listed above	D

Coding and Memory (Test 4)
Coding Section (Step 3)

Questions

	Address	Delivery Route			
1.	55 W. 72nd St.	A	B	C	D
2.	200 Camela St.	A	B	C	D
3.	910 Baldwin Ave.	A	B	C	D
4.	190 Redwood Dr.	A	B	C	D
5.	20 Beckett Pl.	A	B	C	D
6.	423 Redwood Dr.	A	B	C	D
7.	920 Naples Ct.	A	B	C	D
8.	272 Baldwin Ave.	A	B	C	D
9.	240 Beckett Pl.	A	B	C	D
10.	35 Redwood Dr.	A	B	C	D
11.	1050 Naples Ct.	A	B	C	D
12.	120 W. 72nd St.	A	B	C	D
13.	142 Sabal Way	A	B	C	D
14.	79 W. 72nd St.	A	B	C	D
15.	49 E. 72nd St.	A	B	C	D
16.	150 Beckett Pl.	A	B	C	D
17.	29 Baldwin Ave.	A	B	C	D
18.	44 W. 72nd St.	A	B	C	D

Coding and Memory (Test 4)
Coding Section (Step 3)

CODING GUIDE	
Address Range	**Delivery Route**
40-299 Redwood Dr. 30-399 Baldwin Ave.	A
300-500 Redwood Dr. 400-900 Baldwin Ave. 4-50 W. 72nd St.	B
900-2000 Naples Ct. 25-200 Beckett Pl. 51-100 W. 72nd St.	C
All mail that doesn't fall in one of the address range listed above	D

Coding and Memory (Test 4)
Coding Section (Step 3)

Questions

	Address	Delivery Route			
19.	43 N. Harvard Blvd.	A	B	C	D
20.	98 W. 72nd St.	A	B	C	D
21.	850 Naples Ct.	A	B	C	D
22.	390 Redwood Dr.	A	B	C	D
23.	580 Redwood Dr.	A	B	C	D
24.	153 W.72nd St.	A	B	C	D
25.	420 Redwood Dr.	A	B	C	D
26.	76 W. 64th Ave.	A	B	C	D
27.	15 W. 72nd St.	A	B	C	D
28.	79 S. Mcneal Ln.	A	B	C	D
29.	2010 Naples Ct.	A	B	C	D
30.	97 Beckett Pl.	A	B	C	D
31.	27 W. 72nd St.	A	B	C	D
32.	79 S. Lincoln Ave.	A	B	C	D
33.	1021 Naples Ct.	A	B	C	D
34.	401 Baldwin Ave.	A	B	C	D
35	309 Redwood Dr.	A	B	C	D
36.	21 E. 72nd St.	A	B	C	D

Coding and Memory (Test 4)
Memory Section (Step 1)

CODING GUIDE	
Address Range	**Delivery Route**
40-299 Redwood Dr. 30-399 Baldwin Ave.	A
300-500 Redwood Dr. 400-900 Baldwin Ave. 4-50 W. 72nd St.	B
900-2000 Naples Ct. 25-200 Beckett Pl. 51-100 W. 72nd St.	C
All mail that doesn't fall in one of the address range listed above	D

Coding and Memory (Test 4)
Memory Section (Step 2)

Sample Questions

Address	Delivery Route			
1. 149 Beckett Pl.	A	B	C	D
2. 110 W. 72nd St.	A	B	C	D
3. 96 Baldwin Ave.	A	B	C	D
4. 1692 Naples Ct.	A	B	C	D
5. 601 Redwood Dr.	A	B	C	D
6. 2014 Naples Ct.	A	B	C	D
7. 379 Redwood Dr.	A	B	C	D
8. 86 W. 72nd St.	A	B	C	D

Sample Answer Grid

	A	B	C	D
1.	(A)	(B)	(C)	(D)
2.	(A)	(B)	(C)	(D)
3.	(A)	(B)	(C)	(D)
4.	(A)	(B)	(C)	(D)
5.	(A)	(B)	(C)	(D)
6.	(A)	(B)	(C)	(D)
7.	(A)	(B)	(C)	(D)
8.	(A)	(B)	(C)	(D)

The correct answers for sample questions

1. (C) 2.(D) 3.(A) 4.(C) 5.(D) 6.(D) 7.(B) 8.(C)

Coding and Memory (Test 4)
Memory Section (Step 3)

CODING GUIDE	
Address Range	**Delivery Route**
40-299 Redwood Dr. 30-399 Baldwin Ave.	A
300-500 Redwood Dr. 400-900 Baldwin Ave. 4-50 W. 72nd St.	B
900-2000 Naples Ct. 25-200 Beckett Pl. 51-100 W. 72nd St.	C
All mail that doesn't fall in one of the address range listed above	D

Coding and Memory (Test 4)
Memory Section (Step 4)

Questions

	Address	Delivery Route			
37.	867 Baldwin Ave.	A	B	C	D
38.	160 Redwood Dr.	A	B	C	D
39.	12 E. 72nd St.	A	B	C	D
40.	1640 Naples Ct.	A	B	C	D
41.	269 Redwood Dr.	A	B	C	D
42.	47 Walnut St.	A	B	C	D
43.	161 Beckett Pl.	A	B	C	D
44.	290 Baldwin Ave.	A	B	C	D
45.	86 W. 72nd St.	A	B	C	D
46.	714 Almy Ave.	A	B	C	D
47.	2111 Naples Ct.	A	B	C	D
48.	167 Beckett Pl.	A	B	C	D
49.	78 Redwood Dr.	A	B	C	D
50.	41 Rick St.	A	B	C	D
51.	53 W. 72nd St.	A	B	C	D
52.	400 Baldwin Ave.	A	B	C	D
53.	26 Beckett Pl.	A	B	C	D
54.	719 N. Woodside St.	A	B	C	D

Coding and Memory (Test 4)
Memory Section (Step 4)

Questions

	Address	Delivery Route			
55.	927 Naples Ct.	A	B	C	D
56.	400 Beckett Pl.	A	B	C	D
57.	369 Redwood Dr.	A	B	C	D
58.	219 Shelton Rd.	A	B	C	D
59.	48 W.72nd St.	A	B	C	D
60.	879 Baldwin Ave.	A	B	C	D
61.	317 Redwood Dr.	A	B	C	D
62.	269 W. 34th St.	A	B	C	D
63.	76 E. 72nd St.	A	B	C	D
64.	1250 Baldwin Ave.	A	B	C	D
65.	180 Beckett Pl.	A	B	C	D
66.	760 Naples Ct.	A	B	C	D
67.	26 Thom Cir.	A	B	C	D
68.	769 Baldwin Ave.	A	B	C	D
69.	417 Redwood Dr.	A	B	C	D
70.	123 N. Lobo Way	A	B	C	D
71.	124 Beckett Pl.	A	B	C	D
72.	150 W. 72nd St.	A	B	C	D

END

Coding and Memory (Test 5)
Coding Section (Step 1)

CODING GUIDE	
Address Range	**Delivery Route**
1-199 S. Pickens St. 30-300 Brian Ct. 200-500 Carriage Ln.	A
200-400 S. Pickens St. 501-800 Carriage Ln.	B
301-600 Brian Ct. 20000-24000 Tiburon Dr. 1-50 Rosen Ave.	C
All mail that doesn't fall in one of the address range listed above	D

Coding and Memory (Test 5)
Coding Section (Step 1)

Sample Questions

Address	Delivery Route
1. 189 Brian Ct.	A B C D
2. 20419 Tiburon Dr.	A B C D
3. 466 S. Pickens St.	A B C D
4. 600 Carriage Ln.	A B C D

Sample Answer Grid			
1.	Ⓐ	Ⓑ	Ⓒ	Ⓓ
2.	Ⓐ	Ⓑ	Ⓒ	Ⓓ
3.	Ⓐ	Ⓑ	Ⓒ	Ⓓ
4.	Ⓐ	Ⓑ	Ⓒ	Ⓓ

The correct answers for sample questions

1. (A) 2.(C) 3.(D) 4.(B)

Coding and Memory (Test 5)
Coding Section (Step 2)

CODING GUIDE	
Address Range	**Delivery Route**
1-199 S. Pickens St. 30-300 Brian Ct. 200-500 Carriage Ln.	A
200-400 S. Pickens St. 501-800 Carriage Ln.	B
301-600 Brian Ct. 20000-24000 Tiburon Dr. 1-50 Rosen Ave.	C
All mail that doesn't fall in one of the address range listed above	D

Coding and Memory (Test 5)
Coding Section (Step 2)

Sample Questions

	Address	Delivery Route			
1.	292 S. Pickens St.	A	B	C	D
2.	48 Rosen Ave.	A	B	C	D
3.	620 Brian Ct.	A	B	C	D
4.	180 Carriage Ln.	A	B	C	D
5.	20419 Tiburon Dr.	A	B	C	D
6.	801 Carriage Ln.	A	B	C	D
7.	270 Brian Ct.	A	B	C	D
8.	19219 Tiburon Dr.	A	B	C	D

Sample Answer Grid			
1. Ⓐ	Ⓑ	Ⓒ	Ⓓ
2. Ⓐ	Ⓑ	Ⓒ	Ⓓ
3. Ⓐ	Ⓑ	Ⓒ	Ⓓ
4. Ⓐ	Ⓑ	Ⓒ	Ⓓ
5. Ⓐ	Ⓑ	Ⓒ	Ⓓ
6. Ⓐ	Ⓑ	Ⓒ	Ⓓ
7. Ⓐ	Ⓑ	Ⓒ	Ⓓ
8. Ⓐ	Ⓑ	Ⓒ	Ⓓ

The correct answers for sample questions

1. (B) 2.(C) 3.(D) 4.(D) 5.(C) 6.(D) 7.(A) 8.(D)

Coding and Memory (Test 5)
Coding Section (Step 3)

CODING GUIDE	
Address Range	**Delivery Route**
1-199 S. Pickens St. 30-300 Brian Ct. 200-500 Carriage Ln.	A
200-400 S. Pickens St. 501-800 Carriage Ln.	B
301-600 Brian Ct. 20000-24000 Tiburon Dr. 1-50 Rosen Ave.	C
All mail that doesn't fall in one of the address range listed above	D

Coding and Memory (Test 5)
Coding Section (Step 3)

Questions

	Address	Delivery Route			
1.	39 Rosen Ave.	A	B	C	D
2.	24021 Tiburon Dr.	A	B	C	D
3.	321 S. Pickens St.	A	B	C	D
4.	295 Brian Ct.	A	B	C	D
5.	760 Carriage Ln.	A	B	C	D
6.	780 S. Oxford Ave.	A	B	C	D
7.	45 Rosen Ave.	A	B	C	D
8.	412 Carriage Ln.	A	B	C	D
9.	23200 Tiburon Dr.	A	B	C	D
10.	29 Brian Ct.	A	B	C	D
11.	412 S. Pickens St.	A	B	C	D
12.	210 Mitchell Rd.	A	B	C	D
13.	390 Carriage Ln.	A	B	C	D
14.	20049 Tiburon Dr.	A	B	C	D
15.	198 N. Pickens St.	A	B	C	D
16.	601 Brian Ct.	A	B	C	D
17.	712 Carriage Ln.	A	B	C	D
18.	400 N. Gallop Ln.	A	B	C	D

Coding and Memory (Test 5)
Coding Section (Step 3)

CODING GUIDE	
Address Range	**Delivery Route**
1-199 S. Pickens St. 30-300 Brian Ct. 200-500 Carriage Ln.	A
200-400 S. Pickens St. 501-800 Carriage Ln.	B
301-600 Brian Ct. 20000-24000 Tiburon Dr. 1-50 Rosen Ave.	C
All mail that doesn't fall in one of the address range listed above	D

Coding and Memory (Test 5)
Coding Section (Step 3)

Questions

	Address	Delivery Route			
19.	121 Brian Ct.	A	B	C	D
20.	60 Rosen Ave.	A	B	C	D
21.	213 S. Pickens St.	A	B	C	D
22.	25007 Tiburon Dr.	A	B	C	D
23.	769 Falcon Way	A	B	C	D
24.	560 Brian Ct.	A	B	C	D
25.	79 Halsey Dr.	A	B	C	D
26.	25 Brian Ct.	A	B	C	D
27.	248 Carriage Ln.	A	B	C	D
28.	38 Rosen Ave.	A	B	C	D
29.	23619 Tiburon Dr.	A	B	C	D
30.	210 W. Pickens St.	A	B	C	D
31.	419 Patrina Dr.	A	B	C	D
32.	560 S. Pickens St.	A	B	C	D
33.	310 Carriage Ln.	A	B	C	D
34.	914 N. Oakwood Dr.	A	B	C	D
35	799 Carriage Ln.	A	B	C	D
36.	36 Rosen Ave.	A	B	C	D

Coding and Memory (Test 5)
Memory Section (Step 1)

CODING GUIDE	
Address Range	**Delivery Route**
1-199 S. Pickens St. 30-300 Brian Ct. 200-500 Carriage Ln.	A
200-400 S. Pickens St. 501-800 Carriage Ln.	B
301-600 Brian Ct. 20000-24000 Tiburon Dr. 1-50 Rosen Ave.	C
All mail that doesn't fall in one of the address range listed above	D

Coding and Memory (Test 5)
Memory Section (Step 2)

Sample Questions

	Address	Delivery Route			
1.	289 Brian Ct.	A	B	C	D
2.	201 S. Pickens St.	A	B	C	D
3.	469 Carriage Ln.	A	B	C	D
4.	25 Rosen Ave.	A	B	C	D
5.	20046 Tiburon Dr.	A	B	C	D
6.	869 Carriage Ln.	A	B	C	D
7.	369 S. Pickens St.	A	B	C	D
8.	72 Rosen Ave.	A	B	C	D

Sample Answer Grid

1.	Ⓐ	Ⓑ	Ⓒ	Ⓓ
2.	Ⓐ	Ⓑ	Ⓒ	Ⓓ
3.	Ⓐ	Ⓑ	Ⓒ	Ⓓ
4.	Ⓐ	Ⓑ	Ⓒ	Ⓓ
5.	Ⓐ	Ⓑ	Ⓒ	Ⓓ
6.	Ⓐ	Ⓑ	Ⓒ	Ⓓ
7.	Ⓐ	Ⓑ	Ⓒ	Ⓓ
8.	Ⓐ	Ⓑ	Ⓒ	Ⓓ

The correct answers for sample questions

1. (A) 2.(B) 3.(A) 4.(C) 5.(C) 6.(D) 7.(B) 8.(D)

Coding and Memory (Test 5)

Memory Section (Step 3)

CODING GUIDE	
Address Range	**Delivery Route**
1-199 S. Pickens St. 30-300 Brian Ct. 200-500 Carriage Ln.	A
200-400 S. Pickens St. 501-800 Carriage Ln.	B
301-600 Brian Ct. 20000-24000 Tiburon Dr. 1-50 Rosen Ave.	C
All mail that doesn't fall in one of the address range listed above	D

Coding and Memory (Test 5)
Memory Section (Step 4)

Questions

	Address	Delivery Route			
37.	370 Brian Ct.	A	B	C	D
38.	419 S. Pickens St.	A	B	C	D
39.	20010 Tiburon Dr.	A	B	C	D
40.	241 Carriage Ln.	A	B	C	D
41.	768 Eden Ln.	A	B	C	D
42.	310 N. Pickens St.	A	B	C	D
43.	46 Rosen Ave.	A	B	C	D
44.	769 Carriage Ln.	A	B	C	D
45.	25004 Tiburon Dr.	A	B	C	D
46.	32 Brian Ct.	A	B	C	D
47.	291 S. Camisa Cir.	A	B	C	D
48.	65 Rosen Ave.	A	B	C	D
49.	99 S. Pickens St.	A	B	C	D
50.	2194 Chico Ct.	A	B	C	D
51.	910 Carriage Ln.	A	B	C	D
52.	20411 Tiburon Dr.	A	B	C	D
53.	319 Bayview Ave.	A	B	C	D
54.	298 Brian Ct.	A	B	C	D

Coding and Memory (Test 5)
Memory Section (Step 4)

Questions

	Address	Delivery Route			
55.	188 Carriage Ln.	A	B	C	D
56.	20120 Tiburon Dr.	A	B	C	D
57.	294 Brian Ct.	A	B	C	D
58.	3196 Overlook Dr.	A	B	C	D
59.	56 Rosen Ave.	A	B	C	D
60.	319 S. Pickens St.	A	B	C	D
61.	2194 N. 73rd Ave.	A	B	C	D
62.	20045 Tiburon Dr.	A	B	C	D
63.	420 Carriage Ln.	A	B	C	D
64.	42 Rosen Ave.	A	B	C	D
65.	186 S. Pickens St.	A	B	C	D
66.	687 Archer Ln.	A	B	C	D
67.	214 Brian Ct.	A	B	C	D
68.	15 E. Pickens St.	A	B	C	D
69.	720 Carriage Ln.	A	B	C	D
70.	6829 Slaton St.	A	B	C	D
71.	49 Rosen Ave.	A	B	C	D
72.	156 Carriage Ln.	A	B	C	D

END

Coding and Memory (Test 6)
Coding Section (Step 1)

CODING GUIDE	
Address Range	**Delivery Route**
50-250 Harvard Blvd. 300-500 N. Camden Pl. 15500-16999 High Rd.	A
251-450 Harvard Blvd. 501-700 N. Camden Pl.	B
17000-17500 High Rd. 700-1200 W. Pico Blvd. 1-500 Choate St.	C
All mail that doesn't fall in one of the address range listed above	D

Coding and Memory (Test 6)
Coding Section (Step 1)

Sample Questions

Address	Delivery Route			
1. 17420 High Rd.	A	B	C	D
2. 260 Harvard Blvd.	A	B	C	D
3. 350 N. Camden Pl.	A	B	C	D
4. 630 W. Pico Blvd.	A	B	C	D

Sample Answer Grid			
1. Ⓐ	Ⓑ	Ⓒ	Ⓓ
2. Ⓐ	Ⓑ	Ⓒ	Ⓓ
3. Ⓐ	Ⓑ	Ⓒ	Ⓓ
4. Ⓐ	Ⓑ	Ⓒ	Ⓓ

The correct answers for sample questions

1. (C) 2.(B) 3.(A) 4.(D)

Coding and Memory (Test 6)
Coding Section (Step 2)

CODING GUIDE	
Address Range	**Delivery Route**
50-250 Harvard Blvd. 300-500 N. Camden Pl. 15500-16999 High Rd.	A
251-450 Harvard Blvd. 501-700 N. Camden Pl.	B
17000-17500 High Rd. 700-1200 W. Pico Blvd. 1-500 Choate St.	C
All mail that doesn't fall in one of the address range listed above	D

Coding and Memory (Test 6)
Coding Section (Step 2)

Sample Questions

	Address	Delivery Route			
1.	440 Harvard Blvd.	A	B	C	D
2.	129 Choate St.	A	B	C	D
3.	400 N. Camden Pl.	A	B	C	D
4.	16900 High Rd.	A	B	C	D
5.	126 Harvard Blvd.	A	B	C	D
6.	15412 High Rd.	A	B	C	D
7.	567 Choate St.	A	B	C	D
8.	712 N. Camden Pl.	A	B	C	D

Sample Answer Grid			
1. Ⓐ	Ⓑ	Ⓒ	Ⓓ
2. Ⓐ	Ⓑ	Ⓒ	Ⓓ
3. Ⓐ	Ⓑ	Ⓒ	Ⓓ
4. Ⓐ	Ⓑ	Ⓒ	Ⓓ
5. Ⓐ	Ⓑ	Ⓒ	Ⓓ
6. Ⓐ	Ⓑ	Ⓒ	Ⓓ
7. Ⓐ	Ⓑ	Ⓒ	Ⓓ
8. Ⓐ	Ⓑ	Ⓒ	Ⓓ

The correct answers for sample questions

1. (B) 2.(C) 3.(A) 4.(A) 5.(A) 6.(D) 7.(D) 8.(D)

Coding and Memory (Test 6)

Coding Section (Step 3)

CODING GUIDE	
Address Range	**Delivery Route**
50-250 Harvard Blvd. 300-500 N. Camden Pl. 15500-16999 High Rd.	A
251-450 Harvard Blvd. 501-700 N. Camden Pl.	B
17000-17500 High Rd. 700-1200 W. Pico Blvd. 1-500 Choate St.	C
All mail that doesn't fall in one of the address range listed above	D

Coding and Memory (Test 6)
Coding Section (Step 3)

Questions

	Address	Delivery Route			
1.	17503 High Rd.	A	B	C	D
2.	240 Harvard Blvd.	A	B	C	D
3.	870 W. Oxford Ave.	A	B	C	D
4.	324 Harvard Blvd.	A	B	C	D
5.	369 Choate St.	A	B	C	D
6.	460 W. Camden Pl.	A	B	C	D
7.	1245 W. Pico Blvd.	A	B	C	D
8.	860 Alameda Ave.	A	B	C	D
9.	15594 High Rd.	A	B	C	D
10.	264 Harvard Blvd.	A	B	C	D
11.	411 Choate St.	A	B	C	D
12.	650 E. Camden Pl.	A	B	C	D
13.	411 E. Kersey Ct.	A	B	C	D
14.	17260 High Rd.	A	B	C	D
15.	520 Choate St.	A	B	C	D
16.	79 Harvard Blvd.	A	B	C	D
17.	16812 High Rd.	A	B	C	D
18.	1120 W. Pico Blvd.	A	B	C	D

Coding and Memory (Test 6)
Coding Section (Step 3)

CODING GUIDE	
Address Range	**Delivery Route**
50-250 Harvard Blvd. 300-500 N. Camden Pl. 15500-16999 High Rd.	A
251-450 Harvard Blvd. 501-700 N. Camden Pl.	B
17000-17500 High Rd. 700-1200 W. Pico Blvd. 1-500 Choate St.	C
All mail that doesn't fall in one of the address range listed above	D

Coding and Memory (Test 6)
Coding Section (Step 3)

Questions

	Address	Delivery Route			
19.	560 Fletcher St.	A	B	C	D
20.	249 Harvard Blvd.	A	B	C	D
21.	645 W. Pico Blvd.	A	B	C	D
22.	16899 High Rd.	A	B	C	D
23.	710 Wheat Rd.	A	B	C	D
24.	360 Choate St.	A	B	C	D
25.	17260 High Rd.	A	B	C	D
26.	567 N. Camden Pl.	A	B	C	D
27.	469 Bolton Dr.	A	B	C	D
28.	280 N. Camden Pl.	A	B	C	D
29.	465 Harvard Blvd.	A	B	C	D
30.	16817 High Rd.	A	B	C	D
31.	3101 Whitecap Ln.	A	B	C	D
32.	620 N. Camden Pl.	A	B	C	D
33.	445 Harvard Blvd.	A	B	C	D
34.	910 W. Pico Blvd.	A	B	C	D
35	26 Alden Ln.	A	B	C	D
36.	17300 High Rd.	A	B	C	D

Coding and Memory (Test 6)
Memory Section (Step 1)

CODING GUIDE	
Address Range	**Delivery Route**
50-250 Harvard Blvd. 300-500 N. Camden Pl. 15500-16999 High Rd.	A
251-450 Harvard Blvd. 501-700 N. Camden Pl.	B
17000-17500 High Rd. 700-1200 W. Pico Blvd. 1-500 Choate St.	C
All mail that doesn't fall in one of the address range listed above	D

Coding and Memory (Test 6)
Memory Section (Step 2)

Sample Questions

	Address	Delivery Route			
1.	824 W. Pico Blvd.	A	B	C	D
2.	449 Harvard Blvd.	A	B	C	D
3.	267 Choate St.	A	B	C	D
4.	16800 High Rd.	A	B	C	D
5.	412 N. Camden Pl.	A	B	C	D
6.	246 Harvard Blvd.	A	B	C	D
7.	1301 W. Pico Blvd.	A	B	C	D
8.	614 W. Camden Pl.	A	B	C	D

Sample Answer Grid
1. Ⓐ Ⓑ Ⓒ Ⓓ
2. Ⓐ Ⓑ Ⓒ Ⓓ
3. Ⓐ Ⓑ Ⓒ Ⓓ
4. Ⓐ Ⓑ Ⓒ Ⓓ
5. Ⓐ Ⓑ Ⓒ Ⓓ
6. Ⓐ Ⓑ Ⓒ Ⓓ
7. Ⓐ Ⓑ Ⓒ Ⓓ
8. Ⓐ Ⓑ Ⓒ Ⓓ

The correct answers for sample questions

1. (C) 2.(B) 3.(C) 4.(A) 5.(A) 6.(A) 7.(D) 8.(D)

Coding and Memory (Test 6)
Memory Section (Step 3)

CODING GUIDE	
Address Range	**Delivery Route**
50-250 Harvard Blvd. 300-500 N. Camden Pl. 15500-16999 High Rd.	A
251-450 Harvard Blvd. 501-700 N. Camden Pl.	B
17000-17500 High Rd. 700-1200 W. Pico Blvd. 1-500 Choate St.	C
All mail that doesn't fall in one of the address range listed above	D

Coding and Memory (Test 6)
Memory Section (Step 4)

Questions

	Address	Delivery Route			
37.	17200 High Rd.	A	B	C	D
38.	1220 W. Pico Blvd.	A	B	C	D
39.	249 Harvard Blvd.	A	B	C	D
40.	512 N. Camden Pl.	A	B	C	D
41.	3916 Lander Ave.	A	B	C	D
42.	498 Choate St.	A	B	C	D
43.	452 Harvard Blvd.	A	B	C	D
44.	318 S. Camden Pl.	A	B	C	D
45.	545 Choate St.	A	B	C	D
46.	17240 High Rd.	A	B	C	D
47.	364 Forbes Ave.	A	B	C	D
48.	744 W. Pico Blvd.	A	B	C	D
49.	640 N. Camden Pl.	A	B	C	D
50.	2869 Duke Ct.	A	B	C	D
51.	49 Harvard Blvd.	A	B	C	D
52.	15510 High Rd.	A	B	C	D
53.	486 Glade St.	A	B	C	D
54.	260 Harvard Blvd.	A	B	C	D

Coding and Memory (Test 6)
Memory Section (Step 4)

Questions

	Address	Delivery Route			
55.	370 Choate St.	A	B	C	D
56.	16800 High Rd.	A	B	C	D
57.	699 N. Camden Pl.	A	B	C	D
58.	864 Jenner Cir.	A	B	C	D
59.	248 Harvard Blvd.	A	B	C	D
60.	1202 W. Pico Blvd.	A	B	C	D
61.	612 E. Camden Pl.	A	B	C	D
62.	469 Haron Ln.	A	B	C	D
63.	16510 High Rd.	A	B	C	D
64.	840 W. Pico Blvd.	A	B	C	D
65.	442 Harvard Blvd.	A	B	C	D
66.	410 Choate St.	A	B	C	D
67.	38 Formby Ct.	A	B	C	D
68.	301 N. Camden Pl.	A	B	C	D
69.	1091 W. Pico Blvd.	A	B	C	D
70.	469 Sweem St.	A	B	C	D
71.	451 Harvard Blvd.	A	B	C	D
72.	17510 High Rd.	A	B	C	D

END

Coding and Memory (Test 7)
Coding Section (Step 1)

CODING GUIDE	
Address Range	**Delivery Route**
100-600 Terrace Ave. 55-800 W. Powell Dr. 5-25 N. 82nd St.	A
26-50 N. 82nd St. 801-1500 W. Powell Dr.	B
7000-9999 Harmony Way 601-1100 Terrace Ave. 1-100 Farview Ct.	C
All mail that doesn't fall in one of the address range listed above	D

Coding and Memory (Test 7)
Coding Section (Step 1)

Sample Questions

	Address	Delivery Route			
1.	790 W. Powell Dr.	A	B	C	D
2.	120 Farview Ct.	A	B	C	D
3.	39 N. 82nd St.	A	B	C	D
4.	8625 Harmony Way	A	B	C	D

Sample Answer Grid			
1. (A)	(B)	(C)	(D)
2. (A)	(B)	(C)	(D)
3. (A)	(B)	(C)	(D)
4. (A)	(B)	(C)	(D)

The correct answers for sample questions

1. (A) 2.(D) 3.(B) 4.(C)

Coding and Memory (Test 7)
Coding Section (Step 2)

CODING GUIDE	
Address Range	**Delivery Route**
100-600 Terrace Ave. 55-800 W. Powell Dr. 5-25 N. 82nd St.	A
26-50 N. 82nd St. 801-1500 W. Powell Dr.	B
7000-9999 Harmony Way 601-1100 Terrace Ave. 1-100 Farview Ct.	C
All mail that doesn't fall in one of the address range listed above	D

Coding and Memory (Test 7)
Coding Section (Step 2)

Sample Questions

	Address	Delivery Route			
1.	409 Terrace Ave.	A	B	C	D
2.	1329 W. Powell Dr.	A	B	C	D
3.	24 N. 82nd St.	A	B	C	D
4.	82 Farview Ct.	A	B	C	D
5.	6290 Harmony Way	A	B	C	D
6.	1109 Terrace Ave.	A	B	C	D
7.	627 W. Powell Dr.	A	B	C	D
8.	51 N. 82nd St.	A	B	C	D

Sample Answer Grid

1.	Ⓐ	Ⓑ	Ⓒ	Ⓓ
2.	Ⓐ	Ⓑ	Ⓒ	Ⓓ
3.	Ⓐ	Ⓑ	Ⓒ	Ⓓ
4.	Ⓐ	Ⓑ	Ⓒ	Ⓓ
5.	Ⓐ	Ⓑ	Ⓒ	Ⓓ
6.	Ⓐ	Ⓑ	Ⓒ	Ⓓ
7.	Ⓐ	Ⓑ	Ⓒ	Ⓓ
8.	Ⓐ	Ⓑ	Ⓒ	Ⓓ

The correct answers for sample questions

1. (A) 2.(B) 3.(A) 4.(C) 5.(D) 6.(D) 7.(A) 8.(D)

Coding and Memory (Test 7)
Coding Section (Step 3)

CODING GUIDE	
Address Range	**Delivery Route**
100-600 Terrace Ave. 55-800 W. Powell Dr. 5-25 N. 82nd St.	A
26-50 N. 82nd St. 801-1500 W. Powell Dr.	B
7000-9999 Harmony Way 601-1100 Terrace Ave. 1-100 Farview Ct.	C
All mail that doesn't fall in one of the address range listed above	D

Coding and Memory (Test 7)
Coding Section (Step 3)

Questions

	Address	Delivery Route			
1.	45 N. 82nd St.	A	B	C	D
2.	6900 Harmony Way	A	B	C	D
3.	727 W. Powell Dr.	A	B	C	D
4.	79 Farview Ct.	A	B	C	D
5.	600 Terrace Ave.	A	B	C	D
6.	7624 Lauren Ave.	A	B	C	D
7.	1211 W. Powell Dr.	A	B	C	D
8.	76 Farview Ct.	A	B	C	D
9.	1121 Terrace Ave.	A	B	C	D
10.	27 N. 82nd St.	A	B	C	D
11.	154 E. Powell Dr.	A	B	C	D
12.	31 N. 82nd St.	A	B	C	D
13.	419 Elmira St.	A	B	C	D
14.	8600 Harmony Way	A	B	C	D
15.	110 Farview Ct.	A	B	C	D
16.	1611 W. Powell Dr.	A	B	C	D
17.	761 Songbird Ln.	A	B	C	D
18.	16 N. 82nd St.	A	B	C	D

Coding and Memory (Test 7)
Coding Section (Step 3)

CODING GUIDE	
Address Range	**Delivery Route**
100-600 Terrace Ave. 55-800 W. Powell Dr. 5-25 N. 82nd St.	A
26-50 N. 82nd St. 801-1500 W. Powell Dr.	B
7000-9999 Harmony Way 601-1100 Terrace Ave. 1-100 Farview Ct.	C
All mail that doesn't fall in one of the address range listed above	D

Coding and Memory (Test 7)
Coding Section (Step 3)

Questions

	Address	Delivery Route			
19.	89 Farview Ct.	A	B	C	D
20.	517 Terrace Ave.	A	B	C	D
21.	514 Norman Ave.	A	B	C	D
22.	46 S. 82nd St.	A	B	C	D
23.	811 W. Powell Dr.	A	B	C	D
24.	7211 Harmony Way	A	B	C	D
25.	310 Marigold Ave.	A	B	C	D
26.	16 W. 82nd St.	A	B	C	D
27.	86 Farview Ct.	A	B	C	D
28.	416 Terrace Ave.	A	B	C	D
29.	8924 Lucille Ln.	A	B	C	D
30.	890 W. Powell Dr.	A	B	C	D
31.	120 Farview Ct.	A	B	C	D
32.	294 W. 45th Ave.	A	B	C	D
33.	55 N. 82nd St.	A	B	C	D
34.	612 Terrace Ave.	A	B	C	D
35	94 Farview Ct.	A	B	C	D
36.	14 N. 82nd St.	A	B	C	D

Coding and Memory (Test 7)
Memory Section (Step 1)

CODING GUIDE	
Address Range	**Delivery Route**
100-600 Terrace Ave. 55-800 W. Powell Dr. 5-25 N. 82nd St.	A
26-50 N. 82nd St. 801-1500 W. Powell Dr.	B
7000-9999 Harmony Way 601-1100 Terrace Ave. 1-100 Farview Ct.	C
All mail that doesn't fall in one of the address range listed above	D

Coding and Memory (Test 7)
Memory Section (Step 2)

Sample Questions

	Address	Delivery Route			
1.	7249 Harmony Way	A	B	C	D
2.	500 Terrace Ave.	A	B	C	D
3.	802 W. Powell Dr.	A	B	C	D
4.	96 Farview Ct.	A	B	C	D
5.	24 N. 82nd St.	A	B	C	D
6.	927 Terrace Ave.	A	B	C	D
7.	10027 Harmony Way	A	B	C	D
8.	231 Farview Ct.	A	B	C	D

Sample Answer Grid			
1. Ⓐ	Ⓑ	Ⓒ	Ⓓ
2. Ⓐ	Ⓑ	Ⓒ	Ⓓ
3. Ⓐ	Ⓑ	Ⓒ	Ⓓ
4. Ⓐ	Ⓑ	Ⓒ	Ⓓ
5. Ⓐ	Ⓑ	Ⓒ	Ⓓ
6. Ⓐ	Ⓑ	Ⓒ	Ⓓ
7. Ⓐ	Ⓑ	Ⓒ	Ⓓ
8. Ⓐ	Ⓑ	Ⓒ	Ⓓ

The correct answers for sample questions

1. (C) 2.(A) 3.(B) 4.(C) 5.(A) 6.(C) 7.(D) 8.(D)

Coding and Memory (Test 7)
Memory Section (Step 3)

CODING GUIDE	
Address Range	**Delivery Route**
100-600 Terrace Ave. 55-800 W. Powell Dr. 5-25 N. 82nd St.	A
26-50 N. 82nd St. 801-1500 W. Powell Dr.	B
7000-9999 Harmony Way 601-1100 Terrace Ave. 1-100 Farview Ct.	C
All mail that doesn't fall in one of the address range listed above	D

Coding and Memory (Test 7)
Memory Section (Step 4)

Questions

	Address	Delivery Route			
37.	714 E. Powell Dr.	A	B	C	D
38.	128 Farview Ct.	A	B	C	D
39.	420 Terrace Ave.	A	B	C	D
40.	42 N. 82nd St.	A	B	C	D
41.	314 Custer St.	A	B	C	D
42.	8249 Harmony Way	A	B	C	D
43.	694 Terrace Ave.	A	B	C	D
44.	890 W. Powell Dr.	A	B	C	D
45.	24 S. 82nd St.	A	B	C	D
46.	710 Durant Ave.	A	B	C	D
47.	6110 Harmony Way	A	B	C	D
48.	80 Farview Ct.	A	B	C	D
49.	789 Gary Ave.	A	B	C	D
50.	580 Terrace Ave.	A	B	C	D
51.	50 W. Powell Dr.	A	B	C	D
52.	26 Jones Dr.	A	B	C	D
53.	66 Farview Ct.	A	B	C	D
54.	790 W. Powell Dr.	A	B	C	D

Coding and Memory (Test 7)
Memory Section (Step 4)

Questions

	Address	Delivery Route			
55.	71 N. 82nd St.	A	B	C	D
56.	8900 Harmony Way	A	B	C	D
57.	599 Terrace Ave.	A	B	C	D
58.	102 Farview Ct.	A	B	C	D
59.	1400 W. Powell Dr.	A	B	C	D
60.	293 Cottage Ln.	A	B	C	D
61.	7010 Harmony Way	A	B	C	D
62.	86 Farview Ct.	A	B	C	D
63.	590 Terrace Ave.	A	B	C	D
64.	769 Trent Ave.	A	B	C	D
65.	49 W. 82nd St.	A	B	C	D
66.	84 W. Powell Dr.	A	B	C	D
67.	269 Monte St.	A	B	C	D
68.	6 N. 82nd St.	A	B	C	D
69.	10029 Harmony Way	A	B	C	D
70.	98 Terrace Ave.	A	B	C	D
71.	13 N. 82nd St.	A	B	C	D
72.	39 Kader St.	A	B	C	D

END

9. Correct Answers for Coding and Memory

Test 1

1.	C	13.	D	25.	D	37.	C	49.	C	61.	D
2.	B	14.	C	26.	B	38.	B	50.	D	62.	B
3.	B	15.	C	27.	D	39.	D	51.	D	63.	C
4.	B	16.	D	28.	D	40.	D	52.	B	64.	D
5.	D	17.	A	29.	D	41.	A	53.	D	65.	D
6.	D	18.	D	30.	B	42.	D	54.	D	66.	C
7.	D	19.	C	31.	C	43.	B	55.	A	67.	B
8.	A	20.	D	32.	D	44.	D	56.	D	68.	D
9.	D	21.	B	33.	A	45.	D	57.	C	69.	D
10.	D	22.	D	34.	C	46.	D	58.	D	70.	C
11.	D	23.	B	35.	B	47.	B	59.	D	71.	A
12.	B	24.	D	36.	D	48.	D	60.	D	72.	A

Test 2

1.	D	13.	C	25.	C	37.	C	49.	D	61.	B
2.	A	14.	B	26.	A	38.	A	50.	D	62.	C
3.	B	15.	D	27.	B	39.	D	51.	C	63.	D
4.	B	16.	B	28.	D	40.	B	52.	D	64.	C
5.	C	17.	D	29.	D	41.	D	53.	D	65.	A
6.	D	18.	D	30.	B	42.	D	54.	A	66.	D
7.	C	19.	C	31.	A	43.	C	55.	A	67.	C
8.	D	20.	B	32.	D	44.	D	56.	D	68.	D
9.	D	21.	A	33.	C	45.	B	57.	D	69.	B
10.	A	22.	C	34.	D	46.	D	58.	C	70.	D
11.	D	23.	D	35.	B	47.	A	59.	D	71.	C
12.	D	24.	D	36.	D	48.	D	60.	B	72.	D

Correct Answers for Coding and Memory

Test 3

1. B	13. D	25. D	37. C	49. C	61. A
2. C	14. D	26. C	38. A	50. D	62. D
3. D	15. A	27. A	39. A	51. D	63. D
4. A	16. D	28. D	40. D	52. D	64. B
5. C	17. D	29. D	41. D	53. C	65. D
6. D	18. B	30. D	42. C	54. A	66. D
7. B	19. D	31. C	43. D	55. A	67. C
8. C	20. D	32. B	44. D	56. B	68. D
9. D	21. C	33. D	45. C	57. D	69. C
10. B	22. A	34. C	46. C	58. D	70. D
11. D	23. A	35. A	47. D	59. B	71. A
12. B	24. B	36. C	48. B	60. D	72. D

Test 4

1. C	13. D	25. B	37. B	49. A	61. B
2. D	14. C	26. D	38. A	50. D	62. D
3. D	15. D	27. B	39. D	51. C	63. D
4. A	16. C	28. D	40. C	52. B	64. D
5. D	17. D	29. D	41. A	53. C	65. C
6. B	18. B	30. C	42. D	54. D	66. D
7. C	19. D	31. B	43. C	55. C	67. D
8. A	20. C	32. D	44. A	56. D	68. B
9. D	21. D	33. C	45. C	57. B	69. B
10. D	22. B	34. B	46. D	58. D	70. D
11. C	23. D	35. B	47. D	59. B	71. C
12. D	24. D	36. D	48. C	60. B	72. D

Correct Answers for Coding and Memory

Test 5

1. C	13. A	25. D	37. C	49. A	61. D
2. D	14. C	26. D	38. D	50. D	62. C
3. B	15. D	27. A	39. C	51. D	63. A
4. A	16. D	28. C	40. A	52. C	64. C
5. B	17. B	29. C	41. D	53. D	65. A
6. D	18. D	30. D	42. D	54. A	66. D
7. C	19. A	31. D	43. C	55. D	67. A
8. A	20. D	32. D	44. B	56. C	68. D
9. C	21. B	33. A	45. D	57. A	69. B
10. D	22. D	34. D	46. A	58. D	70. D
11. D	23. D	35. B	47. D	59. D	71. C
12. D	24. C	36. C	48. D	60. B	72. D

Test 6

1. D	13. D	25. C	37. C	49. B	61. D
2. A	14. C	26. B	38. D	50. D	62. D
3. D	15. D	27. D	39. A	51. D	63. A
4. B	16. A	28. D	40. B	52. A	64. C
5. C	17. A	29. D	41. D	53. D	65. B
6. D	18. C	30. A	42. C	54. B	66. C
7. D	19. D	31. D	43. D	55. C	67. D
8. D	20. A	32. B	44. D	56. A	68. A
9. A	21. D	33. B	45. D	57. B	69. C
10. B	22. A	34. C	46. C	58. D	70. D
11. C	23. D	35. D	47. D	59. A	71. D
12. D	24. C	36. C	48. C	60. D	72. D

Correct Answers for Coding and Memory

Test 7

1. B	13. D	25. D	37. D	49. D	61. C
2. D	14. C	26. D	38. D	50. A	62. C
3. A	15. D	27. C	39. A	51. D	63. A
4. C	16. D	28. A	40. B	52. D	64. D
5. A	17. D	29. D	41. D	53. C	65. D
6. D	18. A	30. B	42. C	54. A	66. A
7. B	19. C	31. D	43. C	55. D	67. D
8. C	20. A	32. D	44. B	56. C	68. A
9. D	21. D	33. D	45. D	57. A	69. D
10. B	22. D	34. C	46. D	58. D	70. D
11. D	23. B	35. C	47. D	59. B	71. A
12. B	24. C	36. A	48. C	60. D	72. D

10. Memory Tips

10. air, arson
11. ace, arch
12. addition, arguement
13. apple, ant
14. answer, animal
15. access, asian
16. academy, arm
17. account, act
18. advance, admission
19. advice, affair

20. bus, busybee
21. boy, business
22. bank, bumper
23. border, book
24. body, beer
25. bone, benefit
26. ball, bell
27. blanket, bible
28. belly, bean
29. beard, box

30. campus, cancer
31. car, corn
32. chance, channel
33. character, cat
34. cleaning, citizen
35. cake, climate
36. cough, court
37. credit, cross
38. cutting, cure
39. country, coupon

40. distance, duty
41. day, distrust
42. direction, dinner
43. device, destiny
44. dispatch, district
45. dream, drug
46. disorder, delight
47. deficit, dealer
48. data, darkness
49. drum, duck

50. engine, enemy
51. east, enterprise
52. event, evidence
53. engineer, eagle
54. earth, echo
55. economy, egg
56. error, errand
57. exit, exhibition
58. education, editor
59. estate, edge

60. fog, fruit
61. frost, freelance
62. freedom, food
63. force, fortune
64. friend, function
65. fork, format
66. foot, flower
67. freight, fund
68. future, furniture
69. fish, festival

70. golf, grace
71. governor, graduation
72. grape, game
73. gas, grease
74. gold, goat
75. gloom, glove
76. gravy, goodness
77. goal, group
78. guaranty, gun
79. general, garden

80. honor, horse
81. humor, human
82. hurry, house
83. hospital, hunting
84. hope, head
85. hair, hand
86. hall, harbor
87. heart, health
88. helping, height
89. hero, host

90. insurance, iron
91. item, itch
92. island, invoice
93. interview, intern
94. introduce, insect
95. intention, interval
96. inch, impact
97. index, interest
98. industry, ink
99. ingredient, intent

11. Personal Characteristics and Experience Inventory

Refer to the Guide to Post Office Employment

12. List of Post Offices

1   City Of Industry Post Office
Tel; (626) 855-6339 Job Information Line
Address: 15421 Gale Ave
City of Industry, CA 91715

2   L. A. Post Office
Tel; (323) 586-1351 Job Information Line
Address: 7001 S. Central Ave
Los Angeles, CA 90052

3   L. A. Bulk Mail Center
Tel; (562) 435-4529 Job Information Line
Address: 5555 Bandini Blvd
Bell, CA 90201

4   Long Beach Post Office
Tel; (562) 435-4529 Job Information Line
Address: 300 N. Long Beach Blvd
Long Beach, CA 90802

5   Marina Del Rey Processing
Tel; (562) 435-4529 Job Information Line
Address: 13031 W. Jefferson Blvd
Marina Del Rey, CA 90291

6   Pasadena Post Office
Tel; (626) 304-7230 Job Information Line
Address: 600 N. Lincoln Ave
Pasadena, CA 91109

7   San Bernardino Post Office
Tel; (909) 335-4339 Job Information Line
Address: 1900 W. Redlands Blvd
Redlands, CA 92403

8   Santa Ana Post Office
Tel; (714) 662-6375 Job Information Line
Address: 3101 W. Sunflower Ave
Santa Ana, CA 92799

9   Santa Barbara Post Office
Tel; (805) 278-7668 Job Information Line
Address: 836 Anacapa St
Santa Barbara, CA 93102

10   Van Nuys Post Office
Tel; (661) 775-7014 Job Information Line
Address: 15701 Sherman Way
Van Nuys, CA 91409

11   San Diego Post Office
Tel; (858) 674-0577 Job Information Line

12   San Francisco Post Office
Tel; (415) 550-5534 Job Information Line

13   Sacramento Post Office
Tel; (916) 373-8448 Job Information Line

14   New York Post Office
Tel; (518) 452-2445 Job Information Line

15   Texas Post Office
Tel; (713) 226-3872 Job Information Line

13. Forms and Information

Application for Employment
(Shaded Areas for Postal Service Use Only)

The US Postal Service is an Equal Opportunity Employer

Rated Application			Veteran preference has been verified through proof that the separation was under honorable conditions, and other proof as required. (See Section D below.)	Check One:
Rated For	Rating	Date Rcvd.		
				☐ 10 pts. CPS
		Time Rcvd.	Type of Proof Submitted & Date Issued	☐ 10 pts. CP
				☐ 10 pts. XP
Signature & Date			Verifier's Signature, Title & Date	☐ 5 pts. TP

A. General Infomation

1. Name (First, MI, Last)	2. Social Security Number	3. Home Telephone ( )
4. Mailing Address (No., Street, City, State, ZIP)	5. Date of Birth	6. Work Phone ( )
	7. Place of Birth (City & State or City & Country)	

8. Kind of Job Applied for and Postal Facility Name & Location (City & State)	9. Will You Accept: Temporary/Casual (Noncareer) Work ☐ Yes ☐ No	10. When Will You Be Available?	11. Are You Willing to Travel? (Complete only if you are applying for an executive or professional position.) ☐ No ☐ Some ☐ Often

B. Educational History

1. Name and Location (City & State) of Last High School Attended	2. Are You a High School Graduate? Answer "Yes" if you expect to graduate within the next 9 months, or you have an official equivalency certificate of graduation. ☐ Yes - Month & Yesr: ☐ No - Highest Grade Completed:

3a. Name and Location of college or University (City, State, and ZIP Code if known. If you expect to graduate within 9 months. give month and year you expect degree.)	Dates Attended		No. of Credits Completed		Type Degree (BA, etc.)	Year of Degree
	From	To	Semester Hrs.	Quarter Hours		

b. Chief Undergraduate College Subjects	Semester Hrs. Completed	Quarter Hours Completed	c. Chief Graduate College Subject	Semester Hrs. Completed	Quarter Hours Completed

4. Major Field of Study at Highest Level of College Work

5. Other Schools or Training (For example, trade, vacational, armed forces, or business. Give for each; name, city, state, & ZIP Code, if known, of school; dates attended; subjects studied; number of classroom hours of instruction per work; certificates: & any other pertinent infomation.)

6. Honors, Awards, & Fellowships Received

7. Special Qualifications & Skills (License; skills with machines, patents or inventions; publications - do not submit copies unless requested; public speaking; memberships in professional or scientific societies; typing or shorthand speed, etc.)

PS Form 2591, April 1989 (page 1 of 4)

C. Work History

(Start with your present position and go back for 10 years or to your 16th birthday, whichever is later. You may include volunteer work. Account for periods of unemployment in separate blocks in order. Include military service. Use blank sheets if you need more sapce.)

May the US Postal Service ask your present employer about your character, qualifications, and employment record? A "No" will not affect your consideration for employment opportunities.

☐ Yes   ☐ No

1.

Dates of Employment (Month & Year) From To **Present**	Grade If Postal, Civil Service or Military	Starting Salary/Earnings $ per
Exact Position Title	Number & Kind of Employees Supervised	Present Salary/Earnings $ per

Name of Employer and Complete Mailing Address	Kind of Business (Manufacturing, etc.)	Place of Employment (City & STate)
	Name of Supervisor	Telephone No. (If Known) ( )

Reason for Wanting to Leave

Description of Duties, Responsibilities, & Accomplishments

2.

Dates of Employment (Month & Year) From To	Grade If Postal, Civil Service or Military	Starting Salary/Earnings $ per
Exact Position Title	Number & Kind of Employees Supervised	Ending Salary/Earnings $ per

Name of Employer and Complete Mailing Address	Kind of Business (Manufacturing, etc.)	Place of Employment (City & STate)
	Name of Supervisor	Telephone No. (If Known) ( )

Reason for Leaving

Description of Duties, Responsibilities, & Accomplishments

3.

Dates of Employment (Month & Year) From To	Grade If Postal, Civil Service or Military	Starting Salary/Earnings $ per
Exact Position Title	Number & Kind of Employees Supervised	Ending Salary/Earnings $ per

Name of Employer and Complete Mailing Address	Kind of Business (Manufacturing, etc.)	Place of Employment (City & STate)
	Name of Supervisor	Telephone No. (If Known) ( )

Reason for Leaving

Description of Duties, Responsibilities, & Accomplishments

PS Form 2591, April 1989 (page 1 of 4)

4.	Dates of Employment (Month & Year) From To	Grade If Postal, Civil Service or Military	Starting Salary/Earnings $ per
	Exact Position Title	Number & Kind of Employees Supervised	Ending Salary/Earnings $ per
Name of Employer and Complete Mailing Address		Kind of Business (Manufacturing, etc.)	Place of Employment (City & STate)
		Name of Supervisor	Telephone No. (If Known) ( )

Reason for Leaving

Description of Duties, Responsibilities, & Accomplishments

D. Veteran Preference

Answer all parts. If a part does not apply, answer "no".

	Yes	No
1. Have you ever served on active duty in the US military service? (Exclude tours of active duty for trainning as a reservist or guardsman.)		
2. Have you ever been discharged from the armed service under other than honorable condition? You may omit any such discharge changed to honorable by a Discharge Review Board or similar authority. (If "Yes", give details in Section G.)		
3. Do you claim 5-point preference based on active duty in the armed forces? (If "Yes," you will be required to furnish records to support your claim.		
4. Do you claim 10-point preference? If "Yes," check type of preference claimed and attach Standard Form 15, Claim for 10-point Veteran Preference, together with proof called for in that form.		

☐ Compensable Disability (Less than 30%)   ☐ Non-compensable Disability (includes Receipt of the Purple Heart)   ☐ Widow/Widower   ☐ Other:

☐ Compensable Disability (30% or more)   ☐ Wife/Husband   ☐ Mother

5. List for all military service: (Enter N/A if not applicable)

Dates (From - To)	Serial/Service Number	Branch of service	Type of Discharge

E. References

List three persons who are NOT related to you and who have definite knowledge of your qualifications and fitness for the position for which you are applying. Do not repeat names of supervisors listed above.

Full Name	Present Business or Home Address (No., Street, City, State & ZIP Code)	Business or Occupation

F. Other Information

	Yes	No
1. Are you a United States citizen?		
2. Are you a citizen of American Samoa or any other territory owing allegiance to the United States?		
3. Are you an alien with permanent residence status. If "yes," be prepared to show Form I-151 or I-551.		

If you answer "yes" to either of these questions, give details in Section G, below. Give the name, address (including ZIP Code) of employer, approximates date, and reasons in each case. ▶	4. Have you ever been fired from any job for any reason?		
	5. Have you ever quit a job after being notified that you would be fired?		

6. Do you receive or have you applied for retirement pay, pension, or other compensation based upon military, postal, or federal civilian service? (If you answer "yes," give details in Section G.)		

If you answer "yes" to either question, give details in Section G, Show for each offense: (1) Date of Conviction; (2) Charge convicted of; (3) Court and location; (4) Action taken. Note: A conviction does not automatically mean that you cannot be appointed. What you were convicted of, and how long ago, are important. Give all of the facts so that a decision can be made. ▶	7. Have you ever been convicted of a crime or are you now under charges for any offense against the law? You may omit: (1) any charges that were dismissed or resulted in acquittal; (2) any conviction that has been set aside, vacated, annulled, expunged, or sealed; (3) any offense that was finally adjudicated in a juvenile court or juvenile delinquency proceeding; and (4) any charges that resulted only in a conviction of a non-criminal offense. All felony and misdemeanor convictions and all convictions in federal court are criminal convictions and must be disclosed. Disclosure of such convictions are required even if you did not spend any time in jail and/or were not required to pay a fine.		
	8. While in the military service were you ever convicted by special or general court martial?		

9. Are you a former Postal Service or federal employee not now employed by the US Government? If you answer "Yes", give in section G, name of employing agency(s), position title(s), and date(s) employed.		

If you answer "yes" to question 10, give details in Section G; (1) Full name; (2) Present address (include ZIP Code); (3) Relationship; (4) Position title; (5) Name & location of postal installation where employed. ▶	10. Does the US Postal Service employ any relative of yours by blood or marriage? Postal officials may not appoint any of their relatives or recommend them for appointment in the Postal Service. Any relative who is appointed in violation of this restriction can not be paid. Thus it is necessary to have information about your relatives who are working for the USPS. These include; mother, father, daughter, son, sister, brother, aunt, uncle, first cousin, niece, nephew, wife, husband, mother-in-law, father-in-law, daughter-in-law, sister-in-law, brother-in-law, stepfather, stepmother, stepdaughter, stepson, stepsister, stepbrother, half sister, and half brother.		

11. Are you now dependent on or a user of ANY addictive or hallucinogenic drug, including amphetamines, barbiturates, heroin, morphine, cocain, mescaline, LSD, STP, hashish, marijuana, or methadone, other than for medical treatment under the supervision of a doctor?		

G. Use This Space for Detailed Answers (Use blank sheets if you need more space)

H. Certification

I certify that all of the statements made in this application are true, complete, and correct to the best of my knowledge and belief and are in good faith.	Signature of Applicant	Date Signed

Disclosure by you of your Social Security Number (SSN) is mandatory to obtain the services, benefits, or processes that you are seeking. Solicitation of the SSN by the USPS is authorized under provisions of Executive Order 9397. dated November 22, 1943. The information gathered through the use of the number will be used only as necessary in authorized personnel administration processes.

A false or dishonest answer to any question in this application may be grounds for not employing you or for dismissing you after you begin work, and may be punishable by fine or imprisonment. (US Cod, Title 18, Sec. 1001). All the information you give will be considered in reviewing your application and is subject to investigation.

Use blank sheets if you need more space. Your name and SSN must be included on all additional

Table of Disqualification

A. General Disqualifying Factors:

1. Applicant does not have at least 2years of documented driving experience in a passenger car or larger vehicle.
2. Applicant has had driving permit suspended once (or more) in the last 3 years. or twice (or more) in the last 5 years.
3. Applicant has had driving permit revoked once (or more) in the last 5 years.

B. Specific Disqualifying violations:

Type of Violation

	In Last 3 Yrs.	In Last 5 Yrs.
1. Reckless driving or other similar offense (e.g,. careless driving)	1 or more	2 or more
2. Any driving offense involving use of drugs, alcohol, controlled substances	Any conviction	Any conviction
3. All other traffic offenses (but not parking violations)	3 or more (or more than 1 in last 12 months)	5 or more
4. At- fault accidents	2 or more; or any at-fault accident resulting in a fatality.	
5. Hit-and-run offense	Any conviction	Any conviction

Three convictions for the same offense are disqualifying as they indicate a pattern of inadequate responsibility and disregard for law and order which may affect safety.

Notes:

- For purposes of determining disqualifying violations, consider only offenses followed by a conviction (forfeited bond, jailed, fined, "let off with a warning," oedered to attend traffic school).
- For purposes of establishing time frames for disqualification, use the date of the actual violation.
- At-fault accident--if fined, sued and received adverse judgment; applicant's insurance company settled for damages to other party or applicant settled out of court, or otherwise determined to be liable.

00 Month 00 Day, 20_____.

Postmaster
Exam Unit
Address of Post Office

To Whom It May Concern:

My name is ____. I took a written test for the position of ____ on 00 Month 00 Day, 20_____.
My Social Security number is 000-00-0000.

I'd like to request to change my address.

My new address
0 0 0 0 0 0 0 0 0

Sicerely

                                        Thank you

                                        (Signature)

                                        Name

Attachment

A copy of notice of Rating

00 Month 00 Day, 20_____.

Postmaster
Exam Unit
Address of Post Office

To Whom It May Concern:

My name is ____. I took a written test for the position of 0 0 0 on 00 Month 00 Day, 20_____.
My Social Security number is xxx-xx-xxxx.

I'd like to request to extend my eligibility for the above written test for additional year.

Sincerely

Thank you

(Signature)

Name

Attachment

A copy of notice of Rating

NAME	POSITION TITLE	FINAL RATING
KIM JIN S	DISTRIBUTION CLERK, MACHINE	100.0

POST OFFICE OR INSTALLATION	AREA OFFICES SELECTED
LONG BEACH CA 90809-9998	

PART FAILED				TYPE OF EXAMINATION		BASIC RATING	VETERAN POINTS
WRITTEN	EXPERIENCE	TYPING	DICTATION	ENTRANCE	IN SERVICE		
	N/A	N/A	N/A	X		100.0	

SPECIAL NOTES

Kim Jin S.

ADDRESS *(No., Street, City, State and ZIP Code)*

2611 S BRONSON AVE #12
LOS ANGELES   CA   90018

SOCIAL SECURITY NO.	DATE OF BIRTH	DATE OF EXAMINATION	INSTALLATION NO.	DATE NTAC MAILED	DATE NAME ENTERED ON REGISTER
	07-	03/03/8	05-4482	04/13/8	APR 1 8 19

PS Form
June 1979 5912=B

* ALL APPLICANTS IN A COMPETITIVE EXAMINATION MUST ATTAIN
A RATING OF 70 BEFORE VETERAN'S PREFERENCE IS ALLOWED.

(APPLICANT'S COPY)

NAME KIM	POSITION TITLE	FINAL RATING
JIN S	DISTRIBUTION CLERK, MACHINE	100.0

POST OFFICE OR INSTALLATION	AREA OFFICES SELECTED
INGLEWOOD CA 90311-9998	

PART FAILED				TYPE OF EXAMINATION		BASIC RATING	VETERAN POINTS
WRITTEN	EXPERIENCE	TYPING	DICTATION	ENTRANCE	IN SERVICE		
	N/A	N/A	N/A	X		100.0	

SPECIAL NOTES

ELIGIBILITY 2 YRS. ADDITIONAL YR. ON REQUEST TO PM AFTER 18 MOS.

ADDRESS *(No., Street, City, State and ZIP Code)*

2611 S BRONSON AVE #15
LOS ANGELES   CA   90018

SOCIAL SECURITY NO.	DATE OF BIRTH	DATE OF EXAMINATION	INSTALLATION NO.	DATE NTAC MAILED	DATE NAME ENTERED ON REGISTER
	07-	09/24/8	05-3684	10/08/3	OCT 2 2 198

PS Form
June 1979 5912=B

* ALL APPLICANTS IN A COMPETITIVE EXAMINATION MUST ATTAIN
A RATING OF 70 BEFORE VETERAN'S PREFERENCE IS ALLOWED.

(APPLICANT'S COPY)

NAME KIM	POSITION TITLE	FINAL RATING
JIN S	DISTRIBUTION CLERK, MACHINE	100.0

POST OFFICE OR INSTALLATION	AREA OFFICES SELECTED
SANTA ANA CA 92711-9998	

PART FAILED				TYPE OF EXAMINATION		BASIC RATING	VETERAN POINTS
WRITTEN	EXPERIENCE	TYPING	DICTATION	ENTRANCE	IN SERVICE		
	N/A	N/A	N/A	X		100.0	

SPECIAL NOTES

ELIGIBILITY 2 YRS. ADDITIONAL YR. ON REQUEST TO PM AFTER 18 MOS.

ADDRESS *(No., Street, City, State and ZIP Code)*

2611 S BRONSON AVE #15
LOS ANGELES   CA   90018

SOCIAL SECURITY NO.	DATE OF BIRTH	DATE OF EXAMINATION	INSTALLATION NO.	DATE NTAC MAILED	DATE NAME ENTERED ON REGISTER
	07-	06/26/8	05-6936	07/19/8	JUL 2 4 19

PS Form
June 1979 5912=B

* ALL APPLICANTS IN A COMPETITIVE EXAMINATION MUST ATTAIN
A RATING OF 70 BEFORE VETERAN'S PREFERENCE IS ALLOWED.

(APPLICANT'S COPY)

NOTICE OF RATING

NAME	POSITION TITLE	FINAL RATING
KIM JIN S	DISTRIBUTION CLERK, MACHINE	100.0

POST OFFICE OR INSTALLATION	AREA OFFICES SELECTED
SANTA ANA CA 92711-9998	

PART FAILED				TYPE OF EXAMINATION		BASIC RATING	VETERAN POINTS
WRITTEN	EXPERIENCE	TYPING	DICTATION	ENTRANCE	IN SERVICE		
	N/A	N/A	N/A	X		100.0	

SPECIAL NOTES

ELIGIBILITY 2 YRS. ADDITIONAL YR. ON REQUEST TO PM AFTER 18 MOS.

ADDRESS (No., Street, City, State and ZIP Code)

SOCIAL SECURITY NO.	DATE OF BIRTH	DATE OF EXAMINATION	INSTALLATION NO.	DATE NTAC MAILED	DATE NAME ENTERED ON REGISTER
	07-	03/03/	05-6936	04/03/	APR 5 1984

PS Form 5912=B
June 1979

* ALL APPLICANTS IN A COMPETITIVE EXAMINATION MUST ATTAIN
A RATING OF 70 BEFORE VETERAN'S PREFERENCE IS ALLOWED.

(APPLICANT'S) COPY

NOTICE OF RATING

NAME	POSITION TITLE	FINAL RATING
KIM JIN S	CLERK AND CARRIER	100.0

POST OFFICE OR INSTALLATION	AREA OFFICES SELECTED
ARCADIA CA 91006	

PART FAILED				TYPE OF EXAMINATION		BASIC RATING	VETERAN POINTS
WRITTEN	EXPERIENCE	TYPING	DICTATION	ENTRANCE	IN SERVICE		
	N/A	N/A	N/A	X		100.0	

SPECIAL NOTES

ELIGIBILITY 2 YRS. ADDITIONAL YR. ON REQUEST TO PM AFTER 18 MOS.

ADDRESS (No., Street, City, State and ZIP Code)

SOCIAL SECURITY NO.	DATE OF BIRTH	DATE OF EXAMINATION	INSTALLATION NO.	DATE NTAC MAILED	DATE NAME ENTERED ON REGISTER
	07-	05/23/8	05-0294	06/17/8	JUL 25 1984

PS Form 5912=B
June 1979

* ALL APPLICANTS IN A COMPETITIVE EXAMINATION MUST ATTAIN
A RATING OF 70 BEFORE VETERAN'S PREFERENCE IS ALLOWED.

(APPLICANT'S) COPY

NOTICE OF RATING

NAME	POSITION TITLE	FINAL RATING
KIM JIN S	CLERK AND CARRIER	100.0

POST OFFICE OR INSTALLATION	AREA OFFICES SELECTED
SANTA ANA CA 92711-9998	03 10 21

PART FAILED				TYPE OF EXAMINATION		BASIC RATING	VETERAN POINTS
WRITTEN	EXPERIENCE	TYPING	DICTATION	ENTRANCE	IN SERVICE		
	N/A	N/A	N/A	X		100.0	

SPECIAL NOTES

ELIGIBILITY 2 YRS. ADDITIONAL YR. ON REQUEST TO PM AFTER 18 MOS.

ADDRESS (No., Street, City, State and ZIP Code)

SOCIAL SECURITY NO.	DATE OF BIRTH	DATE OF EXAMINATION	INSTALLATION NO.	DATE NTAC MAILED	DATE NAME ENTERED ON REGISTER
	07-	04/20/3	05-6936	06/14/84	JUN 18 1984

PS Form 5912=B
June 1979

* ALL APPLICANTS IN A COMPETITIVE EXAMINATION MUST ATTAIN
A RATING OF 70 BEFORE VETERAN'S PREFERENCE IS ALLOWED.

(APPLICANT'S) COPY

U.S. POSTAL SERVICE
CALL IN NOTICE

POSTAL INSTALLATION PLACENTIA, CALIFONIA 92670-9998					TELEPHONE NO.	
DATE OF NOTICE	RATING	BIRTHDATE	SOCIAL SECURITY NO.	VP	HIRING WORKSHEET	
					NO.	DATE
3-11-85	100.00					

REPORT FOR INTERVIEW

DATE (Month, Day, Year) 3-18-85	Time 2:00 pm	LOCATION(No., Street, City, State and ZIP Code): 1400 N. Kraemer Blvd., Placentia, CA 92670-9998

To:

FAILURE TO REPLY TO CALL-IN NOTICE WILL RESULT IN REMOVAL FROM ALL CITIES IN AREA REGISTERS. Please obtain a copy of your driving record history for the past 5 years from the Dept. Motor Vehicles. You must have 2 years driving experience.

Your name has been reached on our register of eligible for employment consideration. We would like to interview you for the following position.: **City carrier, PTF, PS 5** or **Clerk, PTF, PS 5.**

In order to qualify for this position you must qualify for a government driver's license. If you have 3 or more traffic violations in the past 3 years you will not qualify.

_____
Signature of installation head or designated employee

This notice is not an offer of emplyment. DO NOT resign from your present position at this time.

Bring this notice, record of military service (DD From 214), Social Security card, and the enclosed form(s) properly completed to your interview. If you are foreign born bring proof of naturealization or Alien Registration Receipt Card (Form 1-151 or 551). ZIP Code all addresses. If you wish to decline this position, complete the "Declination Statement" below return this notice to the post office. _Unless you either report or reply, your eligibility will be suspended._

The collection of this information is authorized by 39 USC 401, 1001. AS a routine use, this information may be disclosed to an appropriate law enforcement agency for investigative or prosecutive purpose, to a congressional office at your request, to OMB for review of private relief legislation, to any agency where relevant to hiring, contracting, or licensing, to a labor organization as required by the NLRA to the EEOC when investigating an EEO complaint, and where pertinent, in a legal proceeding to which the USPS is a party.

DECLINATION OF STATEMENT

If you do not indicate your availability for any type of appointment, your name will be removed from the list of eligible. Your name will be restored to the register upon receipt of your written request if the register is still in use and your eligibility is current.

I am not available for the above appointment. My future availability and my reason for declining are shown below:

☐ REMOVE MY NAME FROM REGISTER UNTIL I NOTIFY YOUR OFFICE THAT I AM AVAILABLE

☐ RETAIN MY NAME ON THE REGISTER FOR THE TYPES OF APPOINTMENTS CHECKED BELOW:

    ☐ CAREER APPOINTMENT   ☐ I WILL BE AVAILABLE AFTER

    ☐ CASUAL APPOINTMENT   ☐ OTHER(Specify)
       (Not to excced 89 days)

MY REASON FOR NOT BEING AVAILABLE FOR THIS APPOINTMENT IS:

14. Answer Sheet

Part A (Address Checking)

1 Ⓐ Ⓑ Ⓒ Ⓓ	11 Ⓐ Ⓑ Ⓒ Ⓓ	21 Ⓐ Ⓑ Ⓒ Ⓓ	31 Ⓐ Ⓑ Ⓒ Ⓓ	41 Ⓐ Ⓑ Ⓒ Ⓓ	51 Ⓐ Ⓑ Ⓒ Ⓓ
2 Ⓐ Ⓑ Ⓒ Ⓓ	12 Ⓐ Ⓑ Ⓒ Ⓓ	22 Ⓐ Ⓑ Ⓒ Ⓓ	32 Ⓐ Ⓑ Ⓒ Ⓓ	42 Ⓐ Ⓑ Ⓒ Ⓓ	52 Ⓐ Ⓑ Ⓒ Ⓓ
3 Ⓐ Ⓑ Ⓒ Ⓓ	13 Ⓐ Ⓑ Ⓒ Ⓓ	23 Ⓐ Ⓑ Ⓒ Ⓓ	33 Ⓐ Ⓑ Ⓒ Ⓓ	43 Ⓐ Ⓑ Ⓒ Ⓓ	53 Ⓐ Ⓑ Ⓒ Ⓓ
4 Ⓐ Ⓑ Ⓒ Ⓓ	14 Ⓐ Ⓑ Ⓒ Ⓓ	24 Ⓐ Ⓑ Ⓒ Ⓓ	34 Ⓐ Ⓑ Ⓒ Ⓓ	44 Ⓐ Ⓑ Ⓒ Ⓓ	54 Ⓐ Ⓑ Ⓒ Ⓓ
5 Ⓐ Ⓑ Ⓒ Ⓓ	15 Ⓐ Ⓑ Ⓒ Ⓓ	25 Ⓐ Ⓑ Ⓒ Ⓓ	35 Ⓐ Ⓑ Ⓒ Ⓓ	45 Ⓐ Ⓑ Ⓒ Ⓓ	55 Ⓐ Ⓑ Ⓒ Ⓓ
6 Ⓐ Ⓑ Ⓒ Ⓓ	16 Ⓐ Ⓑ Ⓒ Ⓓ	26 Ⓐ Ⓑ Ⓒ Ⓓ	36 Ⓐ Ⓑ Ⓒ Ⓓ	46 Ⓐ Ⓑ Ⓒ Ⓓ	56 Ⓐ Ⓑ Ⓒ Ⓓ
7 Ⓐ Ⓑ Ⓒ Ⓓ	17 Ⓐ Ⓑ Ⓒ Ⓓ	27 Ⓐ Ⓑ Ⓒ Ⓓ	37 Ⓐ Ⓑ Ⓒ Ⓓ	47 Ⓐ Ⓑ Ⓒ Ⓓ	57 Ⓐ Ⓑ Ⓒ Ⓓ
8 Ⓐ Ⓑ Ⓒ Ⓓ	18 Ⓐ Ⓑ Ⓒ Ⓓ	28 Ⓐ Ⓑ Ⓒ Ⓓ	38 Ⓐ Ⓑ Ⓒ Ⓓ	48 Ⓐ Ⓑ Ⓒ Ⓓ	58 Ⓐ Ⓑ Ⓒ Ⓓ
9 Ⓐ Ⓑ Ⓒ Ⓓ	19 Ⓐ Ⓑ Ⓒ Ⓓ	29 Ⓐ Ⓑ Ⓒ Ⓓ	39 Ⓐ Ⓑ Ⓒ Ⓓ	49 Ⓐ Ⓑ Ⓒ Ⓓ	59 Ⓐ Ⓑ Ⓒ Ⓓ
10 Ⓐ Ⓑ Ⓒ Ⓓ	20 Ⓐ Ⓑ Ⓒ Ⓓ	30 Ⓐ Ⓑ Ⓒ Ⓓ	40 Ⓐ Ⓑ Ⓒ Ⓓ	50 Ⓐ Ⓑ Ⓒ Ⓓ	60 Ⓐ Ⓑ Ⓒ Ⓓ

Part B (Forms Completion)

1 Ⓐ Ⓑ Ⓒ Ⓓ	6 Ⓐ Ⓑ Ⓒ Ⓓ	11 Ⓐ Ⓑ Ⓒ Ⓓ	16 Ⓐ Ⓑ Ⓒ Ⓓ	21 Ⓐ Ⓑ Ⓒ Ⓓ	26 Ⓐ Ⓑ Ⓒ Ⓓ
2 Ⓐ Ⓑ Ⓒ Ⓓ	7 Ⓐ Ⓑ Ⓒ Ⓓ	12 Ⓐ Ⓑ Ⓒ Ⓓ	17 Ⓐ Ⓑ Ⓒ Ⓓ	22 Ⓐ Ⓑ Ⓒ Ⓓ	27 Ⓐ Ⓑ Ⓒ Ⓓ
3 Ⓐ Ⓑ Ⓒ Ⓓ	8 Ⓐ Ⓑ Ⓒ Ⓓ	13 Ⓐ Ⓑ Ⓒ Ⓓ	18 Ⓐ Ⓑ Ⓒ Ⓓ	23 Ⓐ Ⓑ Ⓒ Ⓓ	28 Ⓐ Ⓑ Ⓒ Ⓓ
4 Ⓐ Ⓑ Ⓒ Ⓓ	9 Ⓐ Ⓑ Ⓒ Ⓓ	14 Ⓐ Ⓑ Ⓒ Ⓓ	19 Ⓐ Ⓑ Ⓒ Ⓓ	24 Ⓐ Ⓑ Ⓒ Ⓓ	29 Ⓐ Ⓑ Ⓒ Ⓓ
5 Ⓐ Ⓑ Ⓒ Ⓓ	10 Ⓐ Ⓑ Ⓒ Ⓓ	15 Ⓐ Ⓑ Ⓒ Ⓓ	20 Ⓐ Ⓑ Ⓒ Ⓓ	25 Ⓐ Ⓑ Ⓒ Ⓓ	30 Ⓐ Ⓑ Ⓒ Ⓓ

Part C (Coding & Memory)

Section 1 (Coding)

1 Ⓐ Ⓑ Ⓒ Ⓓ	13 Ⓐ Ⓑ Ⓒ Ⓓ	25 Ⓐ Ⓑ Ⓒ Ⓓ
2 Ⓐ Ⓑ Ⓒ Ⓓ	14 Ⓐ Ⓑ Ⓒ Ⓓ	26 Ⓐ Ⓑ Ⓒ Ⓓ
3 Ⓐ Ⓑ Ⓒ Ⓓ	15 Ⓐ Ⓑ Ⓒ Ⓓ	27 Ⓐ Ⓑ Ⓒ Ⓓ
4 Ⓐ Ⓑ Ⓒ Ⓓ	16 Ⓐ Ⓑ Ⓒ Ⓓ	28 Ⓐ Ⓑ Ⓒ Ⓓ
5 Ⓐ Ⓑ Ⓒ Ⓓ	17 Ⓐ Ⓑ Ⓒ Ⓓ	29 Ⓐ Ⓑ Ⓒ Ⓓ
6 Ⓐ Ⓑ Ⓒ Ⓓ	18 Ⓐ Ⓑ Ⓒ Ⓓ	30 Ⓐ Ⓑ Ⓒ Ⓓ
7 Ⓐ Ⓑ Ⓒ Ⓓ	19 Ⓐ Ⓑ Ⓒ Ⓓ	31 Ⓐ Ⓑ Ⓒ Ⓓ
8 Ⓐ Ⓑ Ⓒ Ⓓ	20 Ⓐ Ⓑ Ⓒ Ⓓ	32 Ⓐ Ⓑ Ⓒ Ⓓ
9 Ⓐ Ⓑ Ⓒ Ⓓ	21 Ⓐ Ⓑ Ⓒ Ⓓ	33 Ⓐ Ⓑ Ⓒ Ⓓ
10 Ⓐ Ⓑ Ⓒ Ⓓ	22 Ⓐ Ⓑ Ⓒ Ⓓ	34 Ⓐ Ⓑ Ⓒ Ⓓ
11 Ⓐ Ⓑ Ⓒ Ⓓ	23 Ⓐ Ⓑ Ⓒ Ⓓ	35 Ⓐ Ⓑ Ⓒ Ⓓ
12 Ⓐ Ⓑ Ⓒ Ⓓ	24 Ⓐ Ⓑ Ⓒ Ⓓ	36 Ⓐ Ⓑ Ⓒ Ⓓ

Section 2 (Memory)

37 Ⓐ Ⓑ Ⓒ Ⓓ	49 Ⓐ Ⓑ Ⓒ Ⓓ	61 Ⓐ Ⓑ Ⓒ Ⓓ
38 Ⓐ Ⓑ Ⓒ Ⓓ	50 Ⓐ Ⓑ Ⓒ Ⓓ	62 Ⓐ Ⓑ Ⓒ Ⓓ
39 Ⓐ Ⓑ Ⓒ Ⓓ	51 Ⓐ Ⓑ Ⓒ Ⓓ	63 Ⓐ Ⓑ Ⓒ Ⓓ
40 Ⓐ Ⓑ Ⓒ Ⓓ	52 Ⓐ Ⓑ Ⓒ Ⓓ	64 Ⓐ Ⓑ Ⓒ Ⓓ
41 Ⓐ Ⓑ Ⓒ Ⓓ	53 Ⓐ Ⓑ Ⓒ Ⓓ	65 Ⓐ Ⓑ Ⓒ Ⓓ
42 Ⓐ Ⓑ Ⓒ Ⓓ	54 Ⓐ Ⓑ Ⓒ Ⓓ	66 Ⓐ Ⓑ Ⓒ Ⓓ
43 Ⓐ Ⓑ Ⓒ Ⓓ	55 Ⓐ Ⓑ Ⓒ Ⓓ	67 Ⓐ Ⓑ Ⓒ Ⓓ
44 Ⓐ Ⓑ Ⓒ Ⓓ	56 Ⓐ Ⓑ Ⓒ Ⓓ	68 Ⓐ Ⓑ Ⓒ Ⓓ
45 Ⓐ Ⓑ Ⓒ Ⓓ	57 Ⓐ Ⓑ Ⓒ Ⓓ	69 Ⓐ Ⓑ Ⓒ Ⓓ
46 Ⓐ Ⓑ Ⓒ Ⓓ	58 Ⓐ Ⓑ Ⓒ Ⓓ	70 Ⓐ Ⓑ Ⓒ Ⓓ
47 Ⓐ Ⓑ Ⓒ Ⓓ	59 Ⓐ Ⓑ Ⓒ Ⓓ	71 Ⓐ Ⓑ Ⓒ Ⓓ
48 Ⓐ Ⓑ Ⓒ Ⓓ	60 Ⓐ Ⓑ Ⓒ Ⓓ	72 Ⓐ Ⓑ Ⓒ Ⓓ

Answer Sheet

Part A (Address Checking)

1 Ⓐ Ⓑ Ⓒ Ⓓ	11 Ⓐ Ⓑ Ⓒ Ⓓ	21 Ⓐ Ⓑ Ⓒ Ⓓ	31 Ⓐ Ⓑ Ⓒ Ⓓ	41 Ⓐ Ⓑ Ⓒ Ⓓ	51 Ⓐ Ⓑ Ⓒ Ⓓ
2 Ⓐ Ⓑ Ⓒ Ⓓ	12 Ⓐ Ⓑ Ⓒ Ⓓ	22 Ⓐ Ⓑ Ⓒ Ⓓ	32 Ⓐ Ⓑ Ⓒ Ⓓ	42 Ⓐ Ⓑ Ⓒ Ⓓ	52 Ⓐ Ⓑ Ⓒ Ⓓ
3 Ⓐ Ⓑ Ⓒ Ⓓ	13 Ⓐ Ⓑ Ⓒ Ⓓ	23 Ⓐ Ⓑ Ⓒ Ⓓ	33 Ⓐ Ⓑ Ⓒ Ⓓ	43 Ⓐ Ⓑ Ⓒ Ⓓ	53 Ⓐ Ⓑ Ⓒ Ⓓ
4 Ⓐ Ⓑ Ⓒ Ⓓ	14 Ⓐ Ⓑ Ⓒ Ⓓ	24 Ⓐ Ⓑ Ⓒ Ⓓ	34 Ⓐ Ⓑ Ⓒ Ⓓ	44 Ⓐ Ⓑ Ⓒ Ⓓ	54 Ⓐ Ⓑ Ⓒ Ⓓ
5 Ⓐ Ⓑ Ⓒ Ⓓ	15 Ⓐ Ⓑ Ⓒ Ⓓ	25 Ⓐ Ⓑ Ⓒ Ⓓ	35 Ⓐ Ⓑ Ⓒ Ⓓ	45 Ⓐ Ⓑ Ⓒ Ⓓ	55 Ⓐ Ⓑ Ⓒ Ⓓ
6 Ⓐ Ⓑ Ⓒ Ⓓ	16 Ⓐ Ⓑ Ⓒ Ⓓ	26 Ⓐ Ⓑ Ⓒ Ⓓ	36 Ⓐ Ⓑ Ⓒ Ⓓ	46 Ⓐ Ⓑ Ⓒ Ⓓ	56 Ⓐ Ⓑ Ⓒ Ⓓ
7 Ⓐ Ⓑ Ⓒ Ⓓ	17 Ⓐ Ⓑ Ⓒ Ⓓ	27 Ⓐ Ⓑ Ⓒ Ⓓ	37 Ⓐ Ⓑ Ⓒ Ⓓ	47 Ⓐ Ⓑ Ⓒ Ⓓ	57 Ⓐ Ⓑ Ⓒ Ⓓ
8 Ⓐ Ⓑ Ⓒ Ⓓ	18 Ⓐ Ⓑ Ⓒ Ⓓ	28 Ⓐ Ⓑ Ⓒ Ⓓ	38 Ⓐ Ⓑ Ⓒ Ⓓ	48 Ⓐ Ⓑ Ⓒ Ⓓ	58 Ⓐ Ⓑ Ⓒ Ⓓ
9 Ⓐ Ⓑ Ⓒ Ⓓ	19 Ⓐ Ⓑ Ⓒ Ⓓ	29 Ⓐ Ⓑ Ⓒ Ⓓ	39 Ⓐ Ⓑ Ⓒ Ⓓ	49 Ⓐ Ⓑ Ⓒ Ⓓ	59 Ⓐ Ⓑ Ⓒ Ⓓ
10 Ⓐ Ⓑ Ⓒ Ⓓ	20 Ⓐ Ⓑ Ⓒ Ⓓ	30 Ⓐ Ⓑ Ⓒ Ⓓ	40 Ⓐ Ⓑ Ⓒ Ⓓ	50 Ⓐ Ⓑ Ⓒ Ⓓ	60 Ⓐ Ⓑ Ⓒ Ⓓ

Part B (Forms Completion)

1 Ⓐ Ⓑ Ⓒ Ⓓ	6 Ⓐ Ⓑ Ⓒ Ⓓ	11 Ⓐ Ⓑ Ⓒ Ⓓ	16 Ⓐ Ⓑ Ⓒ Ⓓ	21 Ⓐ Ⓑ Ⓒ Ⓓ	26 Ⓐ Ⓑ Ⓒ Ⓓ
2 Ⓐ Ⓑ Ⓒ Ⓓ	7 Ⓐ Ⓑ Ⓒ Ⓓ	12 Ⓐ Ⓑ Ⓒ Ⓓ	17 Ⓐ Ⓑ Ⓒ Ⓓ	22 Ⓐ Ⓑ Ⓒ Ⓓ	27 Ⓐ Ⓑ Ⓒ Ⓓ
3 Ⓐ Ⓑ Ⓒ Ⓓ	8 Ⓐ Ⓑ Ⓒ Ⓓ	13 Ⓐ Ⓑ Ⓒ Ⓓ	18 Ⓐ Ⓑ Ⓒ Ⓓ	23 Ⓐ Ⓑ Ⓒ Ⓓ	28 Ⓐ Ⓑ Ⓒ Ⓓ
4 Ⓐ Ⓑ Ⓒ Ⓓ	9 Ⓐ Ⓑ Ⓒ Ⓓ	14 Ⓐ Ⓑ Ⓒ Ⓓ	19 Ⓐ Ⓑ Ⓒ Ⓓ	24 Ⓐ Ⓑ Ⓒ Ⓓ	29 Ⓐ Ⓑ Ⓒ Ⓓ
5 Ⓐ Ⓑ Ⓒ Ⓓ	10 Ⓐ Ⓑ Ⓒ Ⓓ	15 Ⓐ Ⓑ Ⓒ Ⓓ	20 Ⓐ Ⓑ Ⓒ Ⓓ	25 Ⓐ Ⓑ Ⓒ Ⓓ	30 Ⓐ Ⓑ Ⓒ Ⓓ

Part C (Coding & Memory)

Section 1 (Coding)

1 Ⓐ Ⓑ Ⓒ Ⓓ	13 Ⓐ Ⓑ Ⓒ Ⓓ	25 Ⓐ Ⓑ Ⓒ Ⓓ
2 Ⓐ Ⓑ Ⓒ Ⓓ	14 Ⓐ Ⓑ Ⓒ Ⓓ	26 Ⓐ Ⓑ Ⓒ Ⓓ
3 Ⓐ Ⓑ Ⓒ Ⓓ	15 Ⓐ Ⓑ Ⓒ Ⓓ	27 Ⓐ Ⓑ Ⓒ Ⓓ
4 Ⓐ Ⓑ Ⓒ Ⓓ	16 Ⓐ Ⓑ Ⓒ Ⓓ	28 Ⓐ Ⓑ Ⓒ Ⓓ
5 Ⓐ Ⓑ Ⓒ Ⓓ	17 Ⓐ Ⓑ Ⓒ Ⓓ	29 Ⓐ Ⓑ Ⓒ Ⓓ
6 Ⓐ Ⓑ Ⓒ Ⓓ	18 Ⓐ Ⓑ Ⓒ Ⓓ	30 Ⓐ Ⓑ Ⓒ Ⓓ
7 Ⓐ Ⓑ Ⓒ Ⓓ	19 Ⓐ Ⓑ Ⓒ Ⓓ	31 Ⓐ Ⓑ Ⓒ Ⓓ
8 Ⓐ Ⓑ Ⓒ Ⓓ	20 Ⓐ Ⓑ Ⓒ Ⓓ	32 Ⓐ Ⓑ Ⓒ Ⓓ
9 Ⓐ Ⓑ Ⓒ Ⓓ	21 Ⓐ Ⓑ Ⓒ Ⓓ	33 Ⓐ Ⓑ Ⓒ Ⓓ
10 Ⓐ Ⓑ Ⓒ Ⓓ	22 Ⓐ Ⓑ Ⓒ Ⓓ	34 Ⓐ Ⓑ Ⓒ Ⓓ
11 Ⓐ Ⓑ Ⓒ Ⓓ	23 Ⓐ Ⓑ Ⓒ Ⓓ	35 Ⓐ Ⓑ Ⓒ Ⓓ
12 Ⓐ Ⓑ Ⓒ Ⓓ	24 Ⓐ Ⓑ Ⓒ Ⓓ	36 Ⓐ Ⓑ Ⓒ Ⓓ

Section 2 (Memory)

37 Ⓐ Ⓑ Ⓒ Ⓓ	49 Ⓐ Ⓑ Ⓒ Ⓓ	61 Ⓐ Ⓑ Ⓒ Ⓓ
38 Ⓐ Ⓑ Ⓒ Ⓓ	50 Ⓐ Ⓑ Ⓒ Ⓓ	62 Ⓐ Ⓑ Ⓒ Ⓓ
39 Ⓐ Ⓑ Ⓒ Ⓓ	51 Ⓐ Ⓑ Ⓒ Ⓓ	63 Ⓐ Ⓑ Ⓒ Ⓓ
40 Ⓐ Ⓑ Ⓒ Ⓓ	52 Ⓐ Ⓑ Ⓒ Ⓓ	64 Ⓐ Ⓑ Ⓒ Ⓓ
41 Ⓐ Ⓑ Ⓒ Ⓓ	53 Ⓐ Ⓑ Ⓒ Ⓓ	65 Ⓐ Ⓑ Ⓒ Ⓓ
42 Ⓐ Ⓑ Ⓒ Ⓓ	54 Ⓐ Ⓑ Ⓒ Ⓓ	66 Ⓐ Ⓑ Ⓒ Ⓓ
43 Ⓐ Ⓑ Ⓒ Ⓓ	55 Ⓐ Ⓑ Ⓒ Ⓓ	67 Ⓐ Ⓑ Ⓒ Ⓓ
44 Ⓐ Ⓑ Ⓒ Ⓓ	56 Ⓐ Ⓑ Ⓒ Ⓓ	68 Ⓐ Ⓑ Ⓒ Ⓓ
45 Ⓐ Ⓑ Ⓒ Ⓓ	57 Ⓐ Ⓑ Ⓒ Ⓓ	69 Ⓐ Ⓑ Ⓒ Ⓓ
46 Ⓐ Ⓑ Ⓒ Ⓓ	58 Ⓐ Ⓑ Ⓒ Ⓓ	70 Ⓐ Ⓑ Ⓒ Ⓓ
47 Ⓐ Ⓑ Ⓒ Ⓓ	59 Ⓐ Ⓑ Ⓒ Ⓓ	71 Ⓐ Ⓑ Ⓒ Ⓓ
48 Ⓐ Ⓑ Ⓒ Ⓓ	60 Ⓐ Ⓑ Ⓒ Ⓓ	72 Ⓐ Ⓑ Ⓒ Ⓓ

Answer Sheet

Part A (Address Checking)

1 Ⓐ Ⓑ Ⓒ Ⓓ	11 Ⓐ Ⓑ Ⓒ Ⓓ	21 Ⓐ Ⓑ Ⓒ Ⓓ	31 Ⓐ Ⓑ Ⓒ Ⓓ	41 Ⓐ Ⓑ Ⓒ Ⓓ	51 Ⓐ Ⓑ Ⓒ Ⓓ
2 Ⓐ Ⓑ Ⓒ Ⓓ	12 Ⓐ Ⓑ Ⓒ Ⓓ	22 Ⓐ Ⓑ Ⓒ Ⓓ	32 Ⓐ Ⓑ Ⓒ Ⓓ	42 Ⓐ Ⓑ Ⓒ Ⓓ	52 Ⓐ Ⓑ Ⓒ Ⓓ
3 Ⓐ Ⓑ Ⓒ Ⓓ	13 Ⓐ Ⓑ Ⓒ Ⓓ	23 Ⓐ Ⓑ Ⓒ Ⓓ	33 Ⓐ Ⓑ Ⓒ Ⓓ	43 Ⓐ Ⓑ Ⓒ Ⓓ	53 Ⓐ Ⓑ Ⓒ Ⓓ
4 Ⓐ Ⓑ Ⓒ Ⓓ	14 Ⓐ Ⓑ Ⓒ Ⓓ	24 Ⓐ Ⓑ Ⓒ Ⓓ	34 Ⓐ Ⓑ Ⓒ Ⓓ	44 Ⓐ Ⓑ Ⓒ Ⓓ	54 Ⓐ Ⓑ Ⓒ Ⓓ
5 Ⓐ Ⓑ Ⓒ Ⓓ	15 Ⓐ Ⓑ Ⓒ Ⓓ	25 Ⓐ Ⓑ Ⓒ Ⓓ	35 Ⓐ Ⓑ Ⓒ Ⓓ	45 Ⓐ Ⓑ Ⓒ Ⓓ	55 Ⓐ Ⓑ Ⓒ Ⓓ
6 Ⓐ Ⓑ Ⓒ Ⓓ	16 Ⓐ Ⓑ Ⓒ Ⓓ	26 Ⓐ Ⓑ Ⓒ Ⓓ	36 Ⓐ Ⓑ Ⓒ Ⓓ	46 Ⓐ Ⓑ Ⓒ Ⓓ	56 Ⓐ Ⓑ Ⓒ Ⓓ
7 Ⓐ Ⓑ Ⓒ Ⓓ	17 Ⓐ Ⓑ Ⓒ Ⓓ	27 Ⓐ Ⓑ Ⓒ Ⓓ	37 Ⓐ Ⓑ Ⓒ Ⓓ	47 Ⓐ Ⓑ Ⓒ Ⓓ	57 Ⓐ Ⓑ Ⓒ Ⓓ
8 Ⓐ Ⓑ Ⓒ Ⓓ	18 Ⓐ Ⓑ Ⓒ Ⓓ	28 Ⓐ Ⓑ Ⓒ Ⓓ	38 Ⓐ Ⓑ Ⓒ Ⓓ	48 Ⓐ Ⓑ Ⓒ Ⓓ	58 Ⓐ Ⓑ Ⓒ Ⓓ
9 Ⓐ Ⓑ Ⓒ Ⓓ	19 Ⓐ Ⓑ Ⓒ Ⓓ	29 Ⓐ Ⓑ Ⓒ Ⓓ	39 Ⓐ Ⓑ Ⓒ Ⓓ	49 Ⓐ Ⓑ Ⓒ Ⓓ	59 Ⓐ Ⓑ Ⓒ Ⓓ
10 Ⓐ Ⓑ Ⓒ Ⓓ	20 Ⓐ Ⓑ Ⓒ Ⓓ	30 Ⓐ Ⓑ Ⓒ Ⓓ	40 Ⓐ Ⓑ Ⓒ Ⓓ	50 Ⓐ Ⓑ Ⓒ Ⓓ	60 Ⓐ Ⓑ Ⓒ Ⓓ

Part B (Forms Completion)

1 Ⓐ Ⓑ Ⓒ Ⓓ	6 Ⓐ Ⓑ Ⓒ Ⓓ	11 Ⓐ Ⓑ Ⓒ Ⓓ	16 Ⓐ Ⓑ Ⓒ Ⓓ	21 Ⓐ Ⓑ Ⓒ Ⓓ	26 Ⓐ Ⓑ Ⓒ Ⓓ
2 Ⓐ Ⓑ Ⓒ Ⓓ	7 Ⓐ Ⓑ Ⓒ Ⓓ	12 Ⓐ Ⓑ Ⓒ Ⓓ	17 Ⓐ Ⓑ Ⓒ Ⓓ	22 Ⓐ Ⓑ Ⓒ Ⓓ	27 Ⓐ Ⓑ Ⓒ Ⓓ
3 Ⓐ Ⓑ Ⓒ Ⓓ	8 Ⓐ Ⓑ Ⓒ Ⓓ	13 Ⓐ Ⓑ Ⓒ Ⓓ	18 Ⓐ Ⓑ Ⓒ Ⓓ	23 Ⓐ Ⓑ Ⓒ Ⓓ	28 Ⓐ Ⓑ Ⓒ Ⓓ
4 Ⓐ Ⓑ Ⓒ Ⓓ	9 Ⓐ Ⓑ Ⓒ Ⓓ	14 Ⓐ Ⓑ Ⓒ Ⓓ	19 Ⓐ Ⓑ Ⓒ Ⓓ	24 Ⓐ Ⓑ Ⓒ Ⓓ	29 Ⓐ Ⓑ Ⓒ Ⓓ
5 Ⓐ Ⓑ Ⓒ Ⓓ	10 Ⓐ Ⓑ Ⓒ Ⓓ	15 Ⓐ Ⓑ Ⓒ Ⓓ	20 Ⓐ Ⓑ Ⓒ Ⓓ	25 Ⓐ Ⓑ Ⓒ Ⓓ	30 Ⓐ Ⓑ Ⓒ Ⓓ

Part C (Coding & Memory)

Section 1 (Coding)

1 Ⓐ Ⓑ Ⓒ Ⓓ	13 Ⓐ Ⓑ Ⓒ Ⓓ	25 Ⓐ Ⓑ Ⓒ Ⓓ
2 Ⓐ Ⓑ Ⓒ Ⓓ	14 Ⓐ Ⓑ Ⓒ Ⓓ	26 Ⓐ Ⓑ Ⓒ Ⓓ
3 Ⓐ Ⓑ Ⓒ Ⓓ	15 Ⓐ Ⓑ Ⓒ Ⓓ	27 Ⓐ Ⓑ Ⓒ Ⓓ
4 Ⓐ Ⓑ Ⓒ Ⓓ	16 Ⓐ Ⓑ Ⓒ Ⓓ	28 Ⓐ Ⓑ Ⓒ Ⓓ
5 Ⓐ Ⓑ Ⓒ Ⓓ	17 Ⓐ Ⓑ Ⓒ Ⓓ	29 Ⓐ Ⓑ Ⓒ Ⓓ
6 Ⓐ Ⓑ Ⓒ Ⓓ	18 Ⓐ Ⓑ Ⓒ Ⓓ	30 Ⓐ Ⓑ Ⓒ Ⓓ
7 Ⓐ Ⓑ Ⓒ Ⓓ	19 Ⓐ Ⓑ Ⓒ Ⓓ	31 Ⓐ Ⓑ Ⓒ Ⓓ
8 Ⓐ Ⓑ Ⓒ Ⓓ	20 Ⓐ Ⓑ Ⓒ Ⓓ	32 Ⓐ Ⓑ Ⓒ Ⓓ
9 Ⓐ Ⓑ Ⓒ Ⓓ	21 Ⓐ Ⓑ Ⓒ Ⓓ	33 Ⓐ Ⓑ Ⓒ Ⓓ
10 Ⓐ Ⓑ Ⓒ Ⓓ	22 Ⓐ Ⓑ Ⓒ Ⓓ	34 Ⓐ Ⓑ Ⓒ Ⓓ
11 Ⓐ Ⓑ Ⓒ Ⓓ	23 Ⓐ Ⓑ Ⓒ Ⓓ	35 Ⓐ Ⓑ Ⓒ Ⓓ
12 Ⓐ Ⓑ Ⓒ Ⓓ	24 Ⓐ Ⓑ Ⓒ Ⓓ	36 Ⓐ Ⓑ Ⓒ Ⓓ

Section 2 (Memory)

37 Ⓐ Ⓑ Ⓒ Ⓓ	49 Ⓐ Ⓑ Ⓒ Ⓓ	61 Ⓐ Ⓑ Ⓒ Ⓓ
38 Ⓐ Ⓑ Ⓒ Ⓓ	50 Ⓐ Ⓑ Ⓒ Ⓓ	62 Ⓐ Ⓑ Ⓒ Ⓓ
39 Ⓐ Ⓑ Ⓒ Ⓓ	51 Ⓐ Ⓑ Ⓒ Ⓓ	63 Ⓐ Ⓑ Ⓒ Ⓓ
40 Ⓐ Ⓑ Ⓒ Ⓓ	52 Ⓐ Ⓑ Ⓒ Ⓓ	64 Ⓐ Ⓑ Ⓒ Ⓓ
41 Ⓐ Ⓑ Ⓒ Ⓓ	53 Ⓐ Ⓑ Ⓒ Ⓓ	65 Ⓐ Ⓑ Ⓒ Ⓓ
42 Ⓐ Ⓑ Ⓒ Ⓓ	54 Ⓐ Ⓑ Ⓒ Ⓓ	66 Ⓐ Ⓑ Ⓒ Ⓓ
43 Ⓐ Ⓑ Ⓒ Ⓓ	55 Ⓐ Ⓑ Ⓒ Ⓓ	67 Ⓐ Ⓑ Ⓒ Ⓓ
44 Ⓐ Ⓑ Ⓒ Ⓓ	56 Ⓐ Ⓑ Ⓒ Ⓓ	68 Ⓐ Ⓑ Ⓒ Ⓓ
45 Ⓐ Ⓑ Ⓒ Ⓓ	57 Ⓐ Ⓑ Ⓒ Ⓓ	69 Ⓐ Ⓑ Ⓒ Ⓓ
46 Ⓐ Ⓑ Ⓒ Ⓓ	58 Ⓐ Ⓑ Ⓒ Ⓓ	70 Ⓐ Ⓑ Ⓒ Ⓓ
47 Ⓐ Ⓑ Ⓒ Ⓓ	59 Ⓐ Ⓑ Ⓒ Ⓓ	71 Ⓐ Ⓑ Ⓒ Ⓓ
48 Ⓐ Ⓑ Ⓒ Ⓓ	60 Ⓐ Ⓑ Ⓒ Ⓓ	72 Ⓐ Ⓑ Ⓒ Ⓓ

Answer Sheet

Part A (Address Checking)

1 Ⓐ Ⓑ Ⓒ Ⓓ	11 Ⓐ Ⓑ Ⓒ Ⓓ	21 Ⓐ Ⓑ Ⓒ Ⓓ	31 Ⓐ Ⓑ Ⓒ Ⓓ	41 Ⓐ Ⓑ Ⓒ Ⓓ	51 Ⓐ Ⓑ Ⓒ Ⓓ
2 Ⓐ Ⓑ Ⓒ Ⓓ	12 Ⓐ Ⓑ Ⓒ Ⓓ	22 Ⓐ Ⓑ Ⓒ Ⓓ	32 Ⓐ Ⓑ Ⓒ Ⓓ	42 Ⓐ Ⓑ Ⓒ Ⓓ	52 Ⓐ Ⓑ Ⓒ Ⓓ
3 Ⓐ Ⓑ Ⓒ Ⓓ	13 Ⓐ Ⓑ Ⓒ Ⓓ	23 Ⓐ Ⓑ Ⓒ Ⓓ	33 Ⓐ Ⓑ Ⓒ Ⓓ	43 Ⓐ Ⓑ Ⓒ Ⓓ	53 Ⓐ Ⓑ Ⓒ Ⓓ
4 Ⓐ Ⓑ Ⓒ Ⓓ	14 Ⓐ Ⓑ Ⓒ Ⓓ	24 Ⓐ Ⓑ Ⓒ Ⓓ	34 Ⓐ Ⓑ Ⓒ Ⓓ	44 Ⓐ Ⓑ Ⓒ Ⓓ	54 Ⓐ Ⓑ Ⓒ Ⓓ
5 Ⓐ Ⓑ Ⓒ Ⓓ	15 Ⓐ Ⓑ Ⓒ Ⓓ	25 Ⓐ Ⓑ Ⓒ Ⓓ	35 Ⓐ Ⓑ Ⓒ Ⓓ	45 Ⓐ Ⓑ Ⓒ Ⓓ	55 Ⓐ Ⓑ Ⓒ Ⓓ
6 Ⓐ Ⓑ Ⓒ Ⓓ	16 Ⓐ Ⓑ Ⓒ Ⓓ	26 Ⓐ Ⓑ Ⓒ Ⓓ	36 Ⓐ Ⓑ Ⓒ Ⓓ	46 Ⓐ Ⓑ Ⓒ Ⓓ	56 Ⓐ Ⓑ Ⓒ Ⓓ
7 Ⓐ Ⓑ Ⓒ Ⓓ	17 Ⓐ Ⓑ Ⓒ Ⓓ	27 Ⓐ Ⓑ Ⓒ Ⓓ	37 Ⓐ Ⓑ Ⓒ Ⓓ	47 Ⓐ Ⓑ Ⓒ Ⓓ	57 Ⓐ Ⓑ Ⓒ Ⓓ
8 Ⓐ Ⓑ Ⓒ Ⓓ	18 Ⓐ Ⓑ Ⓒ Ⓓ	28 Ⓐ Ⓑ Ⓒ Ⓓ	38 Ⓐ Ⓑ Ⓒ Ⓓ	48 Ⓐ Ⓑ Ⓒ Ⓓ	58 Ⓐ Ⓑ Ⓒ Ⓓ
9 Ⓐ Ⓑ Ⓒ Ⓓ	19 Ⓐ Ⓑ Ⓒ Ⓓ	29 Ⓐ Ⓑ Ⓒ Ⓓ	39 Ⓐ Ⓑ Ⓒ Ⓓ	49 Ⓐ Ⓑ Ⓒ Ⓓ	59 Ⓐ Ⓑ Ⓒ Ⓓ
10 Ⓐ Ⓑ Ⓒ Ⓓ	20 Ⓐ Ⓑ Ⓒ Ⓓ	30 Ⓐ Ⓑ Ⓒ Ⓓ	40 Ⓐ Ⓑ Ⓒ Ⓓ	50 Ⓐ Ⓑ Ⓒ Ⓓ	60 Ⓐ Ⓑ Ⓒ Ⓓ

Part B (Forms Completion)

1 Ⓐ Ⓑ Ⓒ Ⓓ	6 Ⓐ Ⓑ Ⓒ Ⓓ	11 Ⓐ Ⓑ Ⓒ Ⓓ	16 Ⓐ Ⓑ Ⓒ Ⓓ	21 Ⓐ Ⓑ Ⓒ Ⓓ	26 Ⓐ Ⓑ Ⓒ Ⓓ
2 Ⓐ Ⓑ Ⓒ Ⓓ	7 Ⓐ Ⓑ Ⓒ Ⓓ	12 Ⓐ Ⓑ Ⓒ Ⓓ	17 Ⓐ Ⓑ Ⓒ Ⓓ	22 Ⓐ Ⓑ Ⓒ Ⓓ	27 Ⓐ Ⓑ Ⓒ Ⓓ
3 Ⓐ Ⓑ Ⓒ Ⓓ	8 Ⓐ Ⓑ Ⓒ Ⓓ	13 Ⓐ Ⓑ Ⓒ Ⓓ	18 Ⓐ Ⓑ Ⓒ Ⓓ	23 Ⓐ Ⓑ Ⓒ Ⓓ	28 Ⓐ Ⓑ Ⓒ Ⓓ
4 Ⓐ Ⓑ Ⓒ Ⓓ	9 Ⓐ Ⓑ Ⓒ Ⓓ	14 Ⓐ Ⓑ Ⓒ Ⓓ	19 Ⓐ Ⓑ Ⓒ Ⓓ	24 Ⓐ Ⓑ Ⓒ Ⓓ	29 Ⓐ Ⓑ Ⓒ Ⓓ
5 Ⓐ Ⓑ Ⓒ Ⓓ	10 Ⓐ Ⓑ Ⓒ Ⓓ	15 Ⓐ Ⓑ Ⓒ Ⓓ	20 Ⓐ Ⓑ Ⓒ Ⓓ	25 Ⓐ Ⓑ Ⓒ Ⓓ	30 Ⓐ Ⓑ Ⓒ Ⓓ

Part C (Coding & Memory)

Section 1 (Coding)

1 Ⓐ Ⓑ Ⓒ Ⓓ	13 Ⓐ Ⓑ Ⓒ Ⓓ	25 Ⓐ Ⓑ Ⓒ Ⓓ
2 Ⓐ Ⓑ Ⓒ Ⓓ	14 Ⓐ Ⓑ Ⓒ Ⓓ	26 Ⓐ Ⓑ Ⓒ Ⓓ
3 Ⓐ Ⓑ Ⓒ Ⓓ	15 Ⓐ Ⓑ Ⓒ Ⓓ	27 Ⓐ Ⓑ Ⓒ Ⓓ
4 Ⓐ Ⓑ Ⓒ Ⓓ	16 Ⓐ Ⓑ Ⓒ Ⓓ	28 Ⓐ Ⓑ Ⓒ Ⓓ
5 Ⓐ Ⓑ Ⓒ Ⓓ	17 Ⓐ Ⓑ Ⓒ Ⓓ	29 Ⓐ Ⓑ Ⓒ Ⓓ
6 Ⓐ Ⓑ Ⓒ Ⓓ	18 Ⓐ Ⓑ Ⓒ Ⓓ	30 Ⓐ Ⓑ Ⓒ Ⓓ
7 Ⓐ Ⓑ Ⓒ Ⓓ	19 Ⓐ Ⓑ Ⓒ Ⓓ	31 Ⓐ Ⓑ Ⓒ Ⓓ
8 Ⓐ Ⓑ Ⓒ Ⓓ	20 Ⓐ Ⓑ Ⓒ Ⓓ	32 Ⓐ Ⓑ Ⓒ Ⓓ
9 Ⓐ Ⓑ Ⓒ Ⓓ	21 Ⓐ Ⓑ Ⓒ Ⓓ	33 Ⓐ Ⓑ Ⓒ Ⓓ
10 Ⓐ Ⓑ Ⓒ Ⓓ	22 Ⓐ Ⓑ Ⓒ Ⓓ	34 Ⓐ Ⓑ Ⓒ Ⓓ
11 Ⓐ Ⓑ Ⓒ Ⓓ	23 Ⓐ Ⓑ Ⓒ Ⓓ	35 Ⓐ Ⓑ Ⓒ Ⓓ
12 Ⓐ Ⓑ Ⓒ Ⓓ	24 Ⓐ Ⓑ Ⓒ Ⓓ	36 Ⓐ Ⓑ Ⓒ Ⓓ

Section 2 (Memory)

37 Ⓐ Ⓑ Ⓒ Ⓓ	49 Ⓐ Ⓑ Ⓒ Ⓓ	61 Ⓐ Ⓑ Ⓒ Ⓓ
38 Ⓐ Ⓑ Ⓒ Ⓓ	50 Ⓐ Ⓑ Ⓒ Ⓓ	62 Ⓐ Ⓑ Ⓒ Ⓓ
39 Ⓐ Ⓑ Ⓒ Ⓓ	51 Ⓐ Ⓑ Ⓒ Ⓓ	63 Ⓐ Ⓑ Ⓒ Ⓓ
40 Ⓐ Ⓑ Ⓒ Ⓓ	52 Ⓐ Ⓑ Ⓒ Ⓓ	64 Ⓐ Ⓑ Ⓒ Ⓓ
41 Ⓐ Ⓑ Ⓒ Ⓓ	53 Ⓐ Ⓑ Ⓒ Ⓓ	65 Ⓐ Ⓑ Ⓒ Ⓓ
42 Ⓐ Ⓑ Ⓒ Ⓓ	54 Ⓐ Ⓑ Ⓒ Ⓓ	66 Ⓐ Ⓑ Ⓒ Ⓓ
43 Ⓐ Ⓑ Ⓒ Ⓓ	55 Ⓐ Ⓑ Ⓒ Ⓓ	67 Ⓐ Ⓑ Ⓒ Ⓓ
44 Ⓐ Ⓑ Ⓒ Ⓓ	56 Ⓐ Ⓑ Ⓒ Ⓓ	68 Ⓐ Ⓑ Ⓒ Ⓓ
45 Ⓐ Ⓑ Ⓒ Ⓓ	57 Ⓐ Ⓑ Ⓒ Ⓓ	69 Ⓐ Ⓑ Ⓒ Ⓓ
46 Ⓐ Ⓑ Ⓒ Ⓓ	58 Ⓐ Ⓑ Ⓒ Ⓓ	70 Ⓐ Ⓑ Ⓒ Ⓓ
47 Ⓐ Ⓑ Ⓒ Ⓓ	59 Ⓐ Ⓑ Ⓒ Ⓓ	71 Ⓐ Ⓑ Ⓒ Ⓓ
48 Ⓐ Ⓑ Ⓒ Ⓓ	60 Ⓐ Ⓑ Ⓒ Ⓓ	72 Ⓐ Ⓑ Ⓒ Ⓓ

Answer Sheet

Part A (Address Checking)

1 (A)(B)(C)(D)	11 (A)(B)(C)(D)	21 (A)(B)(C)(D)	31 (A)(B)(C)(D)	41 (A)(B)(C)(D)	51 (A)(B)(C)(D)
2 (A)(B)(C)(D)	12 (A)(B)(C)(D)	22 (A)(B)(C)(D)	32 (A)(B)(C)(D)	42 (A)(B)(C)(D)	52 (A)(B)(C)(D)
3 (A)(B)(C)(D)	13 (A)(B)(C)(D)	23 (A)(B)(C)(D)	33 (A)(B)(C)(D)	43 (A)(B)(C)(D)	53 (A)(B)(C)(D)
4 (A)(B)(C)(D)	14 (A)(B)(C)(D)	24 (A)(B)(C)(D)	34 (A)(B)(C)(D)	44 (A)(B)(C)(D)	54 (A)(B)(C)(D)
5 (A)(B)(C)(D)	15 (A)(B)(C)(D)	25 (A)(B)(C)(D)	35 (A)(B)(C)(D)	45 (A)(B)(C)(D)	55 (A)(B)(C)(D)
6 (A)(B)(C)(D)	16 (A)(B)(C)(D)	26 (A)(B)(C)(D)	36 (A)(B)(C)(D)	46 (A)(B)(C)(D)	56 (A)(B)(C)(D)
7 (A)(B)(C)(D)	17 (A)(B)(C)(D)	27 (A)(B)(C)(D)	37 (A)(B)(C)(D)	47 (A)(B)(C)(D)	57 (A)(B)(C)(D)
8 (A)(B)(C)(D)	18 (A)(B)(C)(D)	28 (A)(B)(C)(D)	38 (A)(B)(C)(D)	48 (A)(B)(C)(D)	58 (A)(B)(C)(D)
9 (A)(B)(C)(D)	19 (A)(B)(C)(D)	29 (A)(B)(C)(D)	39 (A)(B)(C)(D)	49 (A)(B)(C)(D)	59 (A)(B)(C)(D)
10 (A)(B)(C)(D)	20 (A)(B)(C)(D)	30 (A)(B)(C)(D)	40 (A)(B)(C)(D)	50 (A)(B)(C)(D)	60 (A)(B)(C)(D)

Part B (Forms Completion)

1 (A)(B)(C)(D)	6 (A)(B)(C)(D)	11 (A)(B)(C)(D)	16 (A)(B)(C)(D)	21 (A)(B)(C)(D)	26 (A)(B)(C)(D)
2 (A)(B)(C)(D)	7 (A)(B)(C)(D)	12 (A)(B)(C)(D)	17 (A)(B)(C)(D)	22 (A)(B)(C)(D)	27 (A)(B)(C)(D)
3 (A)(B)(C)(D)	8 (A)(B)(C)(D)	13 (A)(B)(C)(D)	18 (A)(B)(C)(D)	23 (A)(B)(C)(D)	28 (A)(B)(C)(D)
4 (A)(B)(C)(D)	9 (A)(B)(C)(D)	14 (A)(B)(C)(D)	19 (A)(B)(C)(D)	24 (A)(B)(C)(D)	29 (A)(B)(C)(D)
5 (A)(B)(C)(D)	10 (A)(B)(C)(D)	15 (A)(B)(C)(D)	20 (A)(B)(C)(D)	25 (A)(B)(C)(D)	30 (A)(B)(C)(D)

Part C (Coding & Memory)

Section 1 (Coding)

1 (A)(B)(C)(D)	13 (A)(B)(C)(D)	25 (A)(B)(C)(D)
2 (A)(B)(C)(D)	14 (A)(B)(C)(D)	26 (A)(B)(C)(D)
3 (A)(B)(C)(D)	15 (A)(B)(C)(D)	27 (A)(B)(C)(D)
4 (A)(B)(C)(D)	16 (A)(B)(C)(D)	28 (A)(B)(C)(D)
5 (A)(B)(C)(D)	17 (A)(B)(C)(D)	29 (A)(B)(C)(D)
6 (A)(B)(C)(D)	18 (A)(B)(C)(D)	30 (A)(B)(C)(D)
7 (A)(B)(C)(D)	19 (A)(B)(C)(D)	31 (A)(B)(C)(D)
8 (A)(B)(C)(D)	20 (A)(B)(C)(D)	32 (A)(B)(C)(D)
9 (A)(B)(C)(D)	21 (A)(B)(C)(D)	33 (A)(B)(C)(D)
10 (A)(B)(C)(D)	22 (A)(B)(C)(D)	34 (A)(B)(C)(D)
11 (A)(B)(C)(D)	23 (A)(B)(C)(D)	35 (A)(B)(C)(D)
12 (A)(B)(C)(D)	24 (A)(B)(C)(D)	36 (A)(B)(C)(D)

Section 2 (Memory)

37 (A)(B)(C)(D)	49 (A)(B)(C)(D)	61 (A)(B)(C)(D)
38 (A)(B)(C)(D)	50 (A)(B)(C)(D)	62 (A)(B)(C)(D)
39 (A)(B)(C)(D)	51 (A)(B)(C)(D)	63 (A)(B)(C)(D)
40 (A)(B)(C)(D)	52 (A)(B)(C)(D)	64 (A)(B)(C)(D)
41 (A)(B)(C)(D)	53 (A)(B)(C)(D)	65 (A)(B)(C)(D)
42 (A)(B)(C)(D)	54 (A)(B)(C)(D)	66 (A)(B)(C)(D)
43 (A)(B)(C)(D)	55 (A)(B)(C)(D)	67 (A)(B)(C)(D)
44 (A)(B)(C)(D)	56 (A)(B)(C)(D)	68 (A)(B)(C)(D)
45 (A)(B)(C)(D)	57 (A)(B)(C)(D)	69 (A)(B)(C)(D)
46 (A)(B)(C)(D)	58 (A)(B)(C)(D)	70 (A)(B)(C)(D)
47 (A)(B)(C)(D)	59 (A)(B)(C)(D)	71 (A)(B)(C)(D)
48 (A)(B)(C)(D)	60 (A)(B)(C)(D)	72 (A)(B)(C)(D)

Answer Sheet

Part A (Address Checking)

1 Ⓐ Ⓑ Ⓒ Ⓓ	11 Ⓐ Ⓑ Ⓒ Ⓓ	21 Ⓐ Ⓑ Ⓒ Ⓓ	31 Ⓐ Ⓑ Ⓒ Ⓓ	41 Ⓐ Ⓑ Ⓒ Ⓓ	51 Ⓐ Ⓑ Ⓒ Ⓓ
2 Ⓐ Ⓑ Ⓒ Ⓓ	12 Ⓐ Ⓑ Ⓒ Ⓓ	22 Ⓐ Ⓑ Ⓒ Ⓓ	32 Ⓐ Ⓑ Ⓒ Ⓓ	42 Ⓐ Ⓑ Ⓒ Ⓓ	52 Ⓐ Ⓑ Ⓒ Ⓓ
3 Ⓐ Ⓑ Ⓒ Ⓓ	13 Ⓐ Ⓑ Ⓒ Ⓓ	23 Ⓐ Ⓑ Ⓒ Ⓓ	33 Ⓐ Ⓑ Ⓒ Ⓓ	43 Ⓐ Ⓑ Ⓒ Ⓓ	53 Ⓐ Ⓑ Ⓒ Ⓓ
4 Ⓐ Ⓑ Ⓒ Ⓓ	14 Ⓐ Ⓑ Ⓒ Ⓓ	24 Ⓐ Ⓑ Ⓒ Ⓓ	34 Ⓐ Ⓑ Ⓒ Ⓓ	44 Ⓐ Ⓑ Ⓒ Ⓓ	54 Ⓐ Ⓑ Ⓒ Ⓓ
5 Ⓐ Ⓑ Ⓒ Ⓓ	15 Ⓐ Ⓑ Ⓒ Ⓓ	25 Ⓐ Ⓑ Ⓒ Ⓓ	35 Ⓐ Ⓑ Ⓒ Ⓓ	45 Ⓐ Ⓑ Ⓒ Ⓓ	55 Ⓐ Ⓑ Ⓒ Ⓓ
6 Ⓐ Ⓑ Ⓒ Ⓓ	16 Ⓐ Ⓑ Ⓒ Ⓓ	26 Ⓐ Ⓑ Ⓒ Ⓓ	36 Ⓐ Ⓑ Ⓒ Ⓓ	46 Ⓐ Ⓑ Ⓒ Ⓓ	56 Ⓐ Ⓑ Ⓒ Ⓓ
7 Ⓐ Ⓑ Ⓒ Ⓓ	17 Ⓐ Ⓑ Ⓒ Ⓓ	27 Ⓐ Ⓑ Ⓒ Ⓓ	37 Ⓐ Ⓑ Ⓒ Ⓓ	47 Ⓐ Ⓑ Ⓒ Ⓓ	57 Ⓐ Ⓑ Ⓒ Ⓓ
8 Ⓐ Ⓑ Ⓒ Ⓓ	18 Ⓐ Ⓑ Ⓒ Ⓓ	28 Ⓐ Ⓑ Ⓒ Ⓓ	38 Ⓐ Ⓑ Ⓒ Ⓓ	48 Ⓐ Ⓑ Ⓒ Ⓓ	58 Ⓐ Ⓑ Ⓒ Ⓓ
9 Ⓐ Ⓑ Ⓒ Ⓓ	19 Ⓐ Ⓑ Ⓒ Ⓓ	29 Ⓐ Ⓑ Ⓒ Ⓓ	39 Ⓐ Ⓑ Ⓒ Ⓓ	49 Ⓐ Ⓑ Ⓒ Ⓓ	59 Ⓐ Ⓑ Ⓒ Ⓓ
10 Ⓐ Ⓑ Ⓒ Ⓓ	20 Ⓐ Ⓑ Ⓒ Ⓓ	30 Ⓐ Ⓑ Ⓒ Ⓓ	40 Ⓐ Ⓑ Ⓒ Ⓓ	50 Ⓐ Ⓑ Ⓒ Ⓓ	60 Ⓐ Ⓑ Ⓒ Ⓓ

Part B (Forms Completion)

1 Ⓐ Ⓑ Ⓒ Ⓓ	6 Ⓐ Ⓑ Ⓒ Ⓓ	11 Ⓐ Ⓑ Ⓒ Ⓓ	16 Ⓐ Ⓑ Ⓒ Ⓓ	21 Ⓐ Ⓑ Ⓒ Ⓓ	26 Ⓐ Ⓑ Ⓒ Ⓓ
2 Ⓐ Ⓑ Ⓒ Ⓓ	7 Ⓐ Ⓑ Ⓒ Ⓓ	12 Ⓐ Ⓑ Ⓒ Ⓓ	17 Ⓐ Ⓑ Ⓒ Ⓓ	22 Ⓐ Ⓑ Ⓒ Ⓓ	27 Ⓐ Ⓑ Ⓒ Ⓓ
3 Ⓐ Ⓑ Ⓒ Ⓓ	8 Ⓐ Ⓑ Ⓒ Ⓓ	13 Ⓐ Ⓑ Ⓒ Ⓓ	18 Ⓐ Ⓑ Ⓒ Ⓓ	23 Ⓐ Ⓑ Ⓒ Ⓓ	28 Ⓐ Ⓑ Ⓒ Ⓓ
4 Ⓐ Ⓑ Ⓒ Ⓓ	9 Ⓐ Ⓑ Ⓒ Ⓓ	14 Ⓐ Ⓑ Ⓒ Ⓓ	19 Ⓐ Ⓑ Ⓒ Ⓓ	24 Ⓐ Ⓑ Ⓒ Ⓓ	29 Ⓐ Ⓑ Ⓒ Ⓓ
5 Ⓐ Ⓑ Ⓒ Ⓓ	10 Ⓐ Ⓑ Ⓒ Ⓓ	15 Ⓐ Ⓑ Ⓒ Ⓓ	20 Ⓐ Ⓑ Ⓒ Ⓓ	25 Ⓐ Ⓑ Ⓒ Ⓓ	30 Ⓐ Ⓑ Ⓒ Ⓓ

Part C (Coding & Memory)

Section 1 (Coding)

1 Ⓐ Ⓑ Ⓒ Ⓓ	13 Ⓐ Ⓑ Ⓒ Ⓓ	25 Ⓐ Ⓑ Ⓒ Ⓓ
2 Ⓐ Ⓑ Ⓒ Ⓓ	14 Ⓐ Ⓑ Ⓒ Ⓓ	26 Ⓐ Ⓑ Ⓒ Ⓓ
3 Ⓐ Ⓑ Ⓒ Ⓓ	15 Ⓐ Ⓑ Ⓒ Ⓓ	27 Ⓐ Ⓑ Ⓒ Ⓓ
4 Ⓐ Ⓑ Ⓒ Ⓓ	16 Ⓐ Ⓑ Ⓒ Ⓓ	28 Ⓐ Ⓑ Ⓒ Ⓓ
5 Ⓐ Ⓑ Ⓒ Ⓓ	17 Ⓐ Ⓑ Ⓒ Ⓓ	29 Ⓐ Ⓑ Ⓒ Ⓓ
6 Ⓐ Ⓑ Ⓒ Ⓓ	18 Ⓐ Ⓑ Ⓒ Ⓓ	30 Ⓐ Ⓑ Ⓒ Ⓓ
7 Ⓐ Ⓑ Ⓒ Ⓓ	19 Ⓐ Ⓑ Ⓒ Ⓓ	31 Ⓐ Ⓑ Ⓒ Ⓓ
8 Ⓐ Ⓑ Ⓒ Ⓓ	20 Ⓐ Ⓑ Ⓒ Ⓓ	32 Ⓐ Ⓑ Ⓒ Ⓓ
9 Ⓐ Ⓑ Ⓒ Ⓓ	21 Ⓐ Ⓑ Ⓒ Ⓓ	33 Ⓐ Ⓑ Ⓒ Ⓓ
10 Ⓐ Ⓑ Ⓒ Ⓓ	22 Ⓐ Ⓑ Ⓒ Ⓓ	34 Ⓐ Ⓑ Ⓒ Ⓓ
11 Ⓐ Ⓑ Ⓒ Ⓓ	23 Ⓐ Ⓑ Ⓒ Ⓓ	35 Ⓐ Ⓑ Ⓒ Ⓓ
12 Ⓐ Ⓑ Ⓒ Ⓓ	24 Ⓐ Ⓑ Ⓒ Ⓓ	36 Ⓐ Ⓑ Ⓒ Ⓓ

Section 2 (Memory)

37 Ⓐ Ⓑ Ⓒ Ⓓ	49 Ⓐ Ⓑ Ⓒ Ⓓ	61 Ⓐ Ⓑ Ⓒ Ⓓ
38 Ⓐ Ⓑ Ⓒ Ⓓ	50 Ⓐ Ⓑ Ⓒ Ⓓ	62 Ⓐ Ⓑ Ⓒ Ⓓ
39 Ⓐ Ⓑ Ⓒ Ⓓ	51 Ⓐ Ⓑ Ⓒ Ⓓ	63 Ⓐ Ⓑ Ⓒ Ⓓ
40 Ⓐ Ⓑ Ⓒ Ⓓ	52 Ⓐ Ⓑ Ⓒ Ⓓ	64 Ⓐ Ⓑ Ⓒ Ⓓ
41 Ⓐ Ⓑ Ⓒ Ⓓ	53 Ⓐ Ⓑ Ⓒ Ⓓ	65 Ⓐ Ⓑ Ⓒ Ⓓ
42 Ⓐ Ⓑ Ⓒ Ⓓ	54 Ⓐ Ⓑ Ⓒ Ⓓ	66 Ⓐ Ⓑ Ⓒ Ⓓ
43 Ⓐ Ⓑ Ⓒ Ⓓ	55 Ⓐ Ⓑ Ⓒ Ⓓ	67 Ⓐ Ⓑ Ⓒ Ⓓ
44 Ⓐ Ⓑ Ⓒ Ⓓ	56 Ⓐ Ⓑ Ⓒ Ⓓ	68 Ⓐ Ⓑ Ⓒ Ⓓ
45 Ⓐ Ⓑ Ⓒ Ⓓ	57 Ⓐ Ⓑ Ⓒ Ⓓ	69 Ⓐ Ⓑ Ⓒ Ⓓ
46 Ⓐ Ⓑ Ⓒ Ⓓ	58 Ⓐ Ⓑ Ⓒ Ⓓ	70 Ⓐ Ⓑ Ⓒ Ⓓ
47 Ⓐ Ⓑ Ⓒ Ⓓ	59 Ⓐ Ⓑ Ⓒ Ⓓ	71 Ⓐ Ⓑ Ⓒ Ⓓ
48 Ⓐ Ⓑ Ⓒ Ⓓ	60 Ⓐ Ⓑ Ⓒ Ⓓ	72 Ⓐ Ⓑ Ⓒ Ⓓ

Answer Sheet

Part A (Address Checking)

1 Ⓐ Ⓑ Ⓒ Ⓓ	11 Ⓐ Ⓑ Ⓒ Ⓓ	21 Ⓐ Ⓑ Ⓒ Ⓓ	31 Ⓐ Ⓑ Ⓒ Ⓓ	41 Ⓐ Ⓑ Ⓒ Ⓓ	51 Ⓐ Ⓑ Ⓒ Ⓓ
2 Ⓐ Ⓑ Ⓒ Ⓓ	12 Ⓐ Ⓑ Ⓒ Ⓓ	22 Ⓐ Ⓑ Ⓒ Ⓓ	32 Ⓐ Ⓑ Ⓒ Ⓓ	42 Ⓐ Ⓑ Ⓒ Ⓓ	52 Ⓐ Ⓑ Ⓒ Ⓓ
3 Ⓐ Ⓑ Ⓒ Ⓓ	13 Ⓐ Ⓑ Ⓒ Ⓓ	23 Ⓐ Ⓑ Ⓒ Ⓓ	33 Ⓐ Ⓑ Ⓒ Ⓓ	43 Ⓐ Ⓑ Ⓒ Ⓓ	53 Ⓐ Ⓑ Ⓒ Ⓓ
4 Ⓐ Ⓑ Ⓒ Ⓓ	14 Ⓐ Ⓑ Ⓒ Ⓓ	24 Ⓐ Ⓑ Ⓒ Ⓓ	34 Ⓐ Ⓑ Ⓒ Ⓓ	44 Ⓐ Ⓑ Ⓒ Ⓓ	54 Ⓐ Ⓑ Ⓒ Ⓓ
5 Ⓐ Ⓑ Ⓒ Ⓓ	15 Ⓐ Ⓑ Ⓒ Ⓓ	25 Ⓐ Ⓑ Ⓒ Ⓓ	35 Ⓐ Ⓑ Ⓒ Ⓓ	45 Ⓐ Ⓑ Ⓒ Ⓓ	55 Ⓐ Ⓑ Ⓒ Ⓓ
6 Ⓐ Ⓑ Ⓒ Ⓓ	16 Ⓐ Ⓑ Ⓒ Ⓓ	26 Ⓐ Ⓑ Ⓒ Ⓓ	36 Ⓐ Ⓑ Ⓒ Ⓓ	46 Ⓐ Ⓑ Ⓒ Ⓓ	56 Ⓐ Ⓑ Ⓒ Ⓓ
7 Ⓐ Ⓑ Ⓒ Ⓓ	17 Ⓐ Ⓑ Ⓒ Ⓓ	27 Ⓐ Ⓑ Ⓒ Ⓓ	37 Ⓐ Ⓑ Ⓒ Ⓓ	47 Ⓐ Ⓑ Ⓒ Ⓓ	57 Ⓐ Ⓑ Ⓒ Ⓓ
8 Ⓐ Ⓑ Ⓒ Ⓓ	18 Ⓐ Ⓑ Ⓒ Ⓓ	28 Ⓐ Ⓑ Ⓒ Ⓓ	38 Ⓐ Ⓑ Ⓒ Ⓓ	48 Ⓐ Ⓑ Ⓒ Ⓓ	58 Ⓐ Ⓑ Ⓒ Ⓓ
9 Ⓐ Ⓑ Ⓒ Ⓓ	19 Ⓐ Ⓑ Ⓒ Ⓓ	29 Ⓐ Ⓑ Ⓒ Ⓓ	39 Ⓐ Ⓑ Ⓒ Ⓓ	49 Ⓐ Ⓑ Ⓒ Ⓓ	59 Ⓐ Ⓑ Ⓒ Ⓓ
10 Ⓐ Ⓑ Ⓒ Ⓓ	20 Ⓐ Ⓑ Ⓒ Ⓓ	30 Ⓐ Ⓑ Ⓒ Ⓓ	40 Ⓐ Ⓑ Ⓒ Ⓓ	50 Ⓐ Ⓑ Ⓒ Ⓓ	60 Ⓐ Ⓑ Ⓒ Ⓓ

Part B (Forms Completion)

1 Ⓐ Ⓑ Ⓒ Ⓓ	6 Ⓐ Ⓑ Ⓒ Ⓓ	11 Ⓐ Ⓑ Ⓒ Ⓓ	16 Ⓐ Ⓑ Ⓒ Ⓓ	21 Ⓐ Ⓑ Ⓒ Ⓓ	26 Ⓐ Ⓑ Ⓒ Ⓓ
2 Ⓐ Ⓑ Ⓒ Ⓓ	7 Ⓐ Ⓑ Ⓒ Ⓓ	12 Ⓐ Ⓑ Ⓒ Ⓓ	17 Ⓐ Ⓑ Ⓒ Ⓓ	22 Ⓐ Ⓑ Ⓒ Ⓓ	27 Ⓐ Ⓑ Ⓒ Ⓓ
3 Ⓐ Ⓑ Ⓒ Ⓓ	8 Ⓐ Ⓑ Ⓒ Ⓓ	13 Ⓐ Ⓑ Ⓒ Ⓓ	18 Ⓐ Ⓑ Ⓒ Ⓓ	23 Ⓐ Ⓑ Ⓒ Ⓓ	28 Ⓐ Ⓑ Ⓒ Ⓓ
4 Ⓐ Ⓑ Ⓒ Ⓓ	9 Ⓐ Ⓑ Ⓒ Ⓓ	14 Ⓐ Ⓑ Ⓒ Ⓓ	19 Ⓐ Ⓑ Ⓒ Ⓓ	24 Ⓐ Ⓑ Ⓒ Ⓓ	29 Ⓐ Ⓑ Ⓒ Ⓓ
5 Ⓐ Ⓑ Ⓒ Ⓓ	10 Ⓐ Ⓑ Ⓒ Ⓓ	15 Ⓐ Ⓑ Ⓒ Ⓓ	20 Ⓐ Ⓑ Ⓒ Ⓓ	25 Ⓐ Ⓑ Ⓒ Ⓓ	30 Ⓐ Ⓑ Ⓒ Ⓓ

Part C (Coding & Memory)

Section 1 (Coding)

1 Ⓐ Ⓑ Ⓒ Ⓓ	13 Ⓐ Ⓑ Ⓒ Ⓓ	25 Ⓐ Ⓑ Ⓒ Ⓓ
2 Ⓐ Ⓑ Ⓒ Ⓓ	14 Ⓐ Ⓑ Ⓒ Ⓓ	26 Ⓐ Ⓑ Ⓒ Ⓓ
3 Ⓐ Ⓑ Ⓒ Ⓓ	15 Ⓐ Ⓑ Ⓒ Ⓓ	27 Ⓐ Ⓑ Ⓒ Ⓓ
4 Ⓐ Ⓑ Ⓒ Ⓓ	16 Ⓐ Ⓑ Ⓒ Ⓓ	28 Ⓐ Ⓑ Ⓒ Ⓓ
5 Ⓐ Ⓑ Ⓒ Ⓓ	17 Ⓐ Ⓑ Ⓒ Ⓓ	29 Ⓐ Ⓑ Ⓒ Ⓓ
6 Ⓐ Ⓑ Ⓒ Ⓓ	18 Ⓐ Ⓑ Ⓒ Ⓓ	30 Ⓐ Ⓑ Ⓒ Ⓓ
7 Ⓐ Ⓑ Ⓒ Ⓓ	19 Ⓐ Ⓑ Ⓒ Ⓓ	31 Ⓐ Ⓑ Ⓒ Ⓓ
8 Ⓐ Ⓑ Ⓒ Ⓓ	20 Ⓐ Ⓑ Ⓒ Ⓓ	32 Ⓐ Ⓑ Ⓒ Ⓓ
9 Ⓐ Ⓑ Ⓒ Ⓓ	21 Ⓐ Ⓑ Ⓒ Ⓓ	33 Ⓐ Ⓑ Ⓒ Ⓓ
10 Ⓐ Ⓑ Ⓒ Ⓓ	22 Ⓐ Ⓑ Ⓒ Ⓓ	34 Ⓐ Ⓑ Ⓒ Ⓓ
11 Ⓐ Ⓑ Ⓒ Ⓓ	23 Ⓐ Ⓑ Ⓒ Ⓓ	35 Ⓐ Ⓑ Ⓒ Ⓓ
12 Ⓐ Ⓑ Ⓒ Ⓓ	24 Ⓐ Ⓑ Ⓒ Ⓓ	36 Ⓐ Ⓑ Ⓒ Ⓓ

Section 2 (Memory)

37 Ⓐ Ⓑ Ⓒ Ⓓ	49 Ⓐ Ⓑ Ⓒ Ⓓ	61 Ⓐ Ⓑ Ⓒ Ⓓ
38 Ⓐ Ⓑ Ⓒ Ⓓ	50 Ⓐ Ⓑ Ⓒ Ⓓ	62 Ⓐ Ⓑ Ⓒ Ⓓ
39 Ⓐ Ⓑ Ⓒ Ⓓ	51 Ⓐ Ⓑ Ⓒ Ⓓ	63 Ⓐ Ⓑ Ⓒ Ⓓ
40 Ⓐ Ⓑ Ⓒ Ⓓ	52 Ⓐ Ⓑ Ⓒ Ⓓ	64 Ⓐ Ⓑ Ⓒ Ⓓ
41 Ⓐ Ⓑ Ⓒ Ⓓ	53 Ⓐ Ⓑ Ⓒ Ⓓ	65 Ⓐ Ⓑ Ⓒ Ⓓ
42 Ⓐ Ⓑ Ⓒ Ⓓ	54 Ⓐ Ⓑ Ⓒ Ⓓ	66 Ⓐ Ⓑ Ⓒ Ⓓ
43 Ⓐ Ⓑ Ⓒ Ⓓ	55 Ⓐ Ⓑ Ⓒ Ⓓ	67 Ⓐ Ⓑ Ⓒ Ⓓ
44 Ⓐ Ⓑ Ⓒ Ⓓ	56 Ⓐ Ⓑ Ⓒ Ⓓ	68 Ⓐ Ⓑ Ⓒ Ⓓ
45 Ⓐ Ⓑ Ⓒ Ⓓ	57 Ⓐ Ⓑ Ⓒ Ⓓ	69 Ⓐ Ⓑ Ⓒ Ⓓ
46 Ⓐ Ⓑ Ⓒ Ⓓ	58 Ⓐ Ⓑ Ⓒ Ⓓ	70 Ⓐ Ⓑ Ⓒ Ⓓ
47 Ⓐ Ⓑ Ⓒ Ⓓ	59 Ⓐ Ⓑ Ⓒ Ⓓ	71 Ⓐ Ⓑ Ⓒ Ⓓ
48 Ⓐ Ⓑ Ⓒ Ⓓ	60 Ⓐ Ⓑ Ⓒ Ⓓ	72 Ⓐ Ⓑ Ⓒ Ⓓ

Answer Sheet

Part A (Address Checking)

1 Ⓐ Ⓑ Ⓒ Ⓓ	11 Ⓐ Ⓑ Ⓒ Ⓓ	21 Ⓐ Ⓑ Ⓒ Ⓓ	31 Ⓐ Ⓑ Ⓒ Ⓓ	41 Ⓐ Ⓑ Ⓒ Ⓓ	51 Ⓐ Ⓑ Ⓒ Ⓓ
2 Ⓐ Ⓑ Ⓒ Ⓓ	12 Ⓐ Ⓑ Ⓒ Ⓓ	22 Ⓐ Ⓑ Ⓒ Ⓓ	32 Ⓐ Ⓑ Ⓒ Ⓓ	42 Ⓐ Ⓑ Ⓒ Ⓓ	52 Ⓐ Ⓑ Ⓒ Ⓓ
3 Ⓐ Ⓑ Ⓒ Ⓓ	13 Ⓐ Ⓑ Ⓒ Ⓓ	23 Ⓐ Ⓑ Ⓒ Ⓓ	33 Ⓐ Ⓑ Ⓒ Ⓓ	43 Ⓐ Ⓑ Ⓒ Ⓓ	53 Ⓐ Ⓑ Ⓒ Ⓓ
4 Ⓐ Ⓑ Ⓒ Ⓓ	14 Ⓐ Ⓑ Ⓒ Ⓓ	24 Ⓐ Ⓑ Ⓒ Ⓓ	34 Ⓐ Ⓑ Ⓒ Ⓓ	44 Ⓐ Ⓑ Ⓒ Ⓓ	54 Ⓐ Ⓑ Ⓒ Ⓓ
5 Ⓐ Ⓑ Ⓒ Ⓓ	15 Ⓐ Ⓑ Ⓒ Ⓓ	25 Ⓐ Ⓑ Ⓒ Ⓓ	35 Ⓐ Ⓑ Ⓒ Ⓓ	45 Ⓐ Ⓑ Ⓒ Ⓓ	55 Ⓐ Ⓑ Ⓒ Ⓓ
6 Ⓐ Ⓑ Ⓒ Ⓓ	16 Ⓐ Ⓑ Ⓒ Ⓓ	26 Ⓐ Ⓑ Ⓒ Ⓓ	36 Ⓐ Ⓑ Ⓒ Ⓓ	46 Ⓐ Ⓑ Ⓒ Ⓓ	56 Ⓐ Ⓑ Ⓒ Ⓓ
7 Ⓐ Ⓑ Ⓒ Ⓓ	17 Ⓐ Ⓑ Ⓒ Ⓓ	27 Ⓐ Ⓑ Ⓒ Ⓓ	37 Ⓐ Ⓑ Ⓒ Ⓓ	47 Ⓐ Ⓑ Ⓒ Ⓓ	57 Ⓐ Ⓑ Ⓒ Ⓓ
8 Ⓐ Ⓑ Ⓒ Ⓓ	18 Ⓐ Ⓑ Ⓒ Ⓓ	28 Ⓐ Ⓑ Ⓒ Ⓓ	38 Ⓐ Ⓑ Ⓒ Ⓓ	48 Ⓐ Ⓑ Ⓒ Ⓓ	58 Ⓐ Ⓑ Ⓒ Ⓓ
9 Ⓐ Ⓑ Ⓒ Ⓓ	19 Ⓐ Ⓑ Ⓒ Ⓓ	29 Ⓐ Ⓑ Ⓒ Ⓓ	39 Ⓐ Ⓑ Ⓒ Ⓓ	49 Ⓐ Ⓑ Ⓒ Ⓓ	59 Ⓐ Ⓑ Ⓒ Ⓓ
10 Ⓐ Ⓑ Ⓒ Ⓓ	20 Ⓐ Ⓑ Ⓒ Ⓓ	30 Ⓐ Ⓑ Ⓒ Ⓓ	40 Ⓐ Ⓑ Ⓒ Ⓓ	50 Ⓐ Ⓑ Ⓒ Ⓓ	60 Ⓐ Ⓑ Ⓒ Ⓓ

Part B (Forms Completion)

1 Ⓐ Ⓑ Ⓒ Ⓓ	6 Ⓐ Ⓑ Ⓒ Ⓓ	11 Ⓐ Ⓑ Ⓒ Ⓓ	16 Ⓐ Ⓑ Ⓒ Ⓓ	21 Ⓐ Ⓑ Ⓒ Ⓓ	26 Ⓐ Ⓑ Ⓒ Ⓓ
2 Ⓐ Ⓑ Ⓒ Ⓓ	7 Ⓐ Ⓑ Ⓒ Ⓓ	12 Ⓐ Ⓑ Ⓒ Ⓓ	17 Ⓐ Ⓑ Ⓒ Ⓓ	22 Ⓐ Ⓑ Ⓒ Ⓓ	27 Ⓐ Ⓑ Ⓒ Ⓓ
3 Ⓐ Ⓑ Ⓒ Ⓓ	8 Ⓐ Ⓑ Ⓒ Ⓓ	13 Ⓐ Ⓑ Ⓒ Ⓓ	18 Ⓐ Ⓑ Ⓒ Ⓓ	23 Ⓐ Ⓑ Ⓒ Ⓓ	28 Ⓐ Ⓑ Ⓒ Ⓓ
4 Ⓐ Ⓑ Ⓒ Ⓓ	9 Ⓐ Ⓑ Ⓒ Ⓓ	14 Ⓐ Ⓑ Ⓒ Ⓓ	19 Ⓐ Ⓑ Ⓒ Ⓓ	24 Ⓐ Ⓑ Ⓒ Ⓓ	29 Ⓐ Ⓑ Ⓒ Ⓓ
5 Ⓐ Ⓑ Ⓒ Ⓓ	10 Ⓐ Ⓑ Ⓒ Ⓓ	15 Ⓐ Ⓑ Ⓒ Ⓓ	20 Ⓐ Ⓑ Ⓒ Ⓓ	25 Ⓐ Ⓑ Ⓒ Ⓓ	30 Ⓐ Ⓑ Ⓒ Ⓓ

Part C (Coding & Memory)

Section 1 (Coding)

1 Ⓐ Ⓑ Ⓒ Ⓓ	13 Ⓐ Ⓑ Ⓒ Ⓓ	25 Ⓐ Ⓑ Ⓒ Ⓓ
2 Ⓐ Ⓑ Ⓒ Ⓓ	14 Ⓐ Ⓑ Ⓒ Ⓓ	26 Ⓐ Ⓑ Ⓒ Ⓓ
3 Ⓐ Ⓑ Ⓒ Ⓓ	15 Ⓐ Ⓑ Ⓒ Ⓓ	27 Ⓐ Ⓑ Ⓒ Ⓓ
4 Ⓐ Ⓑ Ⓒ Ⓓ	16 Ⓐ Ⓑ Ⓒ Ⓓ	28 Ⓐ Ⓑ Ⓒ Ⓓ
5 Ⓐ Ⓑ Ⓒ Ⓓ	17 Ⓐ Ⓑ Ⓒ Ⓓ	29 Ⓐ Ⓑ Ⓒ Ⓓ
6 Ⓐ Ⓑ Ⓒ Ⓓ	18 Ⓐ Ⓑ Ⓒ Ⓓ	30 Ⓐ Ⓑ Ⓒ Ⓓ
7 Ⓐ Ⓑ Ⓒ Ⓓ	19 Ⓐ Ⓑ Ⓒ Ⓓ	31 Ⓐ Ⓑ Ⓒ Ⓓ
8 Ⓐ Ⓑ Ⓒ Ⓓ	20 Ⓐ Ⓑ Ⓒ Ⓓ	32 Ⓐ Ⓑ Ⓒ Ⓓ
9 Ⓐ Ⓑ Ⓒ Ⓓ	21 Ⓐ Ⓑ Ⓒ Ⓓ	33 Ⓐ Ⓑ Ⓒ Ⓓ
10 Ⓐ Ⓑ Ⓒ Ⓓ	22 Ⓐ Ⓑ Ⓒ Ⓓ	34 Ⓐ Ⓑ Ⓒ Ⓓ
11 Ⓐ Ⓑ Ⓒ Ⓓ	23 Ⓐ Ⓑ Ⓒ Ⓓ	35 Ⓐ Ⓑ Ⓒ Ⓓ
12 Ⓐ Ⓑ Ⓒ Ⓓ	24 Ⓐ Ⓑ Ⓒ Ⓓ	36 Ⓐ Ⓑ Ⓒ Ⓓ

Section 2 (Memory)

37 Ⓐ Ⓑ Ⓒ Ⓓ	49 Ⓐ Ⓑ Ⓒ Ⓓ	61 Ⓐ Ⓑ Ⓒ Ⓓ
38 Ⓐ Ⓑ Ⓒ Ⓓ	50 Ⓐ Ⓑ Ⓒ Ⓓ	62 Ⓐ Ⓑ Ⓒ Ⓓ
39 Ⓐ Ⓑ Ⓒ Ⓓ	51 Ⓐ Ⓑ Ⓒ Ⓓ	63 Ⓐ Ⓑ Ⓒ Ⓓ
40 Ⓐ Ⓑ Ⓒ Ⓓ	52 Ⓐ Ⓑ Ⓒ Ⓓ	64 Ⓐ Ⓑ Ⓒ Ⓓ
41 Ⓐ Ⓑ Ⓒ Ⓓ	53 Ⓐ Ⓑ Ⓒ Ⓓ	65 Ⓐ Ⓑ Ⓒ Ⓓ
42 Ⓐ Ⓑ Ⓒ Ⓓ	54 Ⓐ Ⓑ Ⓒ Ⓓ	66 Ⓐ Ⓑ Ⓒ Ⓓ
43 Ⓐ Ⓑ Ⓒ Ⓓ	55 Ⓐ Ⓑ Ⓒ Ⓓ	67 Ⓐ Ⓑ Ⓒ Ⓓ
44 Ⓐ Ⓑ Ⓒ Ⓓ	56 Ⓐ Ⓑ Ⓒ Ⓓ	68 Ⓐ Ⓑ Ⓒ Ⓓ
45 Ⓐ Ⓑ Ⓒ Ⓓ	57 Ⓐ Ⓑ Ⓒ Ⓓ	69 Ⓐ Ⓑ Ⓒ Ⓓ
46 Ⓐ Ⓑ Ⓒ Ⓓ	58 Ⓐ Ⓑ Ⓒ Ⓓ	70 Ⓐ Ⓑ Ⓒ Ⓓ
47 Ⓐ Ⓑ Ⓒ Ⓓ	59 Ⓐ Ⓑ Ⓒ Ⓓ	71 Ⓐ Ⓑ Ⓒ Ⓓ
48 Ⓐ Ⓑ Ⓒ Ⓓ	60 Ⓐ Ⓑ Ⓒ Ⓓ	72 Ⓐ Ⓑ Ⓒ Ⓓ

Answer Sheet

Part A (Address Checking)

1 Ⓐ Ⓑ Ⓒ Ⓓ	11 Ⓐ Ⓑ Ⓒ Ⓓ	21 Ⓐ Ⓑ Ⓒ Ⓓ	31 Ⓐ Ⓑ Ⓒ Ⓓ	41 Ⓐ Ⓑ Ⓒ Ⓓ	51 Ⓐ Ⓑ Ⓒ Ⓓ
2 Ⓐ Ⓑ Ⓒ Ⓓ	12 Ⓐ Ⓑ Ⓒ Ⓓ	22 Ⓐ Ⓑ Ⓒ Ⓓ	32 Ⓐ Ⓑ Ⓒ Ⓓ	42 Ⓐ Ⓑ Ⓒ Ⓓ	52 Ⓐ Ⓑ Ⓒ Ⓓ
3 Ⓐ Ⓑ Ⓒ Ⓓ	13 Ⓐ Ⓑ Ⓒ Ⓓ	23 Ⓐ Ⓑ Ⓒ Ⓓ	33 Ⓐ Ⓑ Ⓒ Ⓓ	43 Ⓐ Ⓑ Ⓒ Ⓓ	53 Ⓐ Ⓑ Ⓒ Ⓓ
4 Ⓐ Ⓑ Ⓒ Ⓓ	14 Ⓐ Ⓑ Ⓒ Ⓓ	24 Ⓐ Ⓑ Ⓒ Ⓓ	34 Ⓐ Ⓑ Ⓒ Ⓓ	44 Ⓐ Ⓑ Ⓒ Ⓓ	54 Ⓐ Ⓑ Ⓒ Ⓓ
5 Ⓐ Ⓑ Ⓒ Ⓓ	15 Ⓐ Ⓑ Ⓒ Ⓓ	25 Ⓐ Ⓑ Ⓒ Ⓓ	35 Ⓐ Ⓑ Ⓒ Ⓓ	45 Ⓐ Ⓑ Ⓒ Ⓓ	55 Ⓐ Ⓑ Ⓒ Ⓓ
6 Ⓐ Ⓑ Ⓒ Ⓓ	16 Ⓐ Ⓑ Ⓒ Ⓓ	26 Ⓐ Ⓑ Ⓒ Ⓓ	36 Ⓐ Ⓑ Ⓒ Ⓓ	46 Ⓐ Ⓑ Ⓒ Ⓓ	56 Ⓐ Ⓑ Ⓒ Ⓓ
7 Ⓐ Ⓑ Ⓒ Ⓓ	17 Ⓐ Ⓑ Ⓒ Ⓓ	27 Ⓐ Ⓑ Ⓒ Ⓓ	37 Ⓐ Ⓑ Ⓒ Ⓓ	47 Ⓐ Ⓑ Ⓒ Ⓓ	57 Ⓐ Ⓑ Ⓒ Ⓓ
8 Ⓐ Ⓑ Ⓒ Ⓓ	18 Ⓐ Ⓑ Ⓒ Ⓓ	28 Ⓐ Ⓑ Ⓒ Ⓓ	38 Ⓐ Ⓑ Ⓒ Ⓓ	48 Ⓐ Ⓑ Ⓒ Ⓓ	58 Ⓐ Ⓑ Ⓒ Ⓓ
9 Ⓐ Ⓑ Ⓒ Ⓓ	19 Ⓐ Ⓑ Ⓒ Ⓓ	29 Ⓐ Ⓑ Ⓒ Ⓓ	39 Ⓐ Ⓑ Ⓒ Ⓓ	49 Ⓐ Ⓑ Ⓒ Ⓓ	59 Ⓐ Ⓑ Ⓒ Ⓓ
10 Ⓐ Ⓑ Ⓒ Ⓓ	20 Ⓐ Ⓑ Ⓒ Ⓓ	30 Ⓐ Ⓑ Ⓒ Ⓓ	40 Ⓐ Ⓑ Ⓒ Ⓓ	50 Ⓐ Ⓑ Ⓒ Ⓓ	60 Ⓐ Ⓑ Ⓒ Ⓓ

Part B (Forms Completion)

1 Ⓐ Ⓑ Ⓒ Ⓓ	6 Ⓐ Ⓑ Ⓒ Ⓓ	11 Ⓐ Ⓑ Ⓒ Ⓓ	16 Ⓐ Ⓑ Ⓒ Ⓓ	21 Ⓐ Ⓑ Ⓒ Ⓓ	26 Ⓐ Ⓑ Ⓒ Ⓓ
2 Ⓐ Ⓑ Ⓒ Ⓓ	7 Ⓐ Ⓑ Ⓒ Ⓓ	12 Ⓐ Ⓑ Ⓒ Ⓓ	17 Ⓐ Ⓑ Ⓒ Ⓓ	22 Ⓐ Ⓑ Ⓒ Ⓓ	27 Ⓐ Ⓑ Ⓒ Ⓓ
3 Ⓐ Ⓑ Ⓒ Ⓓ	8 Ⓐ Ⓑ Ⓒ Ⓓ	13 Ⓐ Ⓑ Ⓒ Ⓓ	18 Ⓐ Ⓑ Ⓒ Ⓓ	23 Ⓐ Ⓑ Ⓒ Ⓓ	28 Ⓐ Ⓑ Ⓒ Ⓓ
4 Ⓐ Ⓑ Ⓒ Ⓓ	9 Ⓐ Ⓑ Ⓒ Ⓓ	14 Ⓐ Ⓑ Ⓒ Ⓓ	19 Ⓐ Ⓑ Ⓒ Ⓓ	24 Ⓐ Ⓑ Ⓒ Ⓓ	29 Ⓐ Ⓑ Ⓒ Ⓓ
5 Ⓐ Ⓑ Ⓒ Ⓓ	10 Ⓐ Ⓑ Ⓒ Ⓓ	15 Ⓐ Ⓑ Ⓒ Ⓓ	20 Ⓐ Ⓑ Ⓒ Ⓓ	25 Ⓐ Ⓑ Ⓒ Ⓓ	30 Ⓐ Ⓑ Ⓒ Ⓓ

Part C (Coding & Memory)

Section 1 (Coding)

1 Ⓐ Ⓑ Ⓒ Ⓓ	13 Ⓐ Ⓑ Ⓒ Ⓓ	25 Ⓐ Ⓑ Ⓒ Ⓓ
2 Ⓐ Ⓑ Ⓒ Ⓓ	14 Ⓐ Ⓑ Ⓒ Ⓓ	26 Ⓐ Ⓑ Ⓒ Ⓓ
3 Ⓐ Ⓑ Ⓒ Ⓓ	15 Ⓐ Ⓑ Ⓒ Ⓓ	27 Ⓐ Ⓑ Ⓒ Ⓓ
4 Ⓐ Ⓑ Ⓒ Ⓓ	16 Ⓐ Ⓑ Ⓒ Ⓓ	28 Ⓐ Ⓑ Ⓒ Ⓓ
5 Ⓐ Ⓑ Ⓒ Ⓓ	17 Ⓐ Ⓑ Ⓒ Ⓓ	29 Ⓐ Ⓑ Ⓒ Ⓓ
6 Ⓐ Ⓑ Ⓒ Ⓓ	18 Ⓐ Ⓑ Ⓒ Ⓓ	30 Ⓐ Ⓑ Ⓒ Ⓓ
7 Ⓐ Ⓑ Ⓒ Ⓓ	19 Ⓐ Ⓑ Ⓒ Ⓓ	31 Ⓐ Ⓑ Ⓒ Ⓓ
8 Ⓐ Ⓑ Ⓒ Ⓓ	20 Ⓐ Ⓑ Ⓒ Ⓓ	32 Ⓐ Ⓑ Ⓒ Ⓓ
9 Ⓐ Ⓑ Ⓒ Ⓓ	21 Ⓐ Ⓑ Ⓒ Ⓓ	33 Ⓐ Ⓑ Ⓒ Ⓓ
10 Ⓐ Ⓑ Ⓒ Ⓓ	22 Ⓐ Ⓑ Ⓒ Ⓓ	34 Ⓐ Ⓑ Ⓒ Ⓓ
11 Ⓐ Ⓑ Ⓒ Ⓓ	23 Ⓐ Ⓑ Ⓒ Ⓓ	35 Ⓐ Ⓑ Ⓒ Ⓓ
12 Ⓐ Ⓑ Ⓒ Ⓓ	24 Ⓐ Ⓑ Ⓒ Ⓓ	36 Ⓐ Ⓑ Ⓒ Ⓓ

Section 2 (Memory)

37 Ⓐ Ⓑ Ⓒ Ⓓ	49 Ⓐ Ⓑ Ⓒ Ⓓ	61 Ⓐ Ⓑ Ⓒ Ⓓ
38 Ⓐ Ⓑ Ⓒ Ⓓ	50 Ⓐ Ⓑ Ⓒ Ⓓ	62 Ⓐ Ⓑ Ⓒ Ⓓ
39 Ⓐ Ⓑ Ⓒ Ⓓ	51 Ⓐ Ⓑ Ⓒ Ⓓ	63 Ⓐ Ⓑ Ⓒ Ⓓ
40 Ⓐ Ⓑ Ⓒ Ⓓ	52 Ⓐ Ⓑ Ⓒ Ⓓ	64 Ⓐ Ⓑ Ⓒ Ⓓ
41 Ⓐ Ⓑ Ⓒ Ⓓ	53 Ⓐ Ⓑ Ⓒ Ⓓ	65 Ⓐ Ⓑ Ⓒ Ⓓ
42 Ⓐ Ⓑ Ⓒ Ⓓ	54 Ⓐ Ⓑ Ⓒ Ⓓ	66 Ⓐ Ⓑ Ⓒ Ⓓ
43 Ⓐ Ⓑ Ⓒ Ⓓ	55 Ⓐ Ⓑ Ⓒ Ⓓ	67 Ⓐ Ⓑ Ⓒ Ⓓ
44 Ⓐ Ⓑ Ⓒ Ⓓ	56 Ⓐ Ⓑ Ⓒ Ⓓ	68 Ⓐ Ⓑ Ⓒ Ⓓ
45 Ⓐ Ⓑ Ⓒ Ⓓ	57 Ⓐ Ⓑ Ⓒ Ⓓ	69 Ⓐ Ⓑ Ⓒ Ⓓ
46 Ⓐ Ⓑ Ⓒ Ⓓ	58 Ⓐ Ⓑ Ⓒ Ⓓ	70 Ⓐ Ⓑ Ⓒ Ⓓ
47 Ⓐ Ⓑ Ⓒ Ⓓ	59 Ⓐ Ⓑ Ⓒ Ⓓ	71 Ⓐ Ⓑ Ⓒ Ⓓ
48 Ⓐ Ⓑ Ⓒ Ⓓ	60 Ⓐ Ⓑ Ⓒ Ⓓ	72 Ⓐ Ⓑ Ⓒ Ⓓ

A Guide to Post Office Employment

City Carrier

Mail Processing Clerk

Mail Handler Assistant

Sales, Service, and Distribution Associate

PSE (Postal Supplement Employee)

CCA (City Carrier Assistant)

Rural Carrier Associate

Second Printing
Printed in the United States of America

Table of Contents

1. Address Checking

The USPS has changed the Postal Entrance Exam from Test 470 to Test 473 and Test 473-C. Test 473 is for the City Carrier, Rural Carrier, Mail Processing Clerk, Mail Handler and Sales, and Service and Distribution Associate. Test 473-C is only for the City Carrier.

Turn to page 5. There you will see 60 questions on address checking on pages 5 through 8. You can see two addresses, one in the left-hand box and one in the right-hand box, and you are to compare the two addresses. You are allowed 11 minutes for 60 questions.

- If the two addresses and zip codes are identical, mark (A).
- If the two addresses are different in any way, mark (B).
- If the two zip codes are different, mark (C).
- If both the addresses and zip codes are different in any way, mark (D).

Using a No. 2 pencil: There is the following instruction on how to mark the answer sheet in the worksheet:

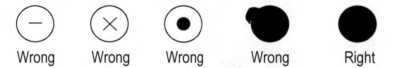

| Wrong | Wrong | Wrong | Wrong | Right |

But not all applicants follow the instruction. Some applicants have reported receiving a high score even though they didn't fill in the entire circle. Your mark needs to be at least three times greater than a dot. You don't have to answer all the questions correctly to get a top score of 100 points. A high-speed scanner scores your test.

As of 2013, the US Postal Service changed to online assessment, so applicants no longer need a pencil.

The monitor will record your name if you are caught looking at another person's test, or if you continue answering questions after the 11-minute time period. If the monitor records your name, you may be disqualified.

The number of questions you answer correctly, minus one-third for every incorrect answer, determines your score.

Here's a method you can use to compare the words and numbers in this portion of the test:

1. Make a slight fist with your left hand, and then straighten out your forefinger and your little finger.

2. Place your little finger under the street number for the left-hand address and your forefinger under the street number for the right-hand address.

    Use your left hand in this manner, as you move through each line of questions.

It is better to compare street number and zip code before comparing street name and city name, because comparing the numbers is easier than comparing street name and city name.

2. Forms Completion

Turn to page 46. There you will see a form followed by six questions on page 47 that refer to the form. There are five forms, with a total of 30 related questions, and you have 15 minutes for the Forms Completion section of the test.

There is no penalty for answering a question wrong, so answer the easy questions first. After you have finished all the questions, return to answer the more difficult ones. If you are running out of time, randomly guess on the remaining questions. You can make notes on the test booklet. Be careful not to spend too much time on a particular question.

3. Coding and Memory

There is a coding section and a memory section in the Coding and Memory subject. The coding section has 3 steps, and the memory section has 4 steps.

A. Coding Section

Step 1

Turn to page 98. There you will see a Coding Guide followed by 4 sample questions on page 99. You have 2 minutes to answer the 4 sample questions on the sample answer sheet. It will not be scored.

Step 2

On page 100, there is a Coding Guide followed by eight sample questions on page 101. You will be given 90 seconds to answer the sample questions on the sample answer sheet. It will not be scored.

Step 3

There is a Coding Guide on page 102 followed by 18 questions on page 103. There is also a Coding Guide on page 104 followed by 18 questions on page 105. On the actual test, you will have 6 minutes to answer all 36 questions. You can see the Coding Guide, and it will be scored. There is a penalty for guessing the answers. The number of questions you answer correctly, minus one-third for every incorrect answer, determines your score.

B. Memory Section

Step 1

There is a Coding Guide on page 106. You will have 3 minutes to memorize the address range to which the delivery route belongs.

Step 2

There are 8 sample questions on page 107. You will have 90 seconds to answer these questions on the sample answer sheet. You cannot see the Coding Guide. The answer sheet will not be scored.

Step 3

There is a Coding Guide on page 108. You will have 5 minutes to memorize the address range to which the delivery route belongs.

Step 4

There are 18 questions on page 109 followed by 18 questions on page 110. You have 7 minutes to answer the 36 questions. You cannot see the Coding Guide. Your answers will be scored and there is a penalty for guessing. The number of questions you answer correctly, minus one-third for every incorrect answer, determines your score.

Memorizing Information on the Test

Here is a way to memorize address ranges for the Coding and Memory Sections of the test. While you answer the sample questions, you can use the time to memorize the address ranges. You can also use the 6 minutes to memorize the address ranges, while you are answering the 36 questions in step 3 of the Coding Guide.

You are not permitted to write anything down in the test pamphlet while you memorize the address range. (These instructions are in the applicant information package that the USPS sends applicants.) However, unless you are instructed differently for a specific section, you may make notes or write anywhere in the test booklet.

Below is a sample Coding Guide and a study method to help you correctly answer the questions in the Coding and Memory Section.

Coding Guide	
Address Range	**Delivery Route**
1-99 Western Ave. 20-300 Redondo St.	A
100-200 Western Ave. 301-400 Redondo St. 15-45 S. 53rd St.	B
2000-5000 Alameda Ave. 1-30 Kingsley St. 46-60 S. 53rd St.	C
All mail that doesn't fall into one of the address ranges listed above.	D

There are streets with a different range of numbers in this Coding Guide. 1-99 Western Ave. is in Delivery Route A, and 100-200 Western Ave. is in Delivery Route B.

To help you remember which address goes with which route, make a phrase or sentence using the street number, the street name and the delivery route.

For example, the address range 1-99 Western Ave. in Route A could be: ***One* (for 1) *wrestler* (for Western) *attack* (for Route A). *The number 99 was omitted to make story easier to remember.***

For another example, 100-200 Western Ave. in Route B could be: ***Arson* (10) *needs a bus* (20) *why (western) for back up* (Route B).**

More examples are as follows:

20-300 Redondo St. in Route A – ***Bus* (20) is *ready* (Redondo) *already* (Route A).**

301-400 Redondo St. in Route B – ***Campus* (30) *one* (1) *dog* (40) is red (Redondo) *bad* (Route B).**

2000-5000 Alameda Ave. in Route C – ***Bus* (20) *engineer* (50) *already* (Alameda) *chanced* (Route C).**

1-30 Kingsley St. in Route C – ***One* (1) *cancer* (30) *king* (Kingsley) *chanced* (Route C).**

15-45 S. 53rd St. in Route A – ***Access* (15) *eagle* (53) *attack* (Route A).**

46-60 S. 53rd St. in Route C – ***Delight* (46) *fruit* (60) is not eagle's (53) choice (Route C).**

Any two-digit number becomes a word by referring to the memory tips on page 199. You need to memorize all the words by two-digit numbers on the list. The street name becomes a word that has a similar pronunciation — *Western* becomes *wrestler*. A word that starts with the same letter as the delivery route helps you remember the route — *Route A* becomes *Asia*, or *Route B* becomes *boy*, or *Route C* becomes *church*.

Here are some addresses. Which delivery routes do they belong in? (Use the sentences or phrase you've made-up to help you memorize the deliver routes.)

1. **87 Western Ave.**
2. **5340 Alameda Ave.**
3. **56 S. 53rd St.**
4. **247 S. Oxford Dr.**
5. **25 Kingsley St.**
6. **127 Redondo St.**
7. **67 S. 53rd St.**
8. **3297 Alameda Ave.**
9. **403 Western Ave.**

The correct answers are

1. (A)	4. (D)	7. (D)
2. (D)	5. (C)	8. (C)
3. (C)	6. (A)	9. (D)

4. Personal Characteristics and Experience Inventory

This part of the test has 236 questions and you will have 90 minutes to answer them. This test has 3 different categories.

You should answer the questions about your personal behavior truthfully. If you respond with an answer that is not true, it will not help your score. Mark only one response for each question. You may see two or more similar questions.

In the first category, you will answer 85 questions, and you have to select among the following:

strongly agree, agree, disagree or *strongly disagree*

In the second category, you will answer 75 questions, and you have to select among the following:

very often, often, sometimes and *rarely*

In the third category, you will answer 76 questions that relate to your personality among the several answers.

There is no exercise for this section. Take less time with the first and second category of questions so that you will have more time to work on the third category, which will take more thoughtful consideration.

You don't need to practice for this part of the test, and it is best to answer the questions thoughtfully and truthfully.

If you finish a section early, you may not return to an earlier section to finish any incomplete questions. Doing so may nullify your test results.

Test Scoring System and Notice of Rating
Seventy points is the passing score.

From this line until page 232, the discussion is for old exam system.

You will receive your score about four weeks after you take the test.

On the notice of rating, it states that your score makes you eligible for two years. Your registry date for your score is written on the bottom right of the page. You can receive third year eligibility if you request it from the Postmaster after 18 months, but before two years from the date of registration. A sample request letter is on page 208.

On your request letter, you must include the name of the lead post office that administered your original test. Send this letter and a copy of your notice of rating to the following address:

> U. S. OOO Post Office
> To: Postmaster
> Attention: Exam Unit
> (Write the address of the lead Post Office here.)

Send the request letter by certified or registered mail with a return receipt required.

On page 207, there is a letter to inform the lead post office of any change of address for their eligibility list. Notifying your local post office is not sufficient. You must notify the Exam Unit of the lead post office. This letter is almost the same as the one used to extend your eligibility for a third year. You need only change some sentences in the letter to extend your eligibility. For example, *I'd like to report that my address has changed. My new address is....*

Even before you get hired, you can transfer your score to another post office. You may do this by writing a letter. This request letter is almost the same as the other two, except for the last sentence. It should say

> *I'd like to request to transfer my score from _____ to _____.*

You need to send the letter, with one copy of your notice of rating, to the Exam Unit of the lead post office. You can do this only during the time when the Postal Service is accepting applications. A letter of request should be sent asking that your scores be transferred to the post office(s) where you are applying for a position.

Though you may not have received your notice of rating, you may still get an interview notice. If several weeks go by, and you do not receive your notice of rating, call the Personnel Office to see if there's a problem. Also, if you scored 75% (or higher) on the exam and you do not hear from the Postal Service within six months, call to find out what your position is on the eligibility list. Even if you don't pass the test, you will receive a notice of rating.

Finding Available Postal Positions

There are 15 job information lines on page 201. But now some have been combined. For example, Line 3 became Lines 2, 5 to 4, 6 to 10, and zip codes 902, 903, 904, 905 in Long Beach combined to 2 and zip codes 906, 907, 908 in Long Beach combined to 8. As a job applicant, you no longer need to call 10 phone lines.

The Long Beach Post Office address on Page 201 is incorrect. The correct address is 300 North Long Beach Blvd. The mailing address of the Van Nuys Post Office has been changed to 28101 Franklin Parkway, Santa Clarita, CA 91354-9461. The above the title "Finding Available Postal Positions" is not old system.

When you file your application, you should receive your test date within three months—though sometimes it can be in as little as two weeks, and sometimes it may take up to six months or even longer. Up to this line, it is old exam system.

Applying for a Position with the Postal Service

The job information web site is www.usps.com/employment. To talk to a person, the phone number for information about the USPS is 1-800-275-8777.

According to the post office, if you are working as a Casual or TE (Transitional Employee) for 180 days or more, the Postal Service will allow you to take the exam two times during a two-year period even if no public test is offered.

You can be hired at age 18. And you can be hired at age 16, if you have a high school diploma or GED.

Lead Post Office

The lead post office used to be called GMF (General Mail Facility) or MSC (Management Sectional Center). Today, it is called the P&DC (Processing & Distribution Center). To get the postal job information phone numbers in the U.S., you must go to a lead post office (district office) of the county. This office is a P&DC. You can ask your local post office for the location of the lead post office. Or, when you go to the lead post office to take an exam or visit the Personnel Office, you can ask about the job information phone number. You may also be able to get other lead post office job information numbers, Personnel Office phone numbers and addresses here, as well. You can also request job information numbers for other counties. On Page 201, there is a list for a portion of the state of California.

The Postal Service has both clerk and carrier positions. It is easier to qualify for the carrier position. For clerk positions, you will need a score of 80% on the exam. With this score, you have a better chance of being called within 6 months. With a score of 74% or less, it may take longer to get hired. You may need to get a score of 80% or above.

Even if you have less than two years driving experience, you can apply for a Carrier position, because you may accumulate driving experience while you are waiting to be hired. Also, you can postpone your interview until you have the necessary two years of driving experience. You will also receive credit for two years of driving experience in other states.

Veteran's Preference Explained

5-Point (tentative): May be awarded to a former member of the Armed Forces who has an honorable discharge (or under honorable conditions), is not disabled and meets one or more of the following criteria:

- Served on active duty in a pre-World War II campaign/expedition, or during World War II (12/7/41-4/28/52)
- Served on active duty during the period beginning 4/28/52 and ending 7/1/55.
- Served on active duty for more than180 consecutive days, other than for training, any part of which occurred between 2/1/55 and 10/14/76.
- Began active duty after 10/14/76 and before 9/8/80 and served in a campaign or expedition for which a campaign badge is authorized.
- Enlisted in the Armed Forces after 9/7/80 or entered active duty through means other than enlistment after 10/14/82 and completed 24 months of continuous service or the full period for which called to active duty and served in a campaign or expedition for which a campaign badge is authorized.

- Enlisted in the Armed Forces after 9/7/80 or entered active duty through means other than enlistment after 10/14/82 and completed 24 months of continuous service or the full period for which called to active duty and served active duty during the period beginning 8/2/90 and ending 1/2/92.
- Served in a campaign or expedition for which a campaign badge is authorized and was discharged early under 10 U.S.C. 1171 or for hardship under 10 U.S.C. 1173.

10 Point — Compensable (Less than 30%): May be awarded to a former member of the Armed Forces with an honorable discharge (or under honorable conditions) and has a service-connected disability that is at least 10% but less than 30% compensable.

10 Point — Compensable (30% or more): May be awarded to a former member of the Armed Forces with an honorable discharge (or under honorable conditions) and has a service-connected disability that is 30% or more compensable.

10 Point (Other): May be awarded to:
- Veterans who were awarded the Purple Heart.
- Veterans who receive compensation or pension from the Dept. of Veterans Affairs or disability retired pay from the Armed Forces.
- Veterans who have a service-connected disability that is not compensable or that is less than 10% compensable.
- The unremarried widow or widower of an honorably separated veteran provided the deceased veteran served in active duty during a war or the veteran died while in the Armed Forces.
- Spouses of certain veterans with a service-connected disability.
- Mothers of certain deceased or disabled veterans.

If you qualify for an additional 5 points as a veteran and another non-veteran applicant has the same score as you, you will be move ahead of that person. And if you qualify an additional 10 points as a veteran, you will move above the other non-veterans, regardless of your final score. But you must get at least 70 points to receive the additional 5 points or 10 points.

5. The Interview Process

It is important to know how to conduct yourself during an interview; how to write your resume; and how to fill out the various forms required.

First take note of the following items:

On page 211, there is a section on "Call in Notice." That "Call in Notice" includes the statement that if you are applying for a carrier position, you must have 2 years of driving experience. <u>Go to the DMV and ask for your driving record H-6</u>. (If you do not ask specifically for an H-6 record, you may receive a record that gives your driving history other than H-6.)

On the interview notice, there is the abbreviation PTF, which stands for Part Time Flexible. This does not mean you can't work 40 hours per week. Rather, it means that the Postal Service doesn't guarantee you 40 hours per week, though new employees usually work 40 hours per week.

After a certain period of time, you will become a full-time regular employee. When that happens, the Postal Service will guarantee you 40 hours of work each week. Most of the benefits for PTF employees are the same as for regular employees. It usually takes from 3 months to 3 years to become a regular full-time worker depending on the post office. In special circumstances, it may take 3 to 5 years or more. Some of the other distinctions between PTF employees and full-time regular employees will be discussed later.

On the bottom of the interview notice, there is a space called the declination statement. This is used only if you can't make your scheduled interview appointment. Before the interview, you must return this notice to the post office. If you do not call, or do not return the call-in notice, <u>you will be dropped from the eligibility list.</u> You must respond before your interview date or on the designated day.

The first box of the declination statement states, "Remove my name from..." If you check this box, it means that your name will be removed from the register until you notify the Postal Service that you are available.

The next box states, "Retain my name on the register..." If you check this box, there are two more boxes to the left and right. If you check the box on the right, it means that you want to receive another call-in notice for a career position in the future. If you check the second box to the left, it means you want to receive another call-in notice for a career position as well as a temporary position in the future. You must mark the first box on the right, and you must also indicate the next available date for an interview. For the second box, you will need to write "for a special situation." Below this box, you must explain why you are not available for an interview at this time.

Casual employees may be hired for a term not to exceed 360 calendar days a year with no benefits, but you may work in a temporary position for more than one year. You can call the job information phone line on page 201, or you can look on your computer to find out what temporary positions are available. You do not have to take a test for temporary positions.

When you get your interview notice, there are many forms included, such as resume, etc. Here is some information to help you fill out these forms. First, turn to page 202 for a sample resume.

Look at the general information in section A. (Applicants should not fill out the upper part of this section.) In Part 7 of Section A, you are required to state your birthplace as documented by your birth certificate, regardless of any variance from the actual situation.

In Part 8 of Section A, you should fill in the job title or the position you are applying for and the specific post office you wish to work at (refer to call-in notice).

In Part 9, you must state whether you will accept temporary employment. If you are not presently working, you may check this box. However, know that if you accept a temporary position and are fired or make a major error in your temporary position, it will adversely affect your chances for a regular position, because it will appear on your record.

Part 10 asks when you can start work. It is best to say "any time."

Part 11 asks whether you can work in different postal locations. This question is usually asked only if you apply for a supervisory position.

Section B covers your educational background. In Part 3a, if you attended a college or university, you should write the name of the school, the years attended and semester or quarter hours achieved. There are separate spaces on the form for semester and quarter hours, depending on the school's system. If you have a Bachelor or Masters Degree, specify it here and state the year it was earned.

In Part 3b, state your major as an undergraduate. In Part 3c, state your major in graduate school, if you earned a graduate degree. In Part 4, state the major in which you earned your final degree. In Part 5, add any other education or training that you have had. "Trade School" means students have learned how to repair some machines or appliances — like cars, televisions or refrigerators. "Technical School" means students have learned to repair specific items — like computers. "Vocational" means students have learned a particular vocation, such as bookkeeping, word-processing, secretarial training, etc. "Armed Forces School means school attended while serving in the United States Armed Forces. "Fellowships received" are grants or monies received by a scientist, artist, or doctor.

In Part 7, indicate any special skills or abilities such as machine or technical skills. These could also include patents, inventions, publications, etc. Verification may be requested. Also you can indicate your public speaking skills, your membership in professional or scientific organizations or any specialized business skills you may have.

Next, turn to page 203 and look at Section C, Work History. According to the Articles of Application for Employment, here you should state your career or work history for the past 10 years. Exclude any work done before you turned 16. Include volunteer work. If you are not presently employed, skip number 1 of Section C. If you have been unemployed, state the times in the proper space. You can include your military service. If you need more space, use an additional page.

The Postal Service will also ask to check your references for accuracy, character, qualifications, etc. If you don't want the Postal Service to check your references and background, you can decline. The Postal Service says it will not affect your job prospects if you deny this background check, however it is better not to decline.

Here are some of the phrases that are used on the form and a look at how you should respond to them. Where it says, "Number and kind of employees supervised," you should state where you worked as a supervisor, and how many people you supervised. The phrase "Kind of Business" refers to the type of business (retail, publishing, manufacturing) where you worked. Other phrases like these include "Name of Employer," "Reasons for Wanting to Leave," "Accomplishments," etc.

If you served in the United States Armed Forces, you must check "yes" in Section D. In Section E, you must give three references (excluding family members and any persons you do not know well). In the reference section, do not repeat any supervisor's name that you have already mentioned in your work history.

Section G is the space to be used for answering questions 4, 5, 6, 7, 8, 9 and 10. Put your answers here only if you answered "yes" to any of the questions. Section H is for your signature and the date.

The question regarding the Selective Service System applies only to male applicants. This is a requirement of the U.S. Government that every male must register within 30 days of his 18th birthday. You must have registered before your 26th birthday, if you were born after December 31, 1959. You will be disqualified for any government job, if you deliberately ignored the Selective Service and you may face a find of $250,000 or five years in prison, or both. If, however, you came to the United States after you turned 26, you do not have to register with the Selective Service. If you came to the U.S.A. before age 26 but you didn't know you had to register, you may need to consult a lawyer.

These instructions will be enclosed with your interview notice and you should fill out this part of the application as indicated above.

Here is some information that will help you proceed with your interview. It is written from personal experience and extensive research. Bring your green card, your driver's license and Social Security card. If you are a U.S. citizen, bring your passport. Do not be late for the interview and bring the appropriate documents and forms.

At your interview, you should convey exactly the same information that is on your resume. A postal interview is a routine situation that covers personal and other information already discussed. If you put some incorrect information in the application for employment and the USPS finds it out later on, you may be fired and prosecuted.

The most commonly asked questions concern the applicants' work history — particularly your current position or last position. You are better preparing some information about your present or last job.

Another common question is why you want to work at the Postal Service. One good answer would be the promise of a good salary, good benefits, and job security and advancement opportunities. Also, have your educational background ready for scrutiny. When asked about the responsibilities of the job your are applying for, you can answer:

1. To be at work on time
2. To be diligent at work
3. To follow postal regulations

It is better not to wear a cap, sunglasses, sports shoes, or anything else that looks sloppy. It is also better not to wear anything "flashy." You will want to appear serious about the job you're applying for. Women should not wear heavy make up. You should be patient and take your time during the interview.

6. Other Tests Required by the Postal Service

Scheme Test

If the Postal Service hires you as a Mail Processing Clerk (for Manual Clerk only), then you must pass a "scheme" test. The Machine Clerk and other positions do not require the scheme test.

To understand what a "scheme" is you first have to understand how a branch post office is set up. Suppose there is a branch post office "B". (The Postal Service uses the term "station" or "association office" for branch.) The delivery area at each branch or station is divided into smaller divisions — one carrier delivers mail to one of the small divisions. As an example, one station may be divided into 50 sub-areas. A sub-area is called a "route." Each route is numbered Route 1, Route 2, Route 3, etc. Station B is responsible for a certain number of addresses; in this case, 600 different addresses, which are divided among the 50 routes.

A "scheme" is the pattern in which these 600 addresses fall into the 50 routes. When there are about 600 addresses, you will be given about 40 hours to memorize all 600 addresses. You will be given one hour or one and half hours each day for scheme training, which will take about two months. You will have to memorize which address goes into which route. The method explained in the Coding and Memory Section of this guide will be helpful to you in memorizing the addresses and the routes. For example, for the address Rosa, which goes into Route 18, you could make up the following sentence, "Russia had wars." "Wars" comes from the number 18 of the memory chart, and Rosa made Russia.

The Postal Service gives a weekly progress test to help you train. This is for you to measure your progress, and the score is not recorded. You are given three chances to pass the "scheme" test. The trainer will select 100 addresses, and you will be given 8 minutes to take the "scheme" test. The passing score is 95%. Most post offices administer the "scheme" test on a computer. You will match the address to the route on the computer. If you don't know the answer, press any key to guess the answer, and move on. Saving time is a crucial strategy for this test, because you only have 8 minutes.

The Driving Test

If you apply for a carrier position, you must also take a driving test, called the "Road Test." It is conducted in the postal vehicle (not a Jeep). You will receive your test date about two weeks before the date of the test.

You will be tested on the following driving skills:

Parking between two cars

1. Use of a seat belt
2. Use of both hands on the wheel
3. Parking on an incline (Don't forget to turn the wheel to the right.)
4. Backing up and parking on the hill
5. Use of the hand brake at any time for parking
6. Parking and backing up on level ground
7. Driving on the freeway (for 3-4 minutes)
8. Turning right, after making a full stop (Remember to start your turn close to the curb.)
9. Turning right on a "No right turn during a red light" situation (Be careful not to turn right until the light is green.)
10. The distance between you and the vehicle in front of you when you stop (Make sure you leave a safe space between the vehicles: you should be able to see the rear tires on the car in front of you.)
11. Right of way at a four-way stop sign
12. Tailgating and speed (Don't tailgate and keep within the speed limits.)
13. Distance between vehicles when moving
14. Stopping at stop signs and intersections (Stop at least three feet before the white line.)
15. U-turns on residential streets (Be sure to make a "3-point U-turn" on narrow streets.)
16. Going through an intersection (Look both ways, even if the light is green.)
17. Normal traffic regulations (Obey the law.)

The Physical Exam

If you pass the interview and driving test, you must then pass a physical exam. It usually takes about two months for the tests to be taken and processed. When the tests have been processed, you will get your job assignment.

The Personnel Office will send you a form for your physical. On the form, you must check any illness you have had. Many of the medical terms are obscure. Usually, if you do not know a term, you do not have that illness. Physical exams are conducted at designated hospitals.

The physical does not include X-rays or blood tests, but it does include a drug test. Your eyes are checked, but you are permitted to wear glasses or corrective lenses. They usually do not check your hearing. There are two tests that are always done: a blood pressure test and a urine test. The urine test is to screen for diabetes and for drugs. If you have a diabetic problem, or very high or low blood pressure, you will be asked to consult your personal doctor and take a second series of tests. If the secondary tests confirm that you are diabetic or have a blood pressure problem, you are still eligible for employment, but you must get a letter from a doctor stating that you are able to work.

If you have your notice of rating and have passed the interview, physical exam, and driving test, and do not hear from the Postal Service within two or three months, call the Personnel Office to see what is happening with your application.

7. Working for the Postal Service

Employee Classifications

There are three classifications of employees.

- PTF (Part Time Flexible)
- Unassigned Regular (Full Time)
- Regular (Full Time)

When first hired, an employee is a PTF. In this case, a PTF worker is not guaranteed 40 hours of work per week, but he or she usually does work 40 hours per week.

There are differences between a PTF and a Full Time Employee:

PTF	Regular (Full Time)
■ Not guaranteed 40 hours per week ■ No bid rights (bid rights are the right to apply for other positions – usually 5 times during a 3-4 year contract.) ■ Post office can change your hours, position and days off, but not the job itself. ■ You can use only the basic vacation days you accumulated. ■ If you don't work on a holiday, you are not paid. ■ You are paid by the hour.	■ 40 hours per week guaranteed ■ Full-bid rights ■ Your position and working conditions cannot be changed, but your starting time can be changed one hour – earlier or later (barring a major reorganization). ■ At the beginning of the year, you can use all vacation days that will be accumulated by the end of that year. ■ If you don't work on holidays, you still get paid. ■ You are paid an annual salary.

When you advance from being a PTF employee, you are known as an "unassigned regular" employee, not a regular employee. To become a regular employee, you must look for open positions within your post office and apply for them. When you are an "unassigned regular," it is a good idea to apply for any open "regular" position that is of interest to you. The Postal Service will usually choose a senior employee — one who has been there for a longer period of time, so seniority is a factor. Most likely, when you are the senior employee at your post office, you will have the opportunity to become a regular employee, if you've applied for a position.

As an unassigned regular, you can be moved from job to job depending on the needs of the Postal Service. One advantage of becoming a regular employee is that you cannot be forced to change position or your work environment. You will have the same fringe benefits whether you are a regular employee or an "unassigned regular" employee.

Regular Rural Carrier

To become a regular rural carrier takes at least one year. At least for the first year, there is no benefit like regular rural carrier. After one year of employment, you are eligible to apply for a full-time career Rural Carrier position with full benefits. In this position, you sell stamps, money orders, deliver packages, collect mail, etc. You use your car, which must have an automatic transmission, and must have liability car insurance. You are paid $0.48 per mile as of June 29, 2007 for the use of your car. In this position, you frequently drive many miles.

As of May 2013, a Rural Carrier's salary is $15.87 per hour.

Applicants must take the Test 473 for this position.

The Orientation Process

After you pass the interview, physical exam, etc., you will probably receive an orientation notice within one to two months. The day your orientation starts is your first day of employment. Orientation for inside workers usually takes 1½ days. For Carriers, it takes about one week. During orientation, you will receive information about benefits, regulations and safety. You may see videos about postal work. After 1½ days, insider workers will receive a photo I.D. Carriers may be trained for one week on how to deliver mail.

Carriers also take a short test mainly covering traffic laws (some post offices don't give out this test) Trainers pose problems and give the answers to them, after which you will take a test on the material covered. You must pass this test. Carriers will also take a driving test with a right-hand steering wheel. In some post offices, applicants are tested on mail classifications, such as 1st class, 2nd class, 3rd class, etc. Before the test, applicants are given a chance to briefly study the different types of mail.

Some post offices require a "casing test." A casing test covers putting of mail in the slot as to the sequence of addresses, such as 1420-1422-1424. When you have correctly inserted all the mail, removed the mail from each slot and bound each bundle together with a rubber band.

After a brief explanation and some practice time, carriers will have to "case" 100 letters in six minutes. Some post offices do not give this test. When you sort "flats", which are magazines or newspapers, sort first by the street names only — not the numbers. Later you can sort by number, address, etc. Today, there is a way to sort everything in one step, instead of two steps. Today, the mail is sorted mostly by machines. After your orientation, you will start work at your assigned post office.

Probation Period

All applicants, after being assigned to a post office, must pass a 90-day probation period. Each month, the supervisor in charge will evaluate you. The supervisor will observe your attendance, job performance, how you follow instructions, etc. After the 90-day probation period, you will be a career employee. During the 90-day probation period, you can be fired by your supervisor, however, once you become a career employee, it is more difficult to be fired. If you are a Mail Processing Clerk (not including machine clerk), you will take the "scheme" test during your 90-day probation period. TE and PSE can join the union during the probation. During probation, if you can't file agreement with union, you can file agreement with EEO.

The Union

As soon as you get hired, join the union. The two union officials in a post office are the Shop Steward and the Chief Steward. There will be a deduction from your paycheck each month of $26 (as of 2013) for your union dues. It is $13 for P.S.E. There are many benefits to joining the union. If an employee has a conflict with his or her supervisor, the union will help settle the dispute. Additionally the EEO may help solve problems about discrimination by race, age, sex, disability and mental problems.

In addition to the job protection you are offered by the union, there are other benefits. You can join health plans such as the APWU Insurance Plan. Other benefits are accidental death Insurance, hospital cash payments and volunteer benefits. You will also receive free magazines — like *Postal Worker*. You can qualify for scholarships and legal services. For legal services, you will pay about $7 per paycheck. The union will also offer you a Master Card.

At the USPS, there has never been a lay-off, and the Postal Service has an EEOC (Equal Employment Opportunity Commission) that deals with complaints of discrimination, etc.

Contracts and Pay Increases

At three or four year intervals, Postal Service employees can renegotiate their contract, which can result in new benefits, such as a salary increase and new policies with regard to your employment. Some policies state that if you work six full years (with 20 or more pay periods per year), you cannot be laid off. You may also put your name on the "overtime desire list" indicating that you want to work overtime hours. This list is updated quarterly.

From 1987 to 1990, Postal Service employees received 13 pay increases. Total amount of the pay increases at the end of the four years was $4,365. This doesn't include individual pay increases by step.

Every three to four years, there is a contract renewal. At this time, future annual pay is determined. Level 4, 5, 6 and 7 employees have to wait 96 weeks for a 1-step increase. The waiting period for the next step increase is 44 weeks, 36 weeks and 24 weeks.

Transfers

When an employee wants to transfer from one post office to another, his or her status can change, depending on whether you are a PTF employee or a regular employee. If you are a P.T. F. employee, you will still be a PTF employee at the new location; however, if you are a regular employee, you will revert to PTF status at the new post office. You will loose your seniority whether you are a PTF employee or a regular employee. However, there is an exception: if you trade places with another employee, both employees will keep their status and their seniority.

However, you should know that the following will occur when you transfer from one post office to another: If you started in 2005, for example, and another employee started in 2007, the senior employee (the one who started in 2005) will have the same seniority as the one who started in 2007. This does not change your actually hire date, benefits, etc. It will only affect your seniority when you apply for new positions within the new post office. An employee can get a position by seniority.

Employees can trade positions between any two post offices in the United States. You can advertise in Postal Worker magazine saying that you are looking for a trade. However, you must get a signature from the President or Vice President of the Union before you place the ad. You must have worked 18 months in a post office, before you can ask to be transferred to another post office in your geographical location, unless your installation head gives you an early release. To move to a post office outside your geographical area, you can apply for a transfer after 12 months, unless released by the installation head earlier. There are exceptions:

- An employee who requests to return to an installation where he or she previously worked

- The opportunity for an employee to substantially increase the number of hours (transferring for over time work) by transferring to another post office. However, if you are seeking a change of job title, you must have worked at the post office for 18 months.)

Don't forget a regular who transfers becomes a PTF.

Work Schedules

A Postal Service employee may be permitted to revise his or her work schedule.

Reinstatement

The rules for reinstatement are different for a non-military veteran than for a military veteran. If you are a military veteran or have worked for the Postal Service for three or more years, you can apply for reinstatement regardless of how long you have been gone from the Postal Service. If you do not fall into either of these categories, you can only apply for reinstatement within three years from the time you left the Postal Service. You will also have to take a non-competitive entrance exam and pass a 90-day probation period. When you apply to be reinstated or to transfer, the amount of sick leave you have used in the past will be taken into consideration.

Community Credit Union

Postal Service employees can join the Community Credit Union. If you join, you may have a checking account, a savings account and a certificate of deposit (CD) with the credit union. Also you can set up a direct deposit so that your salary is sent directly to your bank account.

8. Postal Service Employee Benefits

Health Insurance

One of the many fringe benefits offered by the Postal Service is health insurance. Here is a brief look at what is offered in the Federal Employees Health insurance. The prepaid plan (HMO) covers 100%, while government-wide plans do not.

If you wish to keep your current health insurance after you have retired, you must have been in that health insurance program for at least five years before your retirement. Otherwise you must reapply for health insurance. The health insurance premium will increase some after retirement. For more information, go to www.opm.gov.

Sick Leave

Postal Service employees are allowed 13 sick days leave every year. If you don't use these sick days, you can accumulate them. However, when you retire, the Postal Service will not allow you to add to the service year the accumulated sick leave. If you are sick for three days or less, notify your supervisor by calling. Your supervisor will request a note from your doctor. If you are sick for more than three days, you must have a note from your doctor to give to your supervisor. In special situations, your supervisor may request you to bring a doctor's note even though you took sick days three days or less.

Vacation Time

You can accumulate vacation leave up to 440 hours. When you retire, you can be compensated for unused vacation hours, if you wish. You can request one-week's pay, if you accumulate 440 hours of vacation time.

All carriers receive two days off per week — Sunday and one other day, which is determined by the rotation system. Because of the rotation system, every five weeks, you will get a three-day weekend. However, the following week, you will work six days. The clerks work within a fixed schedule with the same two days off per week.

Sunday Premium

Among the many fringe benefits offered by the Postal Service is one called "Sunday Premium". This means that if you work on a Sunday, you'll be paid 25% more per hour. Also, no matter how many hours you work on a Sunday, you'll be paid for a full eight hours. Usually, at a P&DC (Processing and Distribution Center), there is more overtime available for clerks. A P&DC is a district office. Carriers will have overtime work available at their local post office. Also if you work a P&DC or bigger office, you may become a regular (Full time) more easily. (Shorter period time)

Federal Employees Group Life Insurance

If you're hired by the Postal Service, you can join F.E.G.L.I. (Federal Employees Group Life Insurance). This is basic life insurance, and it is free. You are covered for your annual salary, plus $2,000. Your annual salary is computed by rounding off to the nearest $1,000. For example, an annual salary of $27,690 would be rounded off to $28,000. For more information, refer to the booklet

You have options to your basic coverage. Your can apply to receive up to five times your annual salary in death benefits. This coverage can be used if you die or are dismembered. If a doctor states that you only have 9 months or less to live, you can get the death benefit early. This is called "living benefits." A form is required for this benefit. You can get a booklet from the Personnel Office with more information.

The Federal Employees Retirement System

You can go to the Personnel Office, or visit www.opm.gov/retire. You need to click "FERS retirement"

FERS is short for Federal Employees Retirement System.

FERS is a three-tiered retirement plan. The three components are

> **Social Security Benefits**
>
> **Basic Benefits**
>
> **Savings Plan**

Understanding all aspects of these benefits is difficult, but you must have some knowledge of them, or you may not be able to fully take advantage of all these important benefits.

FERS and CSRS

Anyone hired by the Postal Service after January 1st, 1984 is covered the Federal Employees Retirement System (FERS). Those hired before January 1st, 1984 are covered by the CSRS (Civil Service Retirement System). If you are covered by CSRS, you can contribute up to 9% of your salary to T.S.P as of 2004. There is no agency match. In some cases, there was the opportunity to transfer from CSRS to FERS. There is also an option called CSRS Voluntary Contribution or CSRS employees can contribute up to 10% of their salary without agency match. Social Security is only covered in the FERS program and the CSRS offset.

Social security Benefits

Social Security Tax is deducted from each of your paychecks. This tax is equal to 6.2% of your salary as of April 2008. You pay into the Social Security system in this way so that when you are 62 years of age, you can apply to receive your Social Security Benefits. This is an amount of money based on what you have paid into the Social Security System, and is paid monthly to you until you die. If you wait until your full retirement age, you will receive a higher monthly amount, and those who wait until age 70, receive even more. If your full retirement age is 66, the benefit will be reduced permanently by 25 percent at age 62, 20 percent at age 63, 13 1/3 percent at age 64 and 6 2/3 percent at age 65. You must pay tax into the system for 10 years in order to collect this benefit. If you are working while you are receiving Social Security Benefit, the benefit will reduce before your full retirement age. Your Social Security benefit will increase in some years based on your economic situation. The age to get full Social Security Benefit is determined by the date of your birth.

If you become disabled, the requirement quarters for pay tax will be less than the regular requirement. When a disabled retiree or retiree dies, his or her payment will be transferred to the spouse and certain children for some amount of benefit.

You should always keep a record of your salary payments. After you have paid into the system for a few years, the Social Security Office will send you information about your Social Security Benefits. The more Social Security Tax you pay, the more Social Security Benefit you can collect.

To get information about the Social Security Benefits, visit www.socialsecurity.gov or call 1-800-772-1234.

Applying for Social Security Retirement Benefits and Medicare

You should contact the nearest Social Security Office three months before the month in which you wish to file for retirement benefits, in order to discuss the options that are available to you. In most cases, your choice of the date of your retirement could mean additional benefits for you and your family. Even though you plan to continue working you should sign up for Medicare three months before reaching age 65 regardless of when you will retire. Otherwise, your Medicare medical insurance (Part B) could be delayed and you could be charged a higher premium. It is better to read the Medicare & You book about the limitation of enrollment period for certain situations. If you are disabled, it is possible that even though you have only paid Social Security Tax for as little as two years, you can be eligible for disability payment.

Basic Benefit

If you meet one of the following sets of age and service requirements, you are entitled to an immediate retirement benefit.

Age	Years of Service
62	5
60	20
Minimum Retirement Age	30
Minimum Retirement Age	10 (Reduced Benefits)

The early retirement benefit is available in certain involuntary separation cases, and in case of voluntary separations because of major reorganization or reduction in force.

Age	Years of Service
50	20
Any age	25

If you leave federal service before you meet the age and service requirements for immediate retirement benefit, you may be eligible for deferred retirement benefits. To be eligible, you must have completed at least five years of creditable civilian service, and then receive benefits when you reach one of the following ages.

Age	Years of Service
62	5
60	20
Minimum Retirement Age	30
Minimum Retirement Age	10 (Reduced Benefits)

Reduced benefits are given when you have worked until the minimum retirement age, but less than 30 years, or reach 60 without having worked 20 years. In these cases, your retirement benefit will be reduced by 5%, until you reach age 62.

Deferred retirement benefits occur, if you work the required number years, but have not reached minimum retirement age. In this case, you will receive benefits when you do reach the age of minimum retirement.

Minimum Retirement Age

This is how your minimum retirement age is calculated:

If you were born before	Minimum Retirement Age
1948	55
If you were born in	**Minimum Retirement Age**
1948	55 and 2 months
1949	55 and 4 months
1950	55 and 6 months
1951	55 and 8 months
1952	55 and 10 months
1953 – 1964	56
1965	56 and 2 months
1966	56 and 4 months
1967	56 and 6 months
1968	56 and 8 months
1969	56 and 10 months
1970 and after	57

To compute your retirement benefit, take your highest income for three consecutive years and average them out. If you worked 20 or more years, multiply this average by 1.1%, and then multiply again by the number of years that you worked. If you worked less than 20 years, multiply the average by 1% and then multiply by the number of years that you worked.

If you qualify, a special retirement supplement may be added until you are 62. You will qualify for this supplement, if you

- reach the minimum retirement age, and have worked at least 30 years
- are 60, and have worked at least 20 years
- involuntarily retired, after reaching your minimum retirement age up until age 62
- take early voluntary retirement, after reaching your minimum retirement age until age 62

Thrift Savings Plan (TSP)

The Postal Service has a retirement plan called the "Thrift Savings Plan" (TSP). If you want to know about the TSP in more detail, go to www.tsp.gov. You need to click the "Forms and Publications." And then click "Booklet summary of the Thrift Saving Plan." Some information may change in the future. You may get the booklets about TSP from the Personnel Office.

If you were hired as a PSE after July 31, 2010 and became a full time regular from a PSE, your agency or service will deduct your contribution to the TSP from your pay in the amount you choose (or the automatic enrollment amount of 3%). Your agency or service will continue to do so until you make a new TSP election to change the amount of your contribution or stop it, or until you reach the Internal Revenue Cod (IRC) contribution limit. There is a specific enrollment form, and a phone number to contribute. The plan allows you to contribute up to $16,500 as of 20011 into the plan. There is an automatic 1% contribution by the Postal Service — even if you contribute nothing. However, the more you contribute, the more the Postal Service will contribute. This is called "agency match." If you put in 5%, the Postal Service puts in 5%, which makes a 10% contribution. For example, if the employee contributes 5% on the first 3% of his or her salary, the agency match is $1 for each $1. If the employee contributes 5% on the second 2% of his or her salary, the agency match is $.50 for every $1. If you contribute 10%, the Postal Service contributes 5% for a total of 15%. You can enroll in this plan at any time, and it is wise to enroll, as it will benefit you when you retire.

The IRS limit in 20011 is $16,500/per year

If your contribution reached the IRS limit before end of year, you will miss out the agency matching contribution.

The catch up contribution will not effective the IRS limit contribution.

All TSP money is compounded every day. Your TSP issues quarterly statements in January, April, July, and October, and annual statements for each year in February. There is a phone number where you can check the amount in your account. You can also go to www.tsp.gov and print a statement.

When you invest in the TSP, you pay no income tax on any of the contributions or interest accrued until you withdraw the money. If you stop working before you are eligible for retirement, you can transfer your account balance to an IRA.

Your TSP money can be invested in three different funds:

Name of Fund	Investments made in...	Risk	Year Fund was Established	Average Rate of Return from 1988-1995
G-Fund	Government Securities	No risk	1987	7.9%
F-Fund	Bonds	Some risk	1988	9.8%
C-Fund	Standard & Poor's 500 (S&P 500)	High risk	1988	15.7%

You can see the C-Fund average rate of return was 15.7% for ten years. The reason it is so high is that investment is made in the stocks of many companies. By splitting the investment among many sources, the risk is minimized. It is important to know that in 1995 the C-Fund was as high as 37.4% and the F-fund was as high as 18.3%, however in 1990 the C-Fund was minus 3.2% and in 1990 the F-Fund was minus 3%. In 1992 the C-Fund was 20% of the total of the G-Fund. However by 1996, the total of the G-Fund was $20.9billion and the C-Fund was $13.1 billion and the F-Fund was $2.3 billion.

Those who value their retirement nest egg and are conservative invest in the G-Fund. Those who are more willing to take risks with their money invest in the F-Fund or the C-Fund. The most popular plan is the G-Fund because there is no risk, but some employees contribute the maximum into the C-Fund.

In May 2001, the Thrift Savings Plan added two more funds: S-Fund and I-Fund. The S-Fund is invested in the Barclay's Extended Market Index Fund, which tracks the Wilshire 4500 Stock Index. The Wilshire 4500 Index consists of the stocks that are actively traded in the U.S. stock market, except those in the S&P 500 Index.

The I-Fund is invested in the Barclay's EAFE Index, which tracks EAFE (Europe, Australasia and Far East) Stock Index. The EAFE Index, comprising 21 countries, consists of the stocks of companies that are large relative to the size of the stock markets their countries and industries.

In 2005, the L-Fund was added. The L-Fund is a mixed fund. It is a mix of the G, F, C, S, I-Funds and therefore the investment is spread over five different funds. You can get more information on these funds, at www.tsp.gov.

The Thrift Savings Plan is the same concept as a 401(K) plan, which is a common retirement plan offered by private companies.

You may transfer any part of your account balance from one fund to another. It is called "interfund transfer." For details, go to connect www.tsp.gov and click the Investing Contribution under the Plan Participation.

Eighty percent of Postal Service employees participate in TSP. It is highly advantageous to join TSP as soon as your start working and to contribute the maximum amount available to you. If you do not contribute at least around $6,000, you will not get good benefit from the plan. If you contribute more, you will get more benefit.

Once you stop working for the Postal Service, you cannot contribute to TSP. If you have not worked for the Postal Service for three years and you leave, the 1% automatic match paid will be deducted from your account, and you will lose it. If you can't contribute the maximum amount, it is better to contribute $6,000, or even better to contribute $10,000 per year.

Thrift Savings Plan Withdrawal Options

Partial Withdrawal: You can withdraw part of your account in a single payment, leaving the rest in the TSP until later. (You can use this option only once.)

Note: If you have previously made an age-based-in-service withdrawal, you cannot make a partial withdrawal.

Full Withdrawal:

You can withdraw your entire account in a single payment.

You can withdraw your entire account in a monthly payment

You can have the TSP purchase a life annuity for you with your entire account balance

Mixed Withdrawal: You can withdraw your entire account using any combination of the above three full withdrawal options.

A Life Annuity: A TSP annuity is a monthly benefit paid to you for life. If your account balance has at least $3,500, you can have the TSP use your balance to purchase an annuity for you from the TSP's annuity provider.

A Single Payment: You can withdraw your entire TSP account balance in a single payment.

A Series of Monthly Payments: You can withdraw your account in a series of nearly equal monthly payments. You can choose:

1. A specific dollar amount. You will receive payment in the amount that you request until your entire account balance has been paid to you. The amount of the monthly payments that you request must be $25 or more. (You can change the monthly payment once a year.)
2. Monthly payment computed by the TSP based on IRS Life Expectancy Table 4. Your initial payment amount will be based on your account balance at the time of the first payment and your age. The TSP will recalculate the amount of your monthly payment every year based on your account balance at the end of the preceding year and your age.

At any time while you are receiving monthly payment, you can ask the TSP to stop the monthly payment and pay you your remaining account balance in a single payment. Also, once a year, you have the opportunity to make changes to the dollar amount of the monthly payment you are receiving. You also have the opportunity to make a one-time switch to receiving monthly payments based on a dollar amount rather than monthly payment based on life expectancy.

Thrift Savings Plan after You Retire

If you purchased the TSP annuities, you can collect payments until you die, and you can pass the benefit to your beneficiary if you die. The benefits given to your beneficiary can be either 50% or 100%. If you give your pension and annuity goes to your beneficiary, however, you will receive a lesser amount. You can get additional updated information about TSP and estimate the amount of your pension if you read the TSP *Annuities*.

In case of your purchased the TSP annuities, your TSP payment can be either a fixed amount, or an increasing amount, based on inflation (CPI). The increasing payment can raise your pension by as much as 3% annually. If you choose increasing payment option, only a legal spouse can collect the pension — no other beneficiary. Even if CPI is lower, the pension will be higher. A spouse is entitled to a joint life annuity with 50% survivor benefits, level payment and no cash refund feature unless he or she waives this right before you begin withdrawing your account. To receive a withdrawal option other than an annuity, your spouse must agree to it and sign a form.

When you retire, if you purchased TSP annuities you can choose the interest rate by visiting the website www.tsp.gov. Click "What is New" and then click "Annuity Rate Index." In July 2005, the interest rate was 4.375% and in June 1989, it was 9.25%. The variable rate is based on a three-month moving average of the 10-year U.S. Treasury rate.

Once you choose an interest rate, you will have to keep that option forever.

If you are covered under CSRS, here's how you can calculate the annuity:

> 1.5% x (the highest three-year salary) x (the first five years) (Years 1-5)
>
> 1.75% x (the highest three-year salary x (the next five years) (Years 6-10)
>
> 2% x (the highest three-year salary x (all years of service over 10 years) — including credit for unused sick leave.

Maximum Annuity for CSRS covered employees

Eighty percent of the highest three-year salary (at 41 years and 11 months of service) — although sick leave can increase the annuity over 80%. (There is a limited exception for CSRS employees who transfer to FERS.)

When you retire, you may request a booklet about TSP from the Postal Service Personnel Office or you can download them from www.tsp.gov. These booklets include *The Thrift Savings Plan: Withdrawing Your TSP Account*, and *The Thrift Savings Plan: Annuities, etc.*

New transfer option available

If you have a retirement savings account from a previous employer and you would like to consolidate your retirement investments, you may be able to transfer or roll over that money into your TSP account. The TSP can accept these "eligible rollover distributions" only from qualified retirement plans, or from conduit Individual Retirement Accounts (IRAs) that were set up to accept eligible rollover distributions.

Leaving your money in the TSP

After you leave Federal Service, you can leave your entire account balance in the TSP, until you reach age 70 ½, subject to the restrictions described below.

What is the required withdrawal date?

You are required to withdraw your account balance in a single payment, begin receiving monthly payments, or begin receiving annuity payments by April 1st of the later of

1. The year following the year you become age 70 ½.
2. The year following the year you separate from the Federal Service or Uniform Service.

Requesting an age-based withdrawal before you are 59 ½ (in service withdrawals)

You cannot request an age-based withdrawal before you are 59 ½, but you can request a withdrawal for financial hardship at any time.

TSP Catch-up Contributions

You are eligible if you are a federal employee or a member of the Uniform Service who will be age 50 or older in 2003, and are already contributing the maximum amount of regular TSP contributions for which you are eligible. You can invest up to $5,500 in 2011. Subsequent years will be indexed to inflation.

What is the Roth TSP?

The TSP introduced the Roth TSP in 2012.

For more information, the Thrift Savings Plan website is www.tsp.gov and the phone number is 1-877-968-3778.

If you have enough money, it is wise to participate in an IRA with the Community Credit Union or another bank.

Disability Benefits

There is a disability benefit.

Survivor Benefits

If you have worked over 18 months and die, your spouse can collect a lump sum payment plus either the higher of one-half of your annual pay rate at death, or one-half of the average three consecutive highest annual salary. The lump sum payment, which is increased by a cost of living adjustment each year, was approximately $19,600 in 1994.

If you have 10 years of service or more, the spouse will collect 50% of your accrued basic retirement benefits for life. In addition, the spouse can collect Social Security benefits, life insurance, and your savings plan monies. If a postal worker dies during retirement, the spouse can collect 50% of the basic benefit for life. If the spouse does not qualify for Social Security, the spouse will receive a special supplementary annuity until the age of 60. A former spouse and dependent children are also eligible for survivor benefits. If the retiree dies and his or her spouse remarried before age 55, then the pension stops.

If a retired postal worker wants to give his or her benefits to the beneficiary, the retiree's benefits will be reduced by 10% while the retired postal worker is still alive if the beneficiary is less than 5 years younger. If a spouse doesn't want to receive these benefits, he or she can sign a petition to refuse these survivor benefits. If this petition is not turned in before an employee retires, the pension will be reduced automatically by 10%. If the retiree's spouse dies, the pension reverts to the retiree and all reductions are eliminated.

If you have 18 months of civilian service and die while you are an active Postal Service employee, or if you have retired and die, your children may be eligible to receive an annuity. This benefit is payable to each unmarried child up to the age of 18 and up to the age of 22, if the child is a full-time student. A dependent child, who was disabled before the age of 18, is also entitled to the annuity.

The amount of the Federal Employee Retirement System benefit depends on the number of children and if the children are orphans. In 1994, FERS surviving child benefit was approximately $3,708 per child for each of three children, and $4,464, if orphaned. This is reduced dollar for dollar by any social security that may be payable.

If you applied the retirement, the US Office of Personal Management will send more information about the retirement.

If a retiree gets divorced and remarried, he or she can change his or her designated survivor benefit recipient to the new spouse, as long as he or she does so within two years of the date of the marriage. If this occurs, some money must be deposited into the retirement fund. See the Personnel Office for more details about this.

Cost of Living Adjustments (COLAs)

As a regular retiree, you will receive a Cost-of-Living Adjustment (COLA), if you are age 62 or older. Survivors and disabled retirees receive COLA regardless of their age, however, disabled retirees with 60% of their average pay, do not receive COLA during the first year of retirement. The amount of the annual COLA percentage is based on the Consumer Price Index (CPI).

The special retirement supplement for retirees is not increased by COLA's. The supplement for survivors, however, is increased by COLA's.

If you are a regular retiree, you can collect "cost of living adjustments" when you are 62. However, if you are a survivor/spouse or handicapped retiree, you can collect the "cost of living adjustment" at any time.

Payment of Basic FERS Benefits

Basic FERS benefits are paid in the form of a monthly annuity.

PTR (Part Time Regular)

As a Part Time Regular (PTR) employee, you may work eight hours a day for three days a week, or four hours a day for five days a week. When you retire as a PTR, your basic benefit will be lower, because your basic benefit is computed by averaging your highest salary over any three consecutive years. About four or five years before you retire, you can bid to return to a 40-hour work per week. If you work 40-hours per week, your pay will increase and your benefit will increase, as well. However, it may be difficult to become a full-time employee quickly. You can request anytime the PTR position after probation.

Family and Medical Leave Act of 1995

The Family and Medical Leave Act of 1995 permits a postal worker to take up to 12 weeks leave for a family emergency.

Savings Bond Plan

You can buy savings bonds, and they are tax-deferred.

Long Term Care Program

If you cannot move, eat or go to the restroom, you can join the Long Term Care Program to get help. The term is 2 years or 3 years or five years or for life. Since Federal employees pay Medicare Tax, you will be able to get Medicare when you turn 65. (To be eligible you must have paid Medicare Tax for at least 10 years.)

Flexible Spending Accounts

You can calculate any medical expenses for a certain year and apply to join the FSA (Flexible Spending Account). It will be a payroll deduction. If you pay any medical expenses with the FSA, you do not need to pay any taxes on that money, but if you do not spend all the money in the FSA account and did not reimburse until a certain month of the next year, your money will be forfeited. In 2004, the deadline to reimburse was September 2005. If you use the FSA, when you get a Social Security Benefit, it will be reduced slightly. For more information, read the FSA booklet.

9. Additional Information

Non-Creditable Service

> LWOP (leave without pay) — In excess of six months in a year unless covered by OWCP
>
> Retired Military — Unless combat connected or other exception
>
> Military Lost Time

Partially Creditable Service

Most non-career Rural Service is creditable only for the time of actual employment.

Military Time

If you were in the U.S. military, you can get extra points on your test score (see page 233). If you make a 3% payment on all basic salary in your military career, then your military time will add to your postal time. If you did not make 3% payment on all money received in your military career within 3 years since you were hired, there will be some penalty payment for interest. Because of military service, you can get more vacation time.

Typing Test for Mark-Up Position

If you apply for a Mark-Up position after you are hired, you have to pass a typing test. You have to retype 14 out of 25 lines within one minute on a computer terminal correctly. You need to type each line as shown in the sample exercise using lower case and capital letters. As you practice for this exam, you should use the row of numeric keys near the top of the keyboard just above the QWERTY keys. You cannot use the numeric keypad when taking the exam. When you reach the end of a line, press the "Enter" or "Return" key and begin typing the next line. If you reach the end of the sample items, simply begin again with the first line and continue to type until the five minutes have elapsed. A passing score is 70 correct lines.

The following are sample exercise lines:

KATZ204

CURR907

ADAM101

SONN530

GORD223

OWEN241

SCHN421

HALL375

LOGU779

ROSE995

SHER963

MART895

KATA854

SHAN289

JAME409

CHER103

LINC501

MOSI521

NORM486

SALY541

MCNE326

PATS293

PRIN815

KAPL296

DUNN919

Cash for Suggestions

If you have ideas to improve processing for Postal Service operation, you can submit them. You will receive a cash payment if the Postal Service accepts the ideas.

Postal Service Employees Relief Fund

If you are suffering from a disaster, the Postal Service may give you some money to recover.

APWU Disaster Fund

If you could not get help or could not get enough help from the Postal Service employees Relief Fund when suffering a disaster, the union will help you. But you have to join the union.

If you take a LWOP (leave without pay) for more than 2 years, you have to start again for the no layoff protection. (No lay off with 6 service years)

E.A.P. (Employees Assistance Program)

For help with problems that may occur, there is the E.A.P. You can request to meet with a counselor. The meeting will take place within 48 hours of your request. Before you go to the E.A.P, contact the union for advice.

Miscellaneous Notes

There is a table of disqualification for carrier position on page 206.

It is up to you how often to check the Internet to find out which post offices that are accepting applications. It is good to check once a week, usually on Monday. If you have time, it is also good to check again on Wednesday.

Under certain situations, as in California, as in the case of casual (temporary) position, you will seldom learn about job opening information when you call the local job information phone number, when the information is not on the Internet. The Post Office may change this information in the future.

If you visit any lead post offices (P&DC) or local post offices, you may get some jobs information for casual positions.

At the time of the exam, the examiner will give you a list of post offices that are hiring. You can choose up to 3 post offices to which to apply. (The Post Office may change this information in the future.) It is better to find out which post office is suitable for you before the exam day.

It is easier to advance to full time (Regular) from PTF (Part Time Flexible) at an office with 200 or more employees.

After working at the Post Office for a while, you may want to start preparing for a higher position. To become a postal inspector, you must have a 4-year college degree. And an age limitation does apply.

TE (Transitional Employees) may work up to 359 days in a calendar year. At the end of the 359-day year, you may be reappointed, which would require a five-day break. The health benefit is offered after you have worked a year, but it has a higher cost than for a career employee. You can earn 13 days annual leave (Vacation) per year. TE have to pass the 90 days probation period.

Mail Processing Clerk, City Carrier, and Sale, Service and Distribution Associate belong to Label 6. And Mail Handler belongs to Label 4.

Within 120 days before or after you are discharged from the military, you can request to take the postal exam that the Postal Service gave while you were in the military.

If you call a jobs information line, you may learn about the Casual or TE from the outgoing recorded message. The message will probably say the following:

"The Postal Service will send an application for employment (Resume) within 10 business days."

You have to return the application for employment to the included address. If you return an application for employment, the Postal Service may send a notice for an interview. This information may change in the future. There is no exam for a Casual and a TE.

After you enter the exam room, you have to fill out a form before the test. For filling out the form, you need to write a letter or number in each box. And then go down straightly and darken the space you just wrote in the box. Since online assessment began, this processing is eliminated.

Postal Service employees must have basic competence in speaking and understanding English.

The following is an explanation of the Mark-Up position.

If a resident moves to a new home or apartment, the Post Office will put a yellow sticker on the resident's mail and type a new address. Then the Post Office will deliver the mail to the new address for one year.

In this case, Mark-Up will type a new address on the yellow label.

If you provide incorrect information in the application for employment and the Postal Service finds out later, you may be fired and prosecuted.

The USPS accepts the applications based on city or county of a State.

You can change the investment of your account balance among the five TSP funds while you are receiving monthly payment after you retired. If you have invested in the F fund, C fund, S fund or I fund, remember that investment losses could cause your account balance to decrease, which could reduce either the amount of your monthly payment or duration.

You can also change to a final payment at any time. In addition, you can make a change to the payment amount you are receiving or make a one time only change from TSP computed payments to a specific amount. These last two changes will become effective only once a year — on January 1, if your request is received by December 15 of the preceding year. You can get information about the TSP by reading the booklet "*Withdrawing Your TSP Account after Leaving Federal Service*", the TSP in service Withdrawals and Thrift Saving Plan.

How to Register to Take an Examination Nationwide

This system is effective from August 1, 2008, and it is called eCareer system. With the eCareer system, you can apply to take the examinations. You have to register first to take exams. At the time of registration, you have to provide your eCareer Profile.

How to register: After connecting to www.usps.com/employment, you can see the "Search now" link at the top right-hand corner. You also can see the article "Create an account"" on the same screen. You need to click the article "Create an account" and then follow the instructions to finish the registration. You must have an e-mail address. You also must create a username and a password. There are directions explaining how to create a username and a password on the screen. If you cannot finish the registration at that time, you can save it and finish it later. You need to make note of the username and password, and keep them in a safe place. You also need to keep the candidate number. When you go to the exam room, you need to take the username, password, and candidate number. You also need to take a picture ID, denizenship (for permanent resident), or US citizenship or passport (for US citizen).

You also can create your eCareer profile while you are in processing the "Search jobs & Apply online."

A student told me the following:

He applied to a Post Office more than 50 miles away from his house. The job description said that applicants must live within 50 miles. When he registered to take the exam by the Internet, he wrote a note on the cover letter that he will move within 50 miles from the Post Office if he got the job. He said he passed the interview.

There is another example. A student took an exam for the position of Rural Carrier. Later on, the Post Office allowed that the applicant to apply for any position even though he took the exam for Rural Carrier. The two preceding examples are just anecdotal. They do not guarantee success in other cases.

How to Search the Jobs and to Apply to Take an Exam

Go to www.usps.com/employment.

Click the article "Search now" to search the jobs. Then you can see the screen to search the jobs.

Use the Reset button before every search. If you don't use the Reset button, criteria from a prior search may affect the outcome of your search.

I use the following procedure:

I don't select any city, but instead select a State. I don't use the Functional Area in order to get the broadest selection of jobs. I highlight the blank box just above the "Administrative office services" in the Functional Area.

And if I click "Start," I can see the jobs on the next screen for the State that I selected. I need to click a job to apply for a job. And on the next screen, I can see a job description and "Apply." I need to click the "Apply" and follow the instructions.

Sometimes, if I want to search the jobs from Test 473, Test 473 C, RCA (Rural Carrier Associate), TE (Transitional Employees) Carrier, TE Clerk, Casual Clerk, Casual Carrier and Temporary Relief Carrier, I highlight the Customer Service/Delivery, Operation, Processing and Distribution, Expedited Mail Service, Retail, Sale and others in the Functional Area.

After you have searched, if you see an interesting job on the screen, click that job. Then you can see the job description and the "Apply" button on the next screen. You should read the entire job description. If you click

"Apply," you can see the space for which you need to write your name and e-mail address, etc. You also can see the "Are you already registered?" link. Click to logon. After you have submitted an application to take the exam, you need to check your e-mail everyday."

If you have already taken an exam and have a score and you don't want to take the same exam, you need to select not to take the exam while you are applying for a job. If you want to take an exam, the newest score only will be used. Sometimes the Postal Service indicates that applicants must live within the metropolitan area (i.e., within commuting distance) of the vacancy.

The following articles about the eCareer are from the Postal Service's letter.

Online examination provides instant results with a passing score good for six years in any location of the country.

If an examination is required, applicants without a current score will be referred an assessment vendor to be scheduled and tested within fourteen days of application.

What is the PSE (Postal Supplement Employee)?

The Postal Service created this new position in 2011, called a PSE.

After searching the jobs at www.usps.com/employment, if you click a job on the screen, you can see the job description on the next screen.

HOUR AND NON-SCHEDULED DAYS: Work as needed based on operations needs. No guarantee of work hours. Applicants must be available to work on weekends and holidays.

SALARY RANGE (as of 2016):

$15.63 per hour for PSE Sale & SVCS/Distribution.

BENEFIT INFORMATION: Limited benefits include paid vacation days and access to health benefits after the first 360 days term. PSE has to pay the social security tax. And if the PSE paid the social security tax for 10 years, then the PSE is eligible for the social security benefit. The PSE has to pass a 90-day probation period. Even after passing the probation periods, a PSE still does not have retirement benefit and can't contribute money to the TSP (Thrift Saving Plan). TSP is like the 401k. The Postal Service will make a full-time employee (regular) from the PSE by the seniority. How long will it take to become a full time regular from the PSE? It depends on the post office situation. It may take a month, a year, two years, three years, or four years. There is no guideline for how long it will take to become a full time regular from a PSE. After a PSE becomes a full-time regular Postal Service employee, he or she will have all the benefits of a full-time regular.

To become a PSE, you have to take Test 473 at a home and contract facility. The exam must be completed within 14 days after the date of application submission.

What is CCA (City Carrier Assistant 1)?

CCA is the same as PSE except for the following:

> CCA mainly delivers the mail.
>
> CCA hour rate is $16.06 as of 2016.

What is the Mail Handler Assistant?

Mail Handler Assistant is the same as PSE except for the following:

> Does mostly physical work to hand mail in the post office.
>
> Hour rate is $14.71 asw of 2016.

Information for PSE, CCA, Rural Carrier Associate, etc.

The exam is a two-step process. Upon successful completion of the online assessment (at home), you will be given an opportunity to schedule the final potion of the exam (online assessment) at a contract facility. Instructions for starting the exam process will be sent via email once you successfully submit your application.

You must start this process within three days of the date of your application submission since the second step must be completed within 7 days of your application submission. (It is within 14 days for PSE.) The contract facilities may be outside of the local commuting area and a seat may not be available where requested. You must keep in contact with the email address indicated in your correspondence regarding open seats or you may miss your opportunity to test and would not be considered for position.

There are the HMO and PPO for health insurance. The Blue Cross and Blue Shield Government Wide Plan with PPO. There are the standard option and the basic option.

The basic option covers 100% of the costs, and standard option covers 85%.

What is the out of pocket limit for catastrophic coverage?

For example, with the basic option and the standard option, you make a copayment for a medical expense. If you paid up to $5,000 per year for any copayment, then you don't have to pay any additional amount for that year. There is indication of how much you paid in the explanation of benefits that the insurance company sends you if you go to a medical clinic.

With Blue Cross and Blue Shield, when you reached 65, you can select Medicare Part B. But it is better to just suspend your federal Government health insurance instead of canceling it to join Medicare. If you just suspend your Federal Government health insurance, you can come back to it. You need to call to OPM to get the form.

Some very small post offices are still hiring PTF, instead of the PSE, CCA and Mail Handler Assistant positions.

A student told me the following:

She student took the exam for the Rural Carrier position. Later on, the Post Office allowed her to apply for any position even though she took the Rural Carrier exam which is that same exam between Test 473 and Rural Carrier exam.

This example is just anecdotal. It does not guarantee success in other cases.

Employee Participation

Postal career employees and substitute rural carrier (Designation 72 and 73 only) may apply to take a postal entrance examination noncompetitively at their installation or examination center. Noncompetitive examinations are scheduled consistent with operational needs, but must be scheduled no later than 6 months following date applications are received.

Substitute Rural Carrier, Rural Carrier Associate, and Rural Carrier Relief's

The following employees provide service on established regular and auxiliary rural routes in the absence of regular or auxiliary rural carrier. This service may be as leave replacement or covering vacant regular routes pending the selection of regular rural carriers, as on auxiliary route carrier.

Substitute Rural Carriers - (Designation Code 73)

Substitute Rural Carriers are those employees hired before July 21, 1981, with an appointment without time limitation.

Substitute Rural Carrier - (Designation Code 72)

Substitute Rural Carrier appointed via Form 50 to serve full time on a vacant regular route or in the absence of a Regular Rural Carrier for more than 90 calendar days.

Noncompetitive Selection

Qualified postal career employees and Substitute Rural Carrier (designation 72 and 73) may be selected noncompetitively for entrance-level positions at the option of the installation head.

Promotion to Entrance Level Positions

The preferred action for filling vacancies in entrance-level positions is the noncompetitive promotion of lower-level career Postal Service employee or Substitute Rural Carrier (designation 72 and 73 only) who meet the position qualification requirement (Including any required test), and who are performing satisfactorily.

Any information in this book may be changed in the future.

Ten Retirement Suggestions by American Postal Worker Union (APWU)

1. Begin planning your retirement at the beginning of employment or start today.
2. Attend several pre-retirement seminars.
3. Keep your retirement plan confidential, this allows you to change your mind if retirement plans change.
4. Discuss your plans with your spouse so both your interests can be preserved in your new life style. Know there is a spousal consent requirement.
5. Learn the facts of your many retirement options from the retirement counselor at your post office.
6. Review your life and health insurance needs and figure the cost as you decide which policies to take with you into retirement. Understand how age will impact your life insurance.
7. Stay where you are for about a year after you retire. This will help you make a wise decision on whether to stay close to your family and friends or move to a new area.
8. Take advantage of the various "Thrift Saving Plans" (CSRS-FERS) available to you. Save the maximum you can, even if you will only be in the program for a year or less.
9. Take financial inventory and budget for unexpected expenses like increasing college tuition for your children or medical care for you or your love ones.
10. Take advantage of all the retirement information provided by your APWU Retirement Department, Postal Agency, OPM (Office of Personnel Management) and independent sources.

Lastly, do not live your life for retirement. Retirement is just another stage of life we can look forward to.

Good Luck.

JUL 2019

CPSIA information can be obtained
at www.ICGtesting.com
Printed in the USA
LVHW050919300419
615763LV00022B/222/P

9 781889 057774